THE NEW FOLGER LIBRARY SHAKESPEARE

Designed to make Shakespeare's great plays available to all readers, the New Folger Library edition of Shakespeare's plays provides accurate texts in modern spelling and punctuation, as well as scene-by-scene action summaries, full explanatory notes, many pictures clarifying Shakespeare's language, and notes recording all significant departures from the early printed versions. Each play is prefaced by a brief introduction, by a guide to reading Shakespeare's language, and by accounts of his life and theater. Each play is followed by an annotated list of further readings and by a "Modern Perspective" written by an expert on that particular play.

Barbara A. Mowat is Director of Research *emerita* at the Folger Shakespeare Library, Consulting Editor of *Shakespeare Quarterly*, and author of *The Dramaturgy of Shakespeare's Romances* and of essays on Shakespeare's plays and their editing.

Paul Werstine is Professor of English in the Graduate School and at King's University College at Western University. He is a general editor of the New Variorum Shakespeare and author of *Early Modern Playhouse Manuscripts and the Editing of Shakespeare,* as well as many papers and essays on the printing and editing of Shakespeare's plays.

Folger Shakespeare Library

The Folger Shakespeare Library in Washington, D.C., is a privately funded research library dedicated to Shakespeare and the civilization of early modern Europe. It was founded in 1932 by Henry Clay and Emily Jordan Folger, and incorporated as part of Amherst College in Amherst, Massachusetts, one of the nation's oldest liberal arts colleges, from which Henry Folger had graduated in 1879. In addition to its role as the world's preeminent Shakespeare collection and its emergence as a leading center for Renaissance studies, the Folger Shakespeare Library offers a wide array of cultural and educational programs and services for the general public.

EDITORS

BARBARA A. MOWAT
Director of Research emerita
Folger Shakespeare Library

PAUL WERSTINE
Professor of English
King's University College at the University of Western Ontario, Canada

FOLGER SHAKESPEARE LIBRARY

The Life and Death of

King John

By
WILLIAM SHAKESPEARE

EDITED BY BARBARA A. MOWAT
AND PAUL WERSTINE

SIMON & SCHUSTER PAPERBACKS
New York London Toronto Sydney New Delhi

Simon & Schuster Paperbacks
An Imprint of Simon & Schuster, Inc.
1230 Avenue of the Americas
New York, NY 10020

Washington Square Press New Folger Edition December 2000
This Simon & Schuster paperback edition March 2015

Manufactured in the United States of America

10 9 8 7 6 5

ISBN 978-0-7434-8498-5

From the Director of the Folger Shakespeare Library

It is hard to imagine a world without Shakespeare. Since their composition four hundred years ago, Shakespeare's plays and poems have traveled the globe, inviting those who see and read his works to make them their own.

Readers of the New Folger Editions are part of this ongoing process of "taking up Shakespeare," finding our own thoughts and feelings in language that strikes us as old or unusual and, for that very reason, new. We still struggle to keep up with a writer who could think a mile a minute, whose words paint pictures that shift like clouds. These expertly edited texts, presented here with accompanying explanatory notes and up-to-date critical essays, are distinctive because of what they do: they allow readers not simply to keep up, but to engage deeply with a writer whose works invite us to think, and think again.

These New Folger Editions of Shakespeare's plays are also special because of where they come from. The Folger Shakespeare Library in Washington, DC, where the Editions are produced, is the single greatest documentary source of Shakespeare's works. An unparalleled collection of early modern books, manuscripts, and artwork connected to Shakespeare, the Folger's holdings have been consulted extensively in the preparation of these texts. The Editions also reflect the expertise gained through the regular performance of Shakespeare's works in the Folger's Elizabethan Theater.

I want to express my deep thanks to editors Barbara Mowat and Paul Werstine for creating these indispensable editions of Shakespeare's works, which incorporate the best of textual scholarship with a richness of commentary that is both inspired and engaging. Readers who want to know more about Shakespeare and his plays can follow the paths these distinguished scholars have tread by visiting the Folger itself, where a range of physical and digital resources (available online) exist to supplement the material in these texts. I commend to you these words, and hope that they inspire.

Michael Witmore
Director, Folger Shakespeare Library

Contents

Editors' Preface *ix*
Shakespeare's *King John* *xiii*
Reading Shakespeare's Language: *King John* *xiv*
Shakespeare's Life *xxvi*
Shakespeare's Theater *xxxvi*
The Publication of Shakespeare's Plays *xlvi*
An Introduction to This Text *l*

King John
Text of the Play with Commentary *1*

Longer Notes *211*
Textual Notes *223*
Historical Background
1. King John, Prince Arthur, and "borrowed majesty" *231*
2. King John and the Roman Catholic Church *232*
3. King John and "An Homily against disobedience and willful rebellion" *233*

King John: A Modern Perspective by Deborah T. Curren-Aquino *237*
Further Reading *273*
Key to Famous Lines and Phrases *295*

Editors' Preface

In recent years, ways of dealing with Shakespeare's texts and with the interpretation of his plays have been undergoing significant change. This edition, while retaining many of the features that have always made the Folger Shakespeare so attractive to the general reader, at the same time reflects these current ways of thinking about Shakespeare. For example, modern readers, actors, and teachers have become interested in the differences between, on the one hand, the early forms in which Shakespeare's plays were first published and, on the other hand, the forms in which editors through the centuries have presented them. In response to this interest, we have based our edition on what we consider the best early printed version of a particular play (explaining our rationale in a section called "An Introduction to This Text") and have marked our changes in the text—unobtrusively, we hope, but in such a way that the curious reader can be aware that a change has been made and can consult the "Textual Notes" to discover what appeared in the early printed version.

Current ways of looking at the plays are reflected in our brief prefaces, in many of the commentary notes, in the annotated lists of "Further Reading," and especially in each play's "Modern Perspective," an essay written by an outstanding scholar who brings to the reader his or her fresh assessment of the play in the light of today's interests and concerns.

As in the Folger Library General Reader's Shakespeare, which this edition replaces, we include explanatory notes designed to help make Shakespeare's language clearer to a modern reader, and we place the notes on the page facing the text that they explain. We also follow the earlier edition in including illustrations—of objects, of clothing, of mythological figures—from books and manuscripts in the Folger Library collection. We provide fresh accounts of the life of Shakespeare, of the publishing of his plays, and of the theaters in which his plays were performed, as well as an introduction to the text itself. We also include a section called "Reading Shakespeare's Language," in which we try to help readers learn to "break the code" of Elizabethan poetic language.

For each section of each volume, we are indebted to a host of generous experts and fellow scholars. The "Reading Shakespeare's Language" sections, for example, could not have been written had not Arthur King, of Brigham Young University, and Randall Robinson, author of *Unlocking Shakespeare's Language*, led the way in untangling Shakespearean language puzzles and shared their insights and methodologies generously with us. "Shakespeare's Life" profited by the careful reading given it by the late S. Schoenbaum, "Shakespeare's Theater" was read and strengthened by Andrew Gurr and John Astington, and "The Publication of Shakespeare's Plays" is indebted to the comments of Peter W. M. Blayney. We, as editors, take sole responsibility for any errors in our editions.

We are grateful to the authors of the "Modern Perspectives"; to Gail Kern Paster for her unfailing interest and advice; to Leeds Barroll and David Bevington for their generous encouragement; to the Huntington and Newberry Libraries for fellowship support; to King's College for the grants it has provided to Paul Werstine; to the Social Sciences and Humanities Research Council of Canada, which provided him with a Research Time Stipend for 1990–91; to Deborah Curren-Aquino for helpful suggestions about the text and commentary; to R. J. Shroyer of the University of Western Ontario for essential computer support; to the Folger Institute's

Center for Shakespeare Studies for its sponsorship of a workshop on "Shakespeare's Texts for Students and Teachers" (funded by the National Endowment for the Humanities and led by Richard Knowles of the University of Wisconsin), a workshop from which we learned an enormous amount about what is wanted by college and high-school teachers of Shakespeare today; to Alice Falk for her expert copyediting; and especially to Steve Llano, our production editor at Pocket Books, whose expertise and attention to detail are essential to this project. Among the texts we consulted, we found A. R. Braunmuller's Oxford *King John* (1989) and R. L. Smallwood's New Penguin *King John* (1974) particularly helpful.

Our biggest debt is to the Folger Shakespeare Library—to Werner Gundersheimer, Director of the Library, who made possible our edition; to Deborah Curren-Aquino, who provides extensive editorial and production support; to Jean Miller, the Library's former Art Curator, who combs the Library holdings for illustrations, and to Julie Ainsworth, Head of the Photography Department, who carefully photographs them; to Peggy O'Brien, former Director of Education at the Folger and now Director of Education Programs at the Corporation for Public Broadcasting, who gave us expert advice about the needs being expressed by Shakespeare teachers and students (and to Martha Christian and other "master teachers" who used our texts in manuscript in their classrooms); to Allan Shnerson and Mary Bloodworth for their expert computer support; to the staff of the Academic Programs Division, especially Rachel Kunkle (whose help is crucial), Mary Tonkinson, Kathleen Lynch, Carol Brobeck, Toni Krieger, Liz Pohland, Owen Williams, and Lisa Meyers; and, finally, to the generously supportive staff of the Library's Reading Room.

Barbara A. Mowat and Paul Werstine

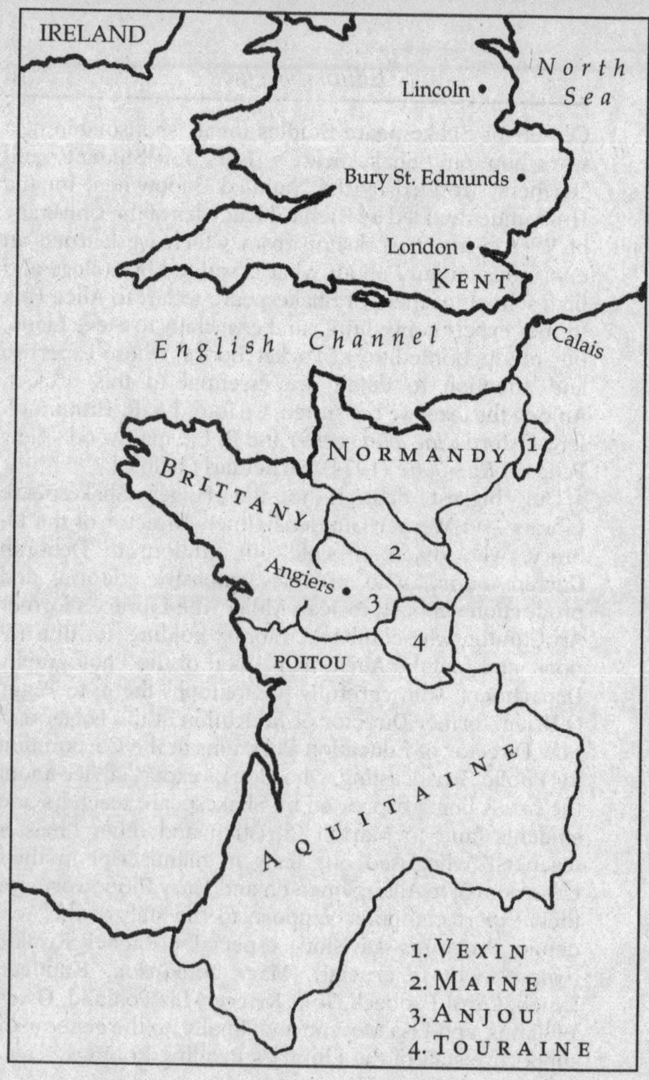

Territories under the dominion of the English monarch in the early years of John's reign.
Stephen Llano, based on William Shepherd, *Historical Atlas*, 8th ed. (1956).

Shakespeare's *King John*

Like most of Shakespeare's history plays, *King John* presents a struggle for the crown of England. In this play, however, the struggle is located much further back in English history than is usual in Shakespeare's plays, and, perhaps for this reason, it is waged with a strikingly cold-blooded brutality. Most of the contestants for the throne are the descendants of King Henry II and Queen Eleanor of Aquitaine. The couple's eldest son, King Richard I or Richard Coeur de Lion, has already been killed before the play begins. The Duke of Austria, presented in the play as Richard's killer, enters wearing as a trophy the lion's skin taken from his victim. The play explains that Richard Coeur de Lion came by the skin and by his name when he ripped out the heart of a lion sent to attack him.

Richard's royal kin who compete to occupy the throne he vacated possess none of Coeur de Lion's legendary heroism; but John, the late Richard's younger brother, who holds the English crown when the play opens, lacks none of Richard's savagery. John's opponent is a boy, Arthur, the son of another of John's elder brothers now deceased. Arthur's cause has been taken up by the King of France and by the fierce-looking Austria, but nonetheless the boy falls into King John's hands among the spoils of victory that King John enjoys when he defeats France and Austria on the battlefield. No sooner has King John captured Arthur than he plots to torture his nephew and thereby put the boy's life at risk. But Arthur's capture fails to secure the throne for King John. Instead, it merely provides the opportunity for Louis, the Dauphin of France, to lay claim to King John's crown—a claim supported by King John's outraged nobles, whom Louis schemes to reward for their assistance with a savage treachery to match King John's against Arthur.

While there are no royal heroes in *King John,* the play finds its hero in the Bastard, Sir Richard Plantagenet, an illegitimate son of Richard Coeur de Lion, who is identified as the Bastard's father in the first place by the Bastard's remarkable physical resemblance to him. By avenging his father through beheading the Duke of Austria in battle, the Bastard adds a chapter to his father's legendary career. Certainly the Bastard has an appetite for warfare and is impatient with any cessation of hostilities: "Cry havoc, kings!" he exclaims. "Back to the stainèd field, / You equal potents, fiery-kindled spirits. / Then let confusion of one part confirm / The other's peace. Till then, blows, blood, and death!" His bloodlust aside, the Bastard is given many attractive features—a trenchant irony that he directs against all kinds of pretension, and a strict conscience that threatens to drive him from his allegiance to King John once the Bastard learns of the plot against Arthur.

After you have read the play, we invite you to turn to the essay printed at the back of this book, "*King John:* A Modern Perspective," written by Dr. Deborah T. Curren-Aquino, a leading scholar of this play.

Reading Shakespeare's Language: *King John*

For many people today, reading Shakespeare's language can be a problem—but it is a problem that can be solved. Those who have studied Latin (or even French or German or Spanish), and those who are used to reading poetry, will have little difficulty understanding the language of Shakespeare's poetic drama. Others, though, need to develop the skills of untangling unusual sentence structures and of recognizing and understanding poetic compressions, omissions, and wordplay. And even those skilled in reading unusual sentence structures may have occasional trouble with Shakespeare's words. Four hundred years of "static" intervene between his speaking and our hearing. Most of his immense vocabulary is still in use, but a few of his words are not, and, worse, some of his words now have meanings quite different from those they had in the sixteenth century. In the theater, most of these difficulties are solved for us by actors who study the language and articulate it for us so that the essential meaning is heard—or, when combined with stage action, is at least *felt*. When reading on one's own, one must do what each actor does: go over the lines (often with a dictionary close at hand) until the puzzles are solved and the lines yield up their poetry and the characters speak in words and phrases that are, suddenly, rewarding and wonderfully memorable.

Shakespeare's Words

As you begin to read the opening scenes of a play by Shakespeare, you may notice occasional unfamiliar words. Some are unfamiliar simply because we no longer use them. In the opening scenes of *King John*, for example, you will find the words "sooth" (i.e., truth), "holp" (i.e., helped), "Zounds" (i.e., by Christ's [or God's] wounds"), and "peisèd" (i.e., balanced). Words of this kind are explained in notes to the text and will become familiar the more of Shakespeare's plays you read.

In *King John*, as in all of Shakespeare's writing, the more problematic are the words that we still use but that we use with a different meaning. In the opening scenes of *King John,* for example, the word *embassy* has the meaning of "message," *warned* is used where we would say "summoned," *fronts* is used where we would say "foreheads," and *likes* where we would say "pleases." Such words will be explained in the notes to the text, but they, too, will become familiar as you continue to read Shakespeare's language.

Some words are strange not because of the "static" introduced by changes in language over the past centuries but because these are words that Shakespeare is using to build dramatic worlds that have their own space, time, and history. *King John* tells the story of a battle for the English crown in the early thirteenth century, a time when much of the land that makes up present-day France was controlled by the monarch of England. It centers on the challenge to the reigning English king, John, by his nephew, Arthur, supported by King Philip of France. The play quickly establishes the geography of John's dominions, with references to such "dominations" as "Poitiers, Anjou, Touraine, Maine" (2.1.183, 1.1.11). It also sets the terms for Arthur's claim against John with charges that John's is a "borrowed majesty," that he "sways usurpingly" his "several titles" (1.1.4, 13), and that, by taking the English throne, he has "cut off the sequence of posterity, / Outfacèd infant state, and done a rape / Upon the maiden virtue of the crown" (2.1.96–98). The earlier history lying behind the play is established with references to "Plantagenet" (1.1.9), to "Geoffrey . . . [John's] elder brother born" (2.1.104), and to "King Richard Coeur de Lion" and the legend of the "aweless lion [who] could not . . . keep his princely heart from Richard's hand" (1.1.261, 274–75).

An additional language world comes into the play with the character who soon becomes known as the Bastard. Philip Faulconbridge, who elects to abandon his legitimacy and announce himself as the bastard son of Richard Coeur de Lion, speaks a language filled with allusions to legend and literature ("Colbrand the Giant," "Philip Sparrow," "Basilisco"), with words that reflect ordinary material life ("half-faced groat," "eel-skins stuffed," "absey-book"), with proverbs ("truth is truth," "have is have," "You are the hare of whom the proverb goes, / Whose valor plucks dead lions by the beard"), and with witty repartee and commentary. (In response to the Citizen's speech proposing a marriage between Louis, the Dauphin of France, and John's niece Blanche, for example, the Bastard comments: "Zounds, I was never so bethumped with words / Since I first called my brother's father Dad" [2.1.487–88].) The Bastard's language serves not only to characterize this unusually vital character but also to enrich a language world that is otherwise relatively one-dimensional. Unusual words that build the play's dramatic worlds will be explained in notes to the text.

Shakespeare's Sentences

In an English sentence, meaning is quite dependent on the place given each word. "The dog bit the boy" and "The boy bit the dog" mean very different things, even though the individual words are the same. Because English places such importance on the positions of words in sentences, on the way words are arranged, unusual arrangements can puzzle a reader. Shakespeare frequently shifts his sentences away from "normal" English arrangements—often to create the rhythm he seeks, sometimes to use a line's poetic rhythm to emphasize a particular word, sometimes to give a character his or her own speech patterns or to allow the character to speak in a special way. When we attend a good performance of the play, the actors will have worked out the sentence structures and will articulate the sentences so that the meaning is clear. In reading for yourself, do as the actor does. That is, when you become puzzled by a character's speech, check to see if words are being presented in an unusual sequence.

Shakespeare often, for example, rearranges subjects and verbs (i.e., instead of "He goes" we find "Goes he"). In *King John,* when Chatillion says "Thus, after greeting, speaks the King of France" (1.1.2), he is using such a construction. So is King John when he says "Here have we war for war" (1.1.19). The "normal" order would be "The King of France speaks" and "We have war for war." Shakespeare also frequently places the object before the subject and verb (i.e., instead of "I hit him," we might find "Him I hit"). King John's command "An honorable conduct let him have" (1.1.29) is an example of such an inversion, as is Robert Faulconbridge's "Th' advantage of his absence took the King" (1.1.105). The "normal" order would be "Let him have an honorable conduct" and "The King took th' advantage of his absence."

Inversions are not the only unusual sentence structures in Shakespeare's language. Often in his sentences words that would normally appear together are separated from each other. Again, this is often done to create a particular rhythm or to stress a particular word. Take, for example, Chatillion's "Philip of France, in right and true behalf / Of thy deceasèd brother Geoffrey's son, / Arthur Plantagenet, lays most lawful claim / To this fair island" (1.1.7–10). Here, the phrase "in right and true behalf of thy deceasèd brother Geoffrey's son, Arthur Plantagenet" separates subject ("Philip of France") from verb ("lays"). Or take Chatillion's description of King John's troops:

And all th' unsettled humors of the land—
Rash, inconsiderate, fiery voluntaries,

With ladies' faces and fierce dragons' spleens—
Have sold their fortunes at their native homes,
Bearing their birthrights proudly on their backs,
To make a hazard of new fortunes here.
(2.1.66–71)

In this sentence the subject ("all th' unsettled humors of the land") and verb ("Have sold") are separated from each other by two lines standing in apposition to the subject. In those two intervening lines the bare appositive ("voluntaries") is modified by a series of adjectives that precede it ("Rash, inconsiderate, fiery") and by the adjective phrase that follows it ("With ladies' faces and fierce dragons' spleens"). In order to create for yourself sentences that seem more like the English of everyday speech, you may wish to rearrange the words, putting together the word clusters ("Philip of France lays most lawful claim" and "all th' unsettled humors of the land have sold their fortunes"). You will usually find that the sentence will gain in clarity but will lose its rhythm or shift its emphasis.

Sometimes, rather than separating basic sentence elements, Shakespeare simply holds them back, delaying them until other material to which he wants to give greater emphasis has been presented. Shakespeare puts this kind of construction in the mouth of the Bastard as he abandons his rights as heir to Sir Robert Faulconbridge's lands, dissociating himself entirely from Faulconbridge and from Faulconbridge's son:

an if my brother had my shape
And I had his, Sir Robert's his like him,
And if my legs were two such riding-rods,
My arms such eel-skins stuffed, my face so thin
That in mine ear I durst not stick a rose,
Lest men should say "Look where three-farthings goes,"

And, to his shape, were heir to all this land,
Would I might never stir from off this place,
I would give it every foot to have this face.
(1.1.141–50)

Holding back the essential sentence elements, the subject and the verb ("I would give"), the Bastard first provides an extensive catalogue of the meager physical features that characterize both the late Sir Robert and his son Robert Faulconbridge (tiny "arms" like "eelskins stuffed," and thin "legs" like "riding-rods"). This prolonged contemptuous description provides the grounds for his final declaration in the last two lines of his speech: that is, if I am not telling the truth, may I never move from where I stand—the truth being that I would give every foot of this land in order to have the face that I have.

Finally, in many of Shakespeare's plays, sentences are sometimes complicated not because of unusual structures or interruptions but because Shakespeare omits words and parts of words that English sentences normally require. (In conversation, we, too, often omit words. We say, "Heard from him yet?" and our hearer supplies the missing "Have you.") Frequent reading of Shakespeare—and of other poets—trains us to supply the words missing from elliptical speeches. This play provides some examples in its very first scene, where King John and his mother, Queen Eleanor, have an exchange so laconic that it may alert an audience to their anxiety about John's ambiguous right to the throne. After Queen Eleanor rebukes John for going immediately to war rather than negotiating with France, John says, using the royal "we," "Our strong possession and our right for us." Queen Eleanor's response matches her son's in its abruptness: "Your strong possession much more than your right" (1.1.39–40). John's line can be expanded as follows: "My strong possession of the throne and my right to the throne are both on my side." And the meaning of Queen Eleanor's elliptical speech is immediately clear: "You will prevail only because you have 'strong possession,' for your right to the throne is not strong." The terseness of this conversation—which depends in part on the familiarity of various proverbs ("possession is nine points of the law," "possession is stronger than an ill charter," etc.)—suggests that John's right to rule is so uncertain that it will not bear extensive discussion, even between himself and his mother.

Shakespearean Wordplay

Shakespeare plays with language so often and so variously that entire books are written on the topic. Here we will mention only two kinds of wordplay, puns and metaphors. Puns in *King John* sometimes play on the multiple meanings of a single word and sometimes on the different meanings of words that sound the same. In the play's first scene, for example, Robert Faulconbridge invokes his father's will, the legal document that names him as heir, as his authority for challenging his brother Philip: "Shall then my father's will be of no force / To dispossess that child which is not his?" Philip, later to be called "the Bastard," replies, "Of no more force to dispossess me, sir, / Than was his will to get me, as I think" (1.1.133–36). Philip's response repeats Robert's use of the word *will,* but puns on the word's meaning of "intention" (with possible wordplay on such other meanings as "carnal desire" and "penis"). In the same scene, when King John wants to know why Robert claims land that by the law of primogeniture should belong to Philip, Philip responds: "Because he hath a half-face like my father. / With half that face would he have all my land" (1.1.95–96). The word "half-face" itself had several possible meanings—a thin or pinched face, an imperfect or unfinished face; or a face in profile, as on a coin. The word "face" in the following line then puns on a second meaning of "face," namely, impudence or insolence.

The Bastard's puns here are of a piece with the many other kinds of wordplay that give his role much of its exuberance and vitality, but puns are also used in many serious contexts in this play. When King Philip accuses John of having "done a rape / Upon the maiden virtue of the crown" (2.1.97–98), his words literally accuse John of having violently stolen the crown; but by attributing "maiden virtue" to the crown, Philip also puns on the word "rape" in its meaning of "sexual assault." And the Bastard, too, carries his use of puns over into serious contexts, as in his speech of advice to the kings at Angiers (2.1.389–412), where England and France are encouraged to "mount / Their battering cannon chargèd to the mouths, / Till their soul-fearing clamors have brawled down / The flinty ribs of this contemptuous city." Here "brawled down" means "driven or forced down by wrangling," but the association of the word "brawled" with the word "clamors" creates a pun on "brawled" as "quarreled noisily."

A metaphor is a play on words in which one object or idea is expressed as if it were something else, something with which it shares common features. For instance, in King John's instructions to Chatillion at line 1.1.27—"Be thou the trumpet of our wrath"—the French ambassador is equated with the musical instrument used to announce a king's approach. This metaphor is strikingly appropriate to the dramatic situation, since John intends to come to France full of "wrath" and hot on Chatillion's heels; indeed, Chatillion arrives in France in time to do little more than announce the approach of John and the army from England. When John arrives in France and finds Philip laying siege to the walled town of Angiers, John's warning to the citizens about the peril they face (2.1.216–41) is expressed in an extended personification—a specific kind of metaphor in which the nonhuman is expressed as if it were human. Here he compares Angiers to a vulnerable, and in some respects feminized, human being exposed to violation. He verbally endows the town first with an "eye," then with "eyes, your winking gates" (lines 217, 224) and with "threatened cheeks" (line 234). In lines 225–29 ("And, but for our approach, those sleeping stones, / That as a waist doth girdle you about, / By the compulsion of their ordinance / By this time from their fixèd beds of lime / Had been dishabited"), John presents the stones that make up the town wall as "sleeping" like people in "beds"; and in a simile (wordplay in which the comparison is made explicit through the use of the words "like" or "as"), he also dresses the personified town in human clothes by figuring the city's wall as encircling the city "as a waist"—that is, a girdle. (The word "dishabited," though primarily meaning "dislodged," continues the clothing comparison by playing on the sense of *habited* as "dressed, attired.") At line 237, the walls are described as threatened with "a shaking fever," and even the cannons aimed at Angiers are given human properties: with "bowels full of wrath," they are ready to "spit forth their . . . indignation" (lines 219–21).

Implied Stage Action

Finally, in reading Shakespeare's plays we should always remember that what we are reading is a performance script. The dialogue is written to be spoken by actors who, at the same time, are moving, gesturing, picking up objects, weeping, shaking their fists. Some stage action is described in what are called "stage directions"; some is suggested within the dialogue itself. We should always try to be alert to such signals as we stage the play in our imaginations.

Consider, for example, the stage action that is suggested in King John's speech addressed to Philip Faulconbridge at 1.1.166–67: "Kneel thou down Philip, but rise more great. / Arise Sir Richard and Plantagenet." We would expect, of course, that Philip would obey the king's order to "kneel"; the ensuing order to "Arise" confirms this expectation. The new name and new title in the command "Arise, Sir Richard" make us fairly certain that as Philip knelt before King John, the king dubbed him a knight by tapping him on the shoulder with a sword. This inference is confirmed a little later in the play when the newly knighted Bastard, Sir Richard, identifies himself to his mother as a knight: "Knight, knight, good mother. . . . / What, I am dubbed! I have it on my shoulder" (1.1.252–53). We have therefore inserted a stage direction into King John's speech at 1.1.166–67, which we print as

> Kneel thou down Philip, but rise more great.
> ⌜*Philip kneels. King John dubs him a knight,*
> *tapping him on the shoulder with his sword.*⌝
> Arise Sir Richard and Plantagenet.

This is one of several places where the dialogue allows us to be reasonably confident in adding, in brackets, a stage direction suggesting the action.

On other occasions in *King John*, the signals for stage action are not so clear. These occasions offer interpretative challenges in the absence of explicit stage directions in the Folio text. One such challenge arises with the entrance of King John together with King Philip in 3.1. Shortly after their entrance, Constance seems to make reference in a pun to the two kings' standing arm in arm when she says to King Philip "You came in arms to spill mine enemies' blood, / But now in arms you strengthen it with yours" (3.1.105–6), where the first "in arms" means "armed, furnished with weapons," and the second apparently means "arm in arm with King John." Later in the scene, there are several indications that the kings are clasping hands. The first of these comes when Cardinal Pandulph, who has excommunicated King John, insists that King Philip "Let go the hand of that arch-heretic" (199). Queen Eleanor counters by ordering King Philip "Do not let go thy hand" (202); and at line 271 Pandulph tells King Philip that he can more safely hold a tiger by the tooth "Than keep in peace that hand which thou dost hold," indicating that the hands are still clasped. By the end of the scene King Philip has dropped King John's hand, perhaps at line 272, when King Philip says "I may disjoin my hand, but not my faith"—or perhaps not until his declaration at lines 334–35, "England, I will fall from thee."

As these quotations indicate, there are a number of different ways of staging this action. Perhaps the kings enter the scene with their hands clasped, and perhaps they sustain the handclasp until King Philip's declaration "England, I will fall from thee." Or they may instead take each other's hands at some point after their entrance together; or they may take and release each other's hands intermittently in the scene. We have chosen to represent them in our stage directions as entering with their hands clasped (since there is no obvious place within the scene where the joining of hands seems an attractive option), and we have chosen to delay the stage direction for King Philip to drop King John's hand until King Philip says "England, I will fall from thee." However, we have, as is our usual practice, placed the stage directions of our own creation in half-square brackets to alert readers that these are only our interpretations, thereby encouraging readers and directors to feel free to work out their own versions of the action.

It is immensely rewarding to work carefully with Shakespeare's language so that the words, the sentences, the wordplay, and the implied stage action all become clear—as readers for the past four centuries have discovered. It may be more pleasurable to attend a good performance of a play—though not everyone has thought so. But the joy of being able to stage one of Shakespeare's plays in one's imagination, to return to passages that continue to yield further meanings (or further questions) the more one reads them—these are pleasures that, for many, rival (or at least augment) those of the performed text, and certainly make it worth considerable effort to "break the code" of Elizabethan poetic drama and let free the remarkable language that makes up a Shakespeare text.

Shakespeare's Life

Surviving documents that give us glimpses into the life of William Shakespeare show us a playwright, poet, and actor who grew up in the market town of Stratford-upon-Avon, spent his professional life in London, and returned to Stratford a wealthy landowner. He was born in April 1564, died in April 1616, and is buried inside the chancel of Holy Trinity Church in Stratford.

We wish we could know more about the life of the world's greatest dramatist. His plays and poems are testaments to his wide reading—especially to his knowledge of Virgil, Ovid, Plutarch, Holinshed's *Chronicles,* and the Bible—and to his mastery of the English language, but we can only speculate about his education. We know that the King's New School in Stratford-upon-Avon was considered excellent. The school was one of the English "grammar schools" established to educate young men, primarily in Latin grammar and literature. As in other schools of the time, students began their studies at the age of four or five in the attached "petty school," and there learned to read and write in English, studying primarily the catechism from the Book of Common Prayer. After two years in the petty school, students entered the lower form (grade) of the grammar school, where they began the serious study of Latin grammar and Latin texts that would occupy most of the remainder of their school days. (Several Latin texts that Shakespeare used repeatedly in writing his plays and poems were texts that schoolboys memorized and recited.) Latin comedies were introduced early in the lower form; in the upper form, which the boys entered at age ten or eleven, students wrote their own Latin orations and declamations, studied Latin historians and rhetoricians, and began the study of Greek using the Greek New Testament.

Since the records of the Stratford "grammar school" do not survive, we cannot prove that William Shakespeare attended the school; however, every indication (his father's position as an alderman and bailiff of Stratford, the playwright's own knowledge of the Latin classics, scenes in the plays that recall grammar-school experiences—for example, *The Merry Wives of Windsor,* 4.1) suggests that he did. We also lack generally accepted documentation about Shakespeare's life after his schooling ended and his professional life in London began. His marriage in 1582 (at age eighteen) to Anne

Hathaway and the subsequent births of his daughter Susanna (1583) and the twins Judith and Hamnet (1585) are recorded, but how he supported himself and where he lived are not known. Nor do we know when and why he left Stratford for the London theatrical world, nor how he rose to be the important figure in that world that he had become by the early 1590s.

We do know that by 1592 he had achieved some prominence in London as both an actor and a playwright. In that year was published a book by the playwright Robert Greene attacking an actor who had the audacity to write blank-verse drama and who was "in his own conceit [i.e., opinion] the only Shake-scene in a country." Since Greene's attack includes a parody of a line from one of Shakespeare's early plays, there is little doubt that it is Shakespeare to whom he refers, a "Shake-scene" who had aroused Greene's fury by successfully competing with university-educated dramatists like Greene himself. It was also in 1593 that Shakespeare became a published poet. In that year he published his long narrative poem *Venus and Adonis;* in 1594, he followed it with *The Rape of Lucrece.* Both poems were dedicated to the young earl of Southampton (Henry Wriothesley), who may have become Shakespeare's patron.

It seems no coincidence that Shakespeare wrote these narrative poems in years in which the theaters were closed because of the plague, a contagious epidemic disease that devastated the population of London. When the theaters reopened late in 1594, Shakespeare apparently resumed his double career of actor and playwright and began his long (and seemingly profitable) service as an acting-company shareholder. Records from the fall of 1594 show him to be a leading member of the Lord Chamberlain's Men. It was this company of actors, later named the King's Men, for whom he would be a principal actor, dramatist, and shareholder for the rest of his career.

So far as we can tell, that career spanned about twenty years. In the 1590s, he wrote his plays on English history as well as several comedies and at least two tragedies (*Titus Andronicus* and *Romeo and Juliet*). These histories, comedies, and tragedies are the plays credited to him in 1598 in a work, *Palladis Tamia,* that in one chapter compares English writers with "Greek, Latin, and Italian Poets." There the author, Francis Meres, claims that Shakespeare is comparable to the Latin dramatists Seneca for tragedy and Plautus for comedy, and calls him "the most excellent in both kinds for the stage." He also names him "Mellifluous and honey-tongued Shakespeare": "I say," writes Meres, "that the Muses would speak with Shakespeare's fine filed phrase, if they would speak English." Since Meres also mentions Shakespeare's "sugared sonnets among his private friends," it is assumed that many of Shakespeare's sonnets (not published until 1609) were also written in the 1590s.

In 1599, Shakespeare's company built a theater for themselves across the river from London, naming it the Globe. The plays that are considered by many to be Shakespeare's major tragedies (*Hamlet, Othello, King Lear,* and *Macbeth*) were written while the company was resident in this theater, as were such comedies as *Twelfth Night* and *Measure for Measure.* Many of Shakespeare's plays were performed at court (both for Queen Elizabeth I and, after her death in 1603, for King James I), some were presented at the Inns of Court (the residences of London's legal societies), and some were doubtless performed in other towns, at the universities, and at great houses when the King's Men went on tour; otherwise, his plays from 1599 to 1608 were, so far as we know, performed only at the Globe.

A stylized representation of the Globe theater.
From Claes Jansz Visscher, *Londinum florentissima Britanniae urbs* . . . [c. 1625].

Between 1608 and 1612, Shakespeare wrote several plays—among them *The Winter's Tale* and *The Tempest*—presumably for the company's new indoor Blackfriars theater, though the plays seem to have been performed also at the Globe and at court. Surviving documents describe a performance of *The Winter's Tale* in 1611 at the Globe, for example, and performances of *The Tempest* in 1611 and 1613 at the royal palace of Whitehall.

Shakespeare wrote very little after 1612, the year in which he probably wrote *King Henry VIII*. (It was at a performance of *Henry VIII* in 1613 that the Globe caught fire and burned to the ground.) Sometime between 1610 and 1613 he seems to have returned to live in Stratford-upon-Avon, where he owned a large house and considerable property, and where his wife and his two daughters and their husbands lived. (His son Hamnet had died in 1596.) During his professional years in London, Shakespeare had presumably derived income from the acting company's profits as well as from his own career as an actor, from the sale of his play manuscripts to the acting company, and, after 1599, from his shares as an owner of the Globe. It was presumably that income, carefully invested in land and other property, which made him the wealthy man that surviving documents show him to have become. It is also assumed that William Shakespeare's growing wealth and reputation played some part in inclining the crown, in 1596, to grant John Shakespeare, William's father, the coat of arms that he had so long sought. William Shakespeare died in Stratford on April 23, 1616 (according to the epitaph carved under his bust in Holy Trinity Church) and was buried on April 25. Seven years after his death, his collected plays were published as *Mr. William Shakespeares Comedies, Histories, & Tragedies* (the work now known as the First Folio).

The years in which Shakespeare wrote were among the most exciting in English history. Intellectually, the discovery, translation, and printing of Greek and Roman classics were making available a set of works and worldviews that interacted complexly with Christian texts and beliefs. The result was a questioning, a vital intellectual ferment, that provided energy for the period's amazing dramatic and literary output and that fed directly into Shakespeare's plays. The Ghost in *Hamlet,* for example, is wonderfully complicated in part because he is a figure from Roman tragedy—the spirit of the dead returning to seek revenge—who at the same time inhabits a Christian hell (or purgatory); Hamlet's description of humankind reflects at one moment the Neoplatonic wonderment at mankind ("What a piece of work is a man!") and, at the next, the Christian disparagement of human sinners ("And yet, to me, what is this quintessence of dust?").

As intellectual horizons expanded, so also did geographical and cosmological horizons. New worlds—both North and South America—were explored, and in them were found human beings who lived and worshiped in ways radically different from those of Renaissance Europeans and Englishmen. The universe during these years also seemed to shift and expand. Copernicus had earlier theorized that the earth was not the center of the cosmos but revolved as a planet around the sun. Galileo's telescope, created in 1609, allowed scientists to see that Copernicus had been correct; the universe was not organized with the earth at the center, nor was it so nicely circumscribed as people had, until that time, thought. In terms of expanding horizons, the impact of these discoveries on people's beliefs—religious, scientific, and philosophical—cannot be overstated.

London, too, rapidly expanded and changed during the years (from the early 1590s to around 1610) that

Shakespeare lived there. London—the center of England's government, its economy, its royal court, its overseas trade—was, during these years, becoming an exciting metropolis, drawing to it thousands of new citizens every year. Troubled by overcrowding, by poverty, by recurring epidemics of the plague, London was also a mecca for the wealthy and the aristocratic, and for those who sought advancement at court, or power in government or finance or trade. One hears in Shakespeare's plays the voices of London—the struggles for power, the fear of venereal disease, the language of buying and selling. One hears as well the voices of Stratford-upon-Avon—references to the nearby Forest of Arden, to sheepherding, to small-town gossip, to village fairs and markets. Part of the richness of Shakespeare's work is the influence felt there of the various worlds in which he lived: the world of metropolitan London, the world of small-town and rural England, the world of the theater, and the worlds of craftsmen and shepherds.

That Shakespeare inhabited such worlds we know from surviving London and Stratford documents, as well as from the evidence of the plays and poems themselves. From such records we can sketch the dramatist's life. We know from his works that he was a voracious reader. We know from legal and business documents that he was a multifaceted theater man who became a wealthy landowner. We know a bit about his family life and a fair amount about his legal and financial dealings. Most scholars today depend upon such evidence as they draw their picture of the world's greatest playwright. Such, however, has not always been the case. Until the late eighteenth century, the William Shakespeare who lived in most biographies was the creation of legend and tradition. This was the Shakespeare who was supposedly caught poaching

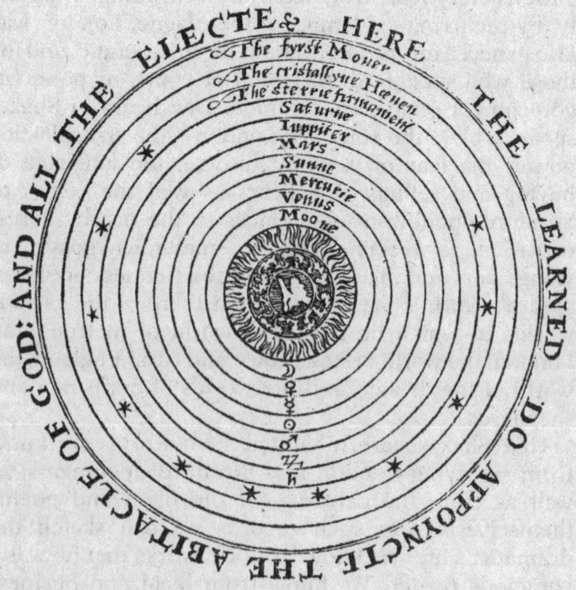

Ptolemaic universe.
From Leonard Digges, *A prognostication* . . . [1556].

deer at Charlecote, the estate of Sir Thomas Lucy close by Stratford; this was the Shakespeare who fled from Sir Thomas' vengeance and made his way in London by taking care of horses outside a playhouse; this was the Shakespeare who reportedly could barely read but whose natural gifts were extraordinary, whose father was a butcher who allowed his gifted son sometimes to help in the butcher shop, where William supposedly killed calves "in a high style," making a speech for the occasion. It was this legendary William Shakespeare whose Falstaff (in *1* and *2 Henry IV*) so pleased Queen Elizabeth that she demanded a play about Falstaff in love, and demanded that it be written in fourteen days (hence the existence of *The Merry Wives of Windsor*). It was this legendary Shakespeare who reached the top of his acting career in the roles of the Ghost in *Hamlet* and old Adam in *As You Like It*—and who died of a fever contracted by drinking too hard at "a merry meeting" with the poets Michael Drayton and Ben Jonson. This legendary Shakespeare is a rambunctious, undisciplined man, as attractively "wild" as his plays were seen by earlier generations to be. Unfortunately, there is no trace of evidence to support these wonderful stories.

Perhaps in response to the disreputable Shakespeare of legend—or perhaps in response to the fragmentary and, for some, all-too-ordinary Shakespeare documented by surviving records—some people since the mid-nineteenth century have argued that William Shakespeare could not have written the plays that bear his name. These persons have put forward some dozen names as more likely authors, among them Queen Elizabeth, Sir Francis Bacon, Edward de Vere (earl of Oxford), and Christopher Marlowe. Such attempts to find what for these people is a more believable author of the plays is a tribute to the regard in which the plays are held. Unfortunately for their claims, the documents that exist that provide evidence for the facts of Shakespeare's life tie him inextricably to the body of plays and poems that bear his name. Unlikely as it seems to those who want the works to have been written by an aristocrat, a university graduate, or an "important" person, the plays and poems seem clearly to have been produced by a man from Stratford-upon-Avon with a very good "grammar-school" education and a life of experience in London and in the world of the London theater. How this particular man produced the works that dominate the cultures of much of the world almost four hundred years after his death is one of life's mysteries—and one that will continue to tease our imaginations as we continue to delight in his plays and poems.

Shakespeare's Theater

The actors of Shakespeare's time are known to have performed plays in a great variety of locations. They played at court (that is, in the great halls of such royal residences as Whitehall, Hampton Court, and Greenwich); they played in halls at the universities of Oxford and Cambridge, and at the Inns of Court (the residences in London of the legal societies); and they also played in the private houses of great lords and civic officials. Sometimes acting companies went on tour from London into the provinces, often (but not only) when outbreaks of bubonic plague in the capital forced the closing of theaters to reduce the possibility of contagion in crowded audiences. In the provinces the actors usually staged their plays in churches (until around 1600) or in guildhalls. While surviving records show only a handful of occasions when actors played at inns while on tour, London inns were important playing places up until the 1590s.

The building of theaters in London had begun only shortly before Shakespeare wrote his first plays in the 1590s. These theaters were of two kinds: outdoor or public playhouses that could accommodate large numbers of playgoers, and indoor or private theaters for much smaller audiences. What is usually regarded as the first London outdoor public playhouse was called simply the Theatre. James Burbage—the father of Richard Burbage, who was perhaps the most famous actor in Shakespeare's company—built it in 1576 in an area north of the city of London called Shoreditch. Among the more famous of the other public playhouses that capitalized on the new fashion were the Curtain and the Fortune (both also built north of the city), the Rose, the Swan, the Globe, and the Hope (all located on the Bankside, a region just across the Thames south of the city of London). All these playhouses had to be built outside the jurisdiction of the city of London because many civic officials were hostile to the performance of drama and repeatedly petitioned the royal council to abolish it.

The theaters erected on the Bankside (a region under the authority of the Church of England, whose head was the monarch) shared the neighborhood with houses of prostitution and with the Paris Garden, where the blood sports of bearbaiting and bullbaiting were carried on. There may have been no clear distinction between playhouses and buildings for such sports, for we know that the Hope was used for both plays and baiting and that Philip Henslowe, owner of the Rose and, later, partner in the ownership of the Fortune, was also a partner in a monopoly on baiting. All these forms of entertainment were easily accessible to Lon-

"As in a theater, whence they gape and point . . ."
(2.1.391)
From [William Alabaster,] *Roxana tragœdia* . . . (1632).

doners by boat across the Thames or over London Bridge.

Evidently Shakespeare's company prospered on the Bankside. They moved there in 1599. Threatened by difficulties in renewing the lease on the land where their first theater (the Theatre) had been built, Shakespeare's company took advantage of the Christmas holiday in 1598 to dismantle the Theatre and transport its timbers across the Thames to the Bankside, where, in 1599, these timbers were used in the building of the Globe. The weather in late December 1598 is recorded as having been especially harsh. It was so cold that the Thames was "nigh [nearly] frozen," and there was heavy snow. Perhaps the weather aided Shakespeare's company in eluding their landlord, the snow hiding their activity and the freezing of the Thames allowing them to slide the timbers across to the Bankside without paying tolls for repeated trips over London Bridge. Attractive as this narrative is, it remains just as likely that the heavy snow hampered transport of the timbers in wagons through the London streets to the river. It also must be remembered that the Thames was, according to report, only "nigh frozen" and therefore as impassable as it ever was. Whatever the precise circumstances of this fascinating event in English theater history, Shakespeare's company was able to begin playing at their new Globe theater on the Bankside in 1599. After the first Globe burned down in 1613 during the staging of Shakespeare's *Henry VIII* (its thatch roof was set alight by cannon fire called for by the performance), Shakespeare's company immediately rebuilt on the same location. The second Globe seems to have been a grander structure than its predecessor. It remained in use until the beginning of the English Civil War in 1642, when Parliament officially closed the theaters. Soon thereafter it was pulled down.

The public theaters of Shakespeare's time were very different buildings from our theaters today. First of all, they were open-air playhouses. As recent excavations of the Rose and the Globe confirm, some were polygonal or roughly circular in shape; the Fortune, however, was square. The most recent estimates of their size put the diameter of these buildings at 72 feet (the Rose) to 100 feet (the Globe), but we know that they held vast audiences of two or three thousand, who must have been squeezed together quite tightly. Some of these spectators paid extra to sit or stand in the two or three levels of roofed galleries that extended, on the upper levels, all the way around the theater and surrounded an open space. In this space were the stage and, perhaps, the tiring house (what we would call dressing rooms), as well as the so-called yard. In the yard stood the spectators who chose to pay less, the ones whom Hamlet contemptuously called "groundlings." For a roof they had only the sky, and so they were exposed to all kinds of weather. They stood on a floor that was sometimes made of mortar and sometimes of ash mixed with the shells of hazelnuts. The latter provided a porous and therefore dry footing for the crowd, and the shells may have been more comfortable to stand on because they were not as hard as mortar. Availability of shells may not have been a problem if hazelnuts were a favorite food for Shakespeare's audiences to munch on as they watched his plays. Archaeologists who are today unearthing the remains of theaters from this period have discovered quantities of these nutshells on theater sites.

Unlike the yard, the stage itself was covered by a roof. Its ceiling, called "the heavens," is thought to have been elaborately painted to depict the sun, moon, stars, and planets. Just how big the stage was remains hard to determine. We have a single sketch of part of the interior of the Swan. A Dutchman named Johannes de Witt visited this theater around 1596 and sent a sketch of it back to his friend, Arend van Buchel. Because van Buchel found de Witt's letter and sketch of interest, he copied both into a book. It is van Buchel's copy, adapted, it seems, to the shape and size of the page in his book, that survives. In this sketch, the stage appears to be a large rectangular platform that thrusts far out into the yard, perhaps even as far as the center of the circle formed by the surrounding galleries. This drawing, combined with the specifications for the size of the stage in the building contract for the Fortune, has led scholars to conjecture that the stage on which Shakespeare's plays were performed must have measured approximately 43 feet in width and 27 feet in depth, a vast acting area. But the digging up of a large part of the Rose by archaeologists has provided evidence of a quite different stage design. The Rose stage was a platform tapered at the corners and much shallower than what seems to be depicted in the van Buchel sketch. Indeed, its measurements seem to be about 37.5 feet across at its widest point and only 15.5 feet deep. Because the surviving indications of stage size and design differ from each other so much, it is possible that the stages in other theaters, like the Theatre, the Curtain, and the Globe (the outdoor playhouses where we know that Shakespeare's plays were performed), were different from those at both the Swan and the Rose.

After about 1608 Shakespeare's plays were staged not only at the Globe but also at an indoor or private playhouse in Blackfriars. This theater had been constructed in 1596 by James Burbage in an upper hall of a former Dominican priory or monastic house. Although Henry VIII had dissolved all English monasteries in the 1530s (shortly after he had founded the Church of

England), the area remained under church, rather than hostile civic, control. The hall that Burbage had purchased and renovated was a large one in which Parliament had once met. In the private theater that he constructed, the stage, lit by candles, was built across the narrow end of the hall, with boxes flanking it. The rest of the hall offered seating room only. Because there was no provision for standing room, the largest audience it could hold was less than a thousand, or about a quarter of what the Globe could accommodate. Admission to Blackfriars was correspondingly more expensive. Instead of a penny to stand in the yard at the Globe, it cost a minimum of sixpence to get into Blackfriars. The best seats at the Globe (in the Lords' Room in the gallery above and behind the stage) cost sixpence; but the boxes flanking the stage at Blackfriars were half a crown, or five times sixpence. Some spectators who were particularly interested in displaying themselves paid even more to sit on stools on the Blackfriars stage.

Whether in the outdoor or indoor playhouses, the stages of Shakespeare's time were different from ours. They were not separated from the audience by the dropping of a curtain between acts and scenes. Therefore the playwrights of the time had to find other ways of signaling to the audience that one scene (to be imagined as occurring in one location at a given time) had ended and the next (to be imagined at perhaps a different location at a later time) had begun. The customary way used by Shakespeare and many of his contemporaries was to have everyone onstage exit at the end of one scene and have one or more different characters enter to begin the next. In a few cases, where characters remain onstage from one scene to another, the dialogue or stage action makes the change of location clear, and the characters are generally to be imagined as having moved from one place to another. For example, in *Romeo and Juliet,* Romeo and his friends remain onstage in Act 1 from scene 4 to scene 5, but they are represented as having moved between scenes from the street that leads to Capulet's house into Capulet's house itself. The new location is signaled in part by the appearance onstage of Capulet's servingmen carrying napkins, something they would not take into the streets. Playwrights had to be quite resourceful in the use of hand properties, like the napkin, or in the use of dialogue to specify where the action was taking place in their plays because, in contrast to most of today's theaters, the playhouses of Shakespeare's time did not use movable scenery to dress the stage and make the setting precise. As another consequence of this difference, however, the playwrights of Shakespeare's time did not have to specify exactly where the action of their plays was set when they did not choose to do so, and much of the action of their plays is tied to no specific place.

Usually Shakespeare's stage is referred to as a "bare stage," to distinguish it from the stages of the last two or three centuries with their elaborate sets. But the stage in Shakespeare's time was not completely bare. Philip Henslowe, owner of the Rose, lists in his inventory of stage properties a rock, three tombs, and two mossy banks. Stage directions in plays of the time also call for such things as thrones (or "states"), banquets (presumably tables with plaster replicas of food on them), and beds and tombs to be pushed onto the stage. Thus the stage often held more than the actors.

The actors did not limit their performing to the stage alone. Occasionally they went beneath the stage, as the Ghost appears to do in the first act of *Hamlet.* From there they could emerge onto the stage through a trapdoor. They could retire behind the hangings across the back of the stage (or the front of the tiring house), as, for example, the actor playing Polonius does when he hides behind the arras. Sometimes the hangings could be drawn back during a performance to "discover" one or more actors behind them. When performance required that an actor appear "above," as when Juliet is imagined to stand at the window of her chamber in the famous and misnamed "balcony scene," then the actor probably climbed the stairs to the gallery over the back of the stage and temporarily shared it with some of the spectators. The stage was also provided with ropes and winches so that actors could descend from, and reascend to, the "heavens."

Perhaps the greatest difference between dramatic performances in Shakespeare's time and ours was that in Shakespeare's England the roles of women were played by boys. (Some of these boys grew up to take male roles in their maturity.) There were no women in the acting companies, only in the audience. It had not always been so in the history of the English stage. There are records of women on English stages in the thirteenth and fourteenth centuries, two hundred years before Shakespeare's plays were performed. After the accession of James I in 1603, the queen of England and her ladies took part in entertainments at court called masques, and with the reopening of the theaters in 1660 at the restoration of Charles II, women again took their place on the public stage.

The chief competitors for the companies of adult actors such as the one to which Shakespeare belonged and for which he wrote were companies of exclusively boy actors. The competition was most intense in the early 1600s. There were then two principal children's companies: the Children of Paul's (the choirboys from St. Paul's Cathedral, whose private playhouse was near the cathedral); and the Children of the Chapel Royal (the choirboys from the monarch's private chapel, who performed at the Blackfriars theater built by Burbage in 1596, which Shakespeare's company had been stopped from using by local residents who objected to crowds). In *Hamlet* Shakespeare writes of "an aerie [nest] of children, little eyases [hawks], that cry out on the top of question and are most tyrannically clapped for 't. These are now the fashion and . . . berattle the common stages [attack the public theaters]." In the long run, the adult actors prevailed. The Children of Paul's dissolved around 1606. By about 1608 the Children of the Chapel Royal had been forced to stop playing at the Blackfriars theater, which was then taken over by the King's Men, Shakespeare's own troupe.

Acting companies and theaters of Shakespeare's time were organized in different ways. For example, Philip Henslowe owned the Rose and leased it to companies of actors, who paid him from their takings. Henslowe would act as manager of these companies, initially paying playwrights for their plays and buying properties, recovering his outlay from the actors. Shakespeare's company, however, managed itself, with the principal actors, Shakespeare among them, having the status of "sharers" and the right to a share in the takings, as well as the responsibility for a part of the expenses. Five of the sharers themselves, Shakespeare among them, owned the Globe. As actor, as sharer in an acting company and in ownership of theaters, and as playwright, Shakespeare was about as involved in the theatrical industry as one could imagine. Although Shakespeare and his fellows prospered, their status under the law was conditional upon the protection of powerful patrons. "Common players"—those who did not have patrons or masters—were classed in the language of the law with "vagabonds and sturdy beggars." So the actors had to secure for themselves the official rank of servants of patrons. Among the patrons under whose protection Shakespeare's company worked were the lord chamberlain and, after the accession of King James in 1603, the king himself.

We are now perhaps on the verge of learning a great deal more about the theaters in which Shakespeare and his contemporaries performed—or at least of opening up new questions about them. Already about 70 percent of the Rose has been excavated, as has about 10 percent of the second Globe, the one built in 1614. It is to be hoped that soon more will be available for study. These are exciting times for students of Shakespeare's stage.

The Publication of Shakespeare's Plays

Eighteen of Shakespeare's plays found their way into print during the playwright's lifetime, but there is nothing to suggest that he took any interest in their publication. These eighteen appeared separately in editions called quartos. Their pages were not much larger than the one you are now reading, and these little books were sold unbound for a few pence. The earliest of the quartos that still survive were printed in 1594, the year that both *Titus Andronicus* and a version of the play now called *2 King Henry VI* became available. While almost every one of these early quartos displays on its title page the name of the acting company that performed the play, only about half provide the name of the playwright, Shakespeare. The first quarto edition to bear the name Shakespeare on its title page is *Love's Labor's Lost* of 1598. A few of these quartos were popular with the book-buying public of Shakespeare's lifetime; for example, quarto *Richard II* went through five editions between 1597 and 1615. But most of the quartos were far from best-sellers; *Love's Labor's Lost* (1598), for instance, was not reprinted in quarto until 1631. After Shakespeare's death, two more of his plays appeared in quarto format: *Othello* in 1622 and *The Two Noble Kinsmen,* coauthored with John Fletcher, in 1634.

In 1623, seven years after Shakespeare's death, *Mr. William Shakespeares Comedies, Histories, & Tragedies* was published. This printing offered readers in a single book thirty-six of the thirty-eight plays now thought to have been written by Shakespeare, including eighteen that had never been printed before. And it offered them in a style that was then reserved for serious literature and scholarship. The plays were arranged in double columns on pages nearly a foot high. This large page size is called "folio," as opposed to the smaller "quarto," and the 1623 volume is usually called the Shakespeare First Folio. It is reputed to have sold for the lordly price of a pound. (One copy at the Folger Library is marked fifteen shillings—that is, three-quarters of a pound.)

In a preface to the First Folio entitled "To the great Variety of Readers," two of Shakespeare's former fellow actors in the King's Men, John Heminge and Henry Condell, wrote that they themselves had collected their dead companion's plays. They suggested that they had seen his own papers: "we have scarce received from him a blot in his papers." The title page of the Folio declared that the plays within it had been printed "according to the True Original Copies." Comparing the Folio to the quartos, Heminge and Condell disparaged the quartos, advising their readers that "before you were abused with divers stolen and surreptitious copies, maimed, and deformed by the frauds and stealths of injurious impostors." Many Shakespeareans of the eighteenth and nineteenth centuries believed Heminge and Condell and regarded the Folio plays as superior to anything in the quartos.

Once we begin to examine the Folio plays in detail, it becomes less easy to take at face value the word of Heminge and Condell about the superiority of the Folio texts. For example, of the first nine plays in the Folio (one-quarter of the entire collection), four were essentially reprinted from earlier quarto printings that Heminge and Condell had disparaged; and four have now been identified as printed from copies written in the hand of a professional scribe of the 1620s named Ralph Crane; the ninth, *The Comedy of Errors,* was apparently also printed from a manuscript, but one whose origin cannot be readily identified. Evidently then, eight of the first nine plays in the First Folio were not printed, in spite of what the Folio title page announces, "according to the True Original Copies," or Shakespeare's own papers, and the source of the ninth is unknown. Since today's editors have been forced to treat Heminge and Condell's pronouncements with skepticism, they must choose whether to base their own editions upon quartos or the Folio on grounds other than Heminge and Condell's story of where the quarto and Folio versions originated.

Editors have often fashioned their own narratives to explain what lies behind the quartos and Folio. They have said that Heminge and Condell meant to criticize only a few of the early quartos, the ones that offer much shorter and sometimes quite different, often garbled, versions of plays. Among the examples of these are the 1600 quarto of *Henry V* (the Folio offers a much fuller version) or the 1603 *Hamlet* quarto (in 1604 a different, much longer form of the play got into print as a quarto).

Early-twentieth-century editors speculated that these questionable texts were produced when someone in the audience took notes from the plays' dialogue during performances and then employed "hack poets" to fill out the notes. The poor results were then sold to a publisher and presented in print as Shakespeare's plays. More recently this story has given way to another in which the shorter versions are said to be re-creations from memory of Shakespeare's plays by actors who wanted to stage them in the provinces but lacked manuscript copies. Most of the quartos offer much better texts than these so-called bad quartos. Indeed, in most of the quartos we find texts that are at least equal to or better than what is printed in the Folio. Many Shakespeare enthusiasts persuaded themselves that most of the quartos were set into type directly from Shakespeare's own papers, although there is nothing on which to base this conclusion except the desire for it to be true. Thus speculation continues about how the Shakespeare plays got to be printed. All that we have are the printed texts.

The book collector who was most successful in bringing together copies of the quartos and the First Folio was Henry Clay Folger, founder of the Folger Shakespeare Library in Washington, D.C. While it is estimated that there survive around the world only about 230 copies of the First Folio, Mr. Folger was able to acquire more than seventy-five copies, as well as a large number of fragments, for the library that bears his name. He also amassed a substantial number of quartos. For example, only fourteen copies of the First Quarto of *Love's Labor's Lost* are known to exist, and three are at the Folger Shakespeare Library. As a consequence of Mr. Folger's labors, scholars visiting the Folger Library have been able to learn a great deal about sixteenth- and seventeenth-century printing and, particularly, about the printing of Shakespeare's plays. And Mr. Folger did not stop at the First Folio, but collected many copies of later editions of Shakespeare, beginning with the Second Folio (1632), the Third (1663–64), and the Fourth (1685). Each of these later folios was based on its immediate predecessor and was edited anonymously. The first editor of Shakespeare whose name we know was Nicholas Rowe, whose first edition came out in 1709. Mr. Folger collected this edition and many, many more by Rowe's successors.

An Introduction to This Text

King John was first printed in the 1623 collection of Shakespeare's plays now known as the First Folio. The present edition is based directly upon that printing.* There was an earlier dramatic version of the events in *King John*. This two-part play, called *The Troublesome Raigne of Iohn, King of England,* was first published in 1591. While the action of *The Troublesome Raigne* is, in most respects, the image of the action in Shakespeare's *King John,* there is practically no verbal resemblance between the two plays. They also differ in that Shakespeare's version omits most of the savage satire on Roman Catholicism that is a large part of *The Troublesome Raigne*. As is always the case with things Shakespearean, there has been controversy over the possibility of reconstructing the chronology and rela-

*We have also consulted the computerized text of the First Folio provided by the Text Archive of the Oxford University Computing Centre, to which we are grateful.

tionship of *King John* and *The Troublesome Raigne.* In the opinion of most scholars, the 1591 play served as Shakespeare's source; other scholars believe that the 1591 play somehow derives from Shakespeare's text—perhaps, according to a small minority of scholars, through the agency of actors' memories of Shakespeare's play. Because there is no way to verify any of this speculation, it cannot be used in the editing of the First Folio text of *King John.* (For more on *King John* and *The Troublesome Raigne,* see our "Further Reading" under the entry "Bullough," p. 274.)

For the convenience of the reader, we have modernized the punctuation and the spelling of the Folio. Sometimes we go so far as to modernize certain old forms of words; for example, usually when *a* means *he,* we change it to *he;* we change *mo* to *more,* and *ye* to *you.* But it is not our practice in editing any of the plays to modernize words that sound distinctly different from modern forms. For example, when the early printed texts read *sith* or *apricocks* or *porpentine,* we have not modernized to *since, apricots, porcupine.* When the forms *an, and,* or *and if* appear instead of the modern form *if,* we have reduced *and* to *an* but have not changed any of these forms to their modern equivalent, *if.* We also modernize and, where necessary, correct passages in foreign languages, unless an error in the early printed text can be reasonably explained as a joke.

Whenever we change the wording of the First Folio or add anything to its stage directions, we mark the change by enclosing it in superior half-brackets (⌜ ⌝). We want our readers to be immediately aware when we have intervened. (Only when we correct an obvious typographical error in the First Folio does the change not get marked.) Whenever we change either the First Folio's wording or its punctuation so that meaning changes, we list the change in the textual notes at the back of the book, even if all we have done is fix an obvious error.

We regularize spellings of a number of the proper names, as is the usual practice in editions of the play. For example, the Folio sometimes calls *Eleanor* by the name "Elinor" but we use the spelling "Eleanor" throughout the text.

This edition differs from many earlier ones in its efforts to aid the reader in imagining the play as a performance rather than as a series of actual events. Thus stage directions that we as editors add to the play's text are written, like those printed in the Folio, with reference to the stage. For example, the Folio's stage directions sometimes specify that armies meeting each other should enter by separate stage doors: "*Enter the two Kings with their powers, at seuerall* [i.e., separate] *doores*" (2.1.347 SD). However, when the King of France and his army meet the Duke of Austria with his forces at the beginning of the second act, it is clear that they must enter separately, but the Folio does not specifically indicate such a staging. In this case, to aid the reader in imagining the play as a performance, we supplement the Folio's stage directions: "*Enter, before Angiers,* ⌜*at one side, with Forces,*⌝ *Philip King of France, Louis* ⌜*the*⌝ *Dauphin, Constance, Arthur,* ⌜*and Attendants; at the other side, with Forces,*⌝ *Austria,* ⌜*wearing a lion's skin.*⌝ Whenever it is reasonably certain, in our view, that a speech is accompanied by a particular action, we provide a stage direction describing the action, setting the added direction in brackets to signal that it is not found in the Folio. (Occasional exceptions to this rule occur when the action is so obvious that to add a stage direction would insult the reader.) Stage directions for the entrance of a character in mid-scene are, with rare exceptions, placed so that they immediately precede the character's participation in the scene, even though these entrances may appear somewhat earlier in the early printed texts. Whenever we move a stage direction, we record this change in the textual notes. Latin stage directions (e.g., *Exeunt*) are translated into English (e.g., *They exit*).

We expand the often severely abbreviated forms of names used as speech headings in early printed texts into the full names of the characters. We also regularize the speakers' names in speech headings, using only a single designation for each character, even though the early printed texts sometimes use a variety of designations. Variations in the speech headings of the early printed texts are recorded in the textual notes.

In the present edition, as well, we mark with a dash any change of address within a speech, unless a stage direction intervenes. When the *-ed* ending of a word is to be pronounced, we mark it with an accent. Like editors for the past two centuries, we print metrically linked lines in the following way:

KING PHILIP
'Tis France, for England.
KING JOHN   England, for itself.
(2.1.210–11)

However, when there are a number of short verse-lines that can be linked in more than one way, we do not, with rare exceptions, indent any of them.

The Explanatory Notes

The notes that appear on the pages facing the text are designed to provide readers with the help that they may need to enjoy the play. Whenever the meaning of a word in the text is not readily accessible in a good contemporary dictionary, we offer the meaning in a note. Sometimes we provide a note even when the relevant meaning is to be found in the dictionary but when the word has acquired since Shakespeare's time other potentially confusing meanings. In our notes, we try to offer modern synonyms for Shakespeare's words. We also try to indicate to the reader the connection between the word in the play and the modern synonym. For example, Shakespeare sometimes uses the word *head* to mean *source*, but, for modern readers, there may be no connection evident between these two words. We provide the connection by explaining Shakespeare's usage as follows: "**head**: fountainhead, source." On some occasions, a whole phrase or clause needs explanation. Then we rephrase in our own words the difficult passage, and add at the end synonyms for individual words in the passage. When scholars have been unable to determine the meaning of a word or phrase, we acknowledge the uncertainty.

The Life and Death of

KING JOHN

Early Descendants of William the Conqueror

(Names of kings appear in bold, with the dates of their reigns in brackets)

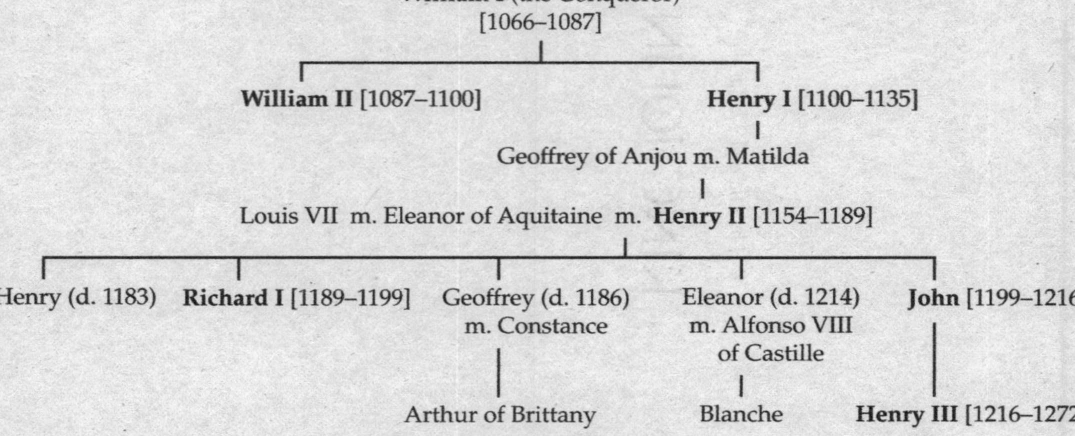

Characters in the Play

JOHN, King of England, with dominion over assorted Continental territories
QUEEN ELEANOR, King John's mother, widow of King Henry II
BLANCHE of Spain, niece to King John
PRINCE HENRY, son to King John

CONSTANCE, widow of Geoffrey, King John's elder brother
ARTHUR, Duke of Brittany, her son

KING PHILIP II of France
LOUIS THE DAUPHIN, his son
DUKE OF AUSTRIA (also called LIMOGES)
CHATILLION, ambassador from France to King John
COUNT MELUN
A FRENCH HERALD

CARDINAL PANDULPH, Papal Legate

LADY FAULCONBRIDGE
The BASTARD, PHILIP FAULCONBRIDGE, her son by King Richard I
ROBERT FAULCONBRIDGE, her son by Sir Robert Faulconbridge
JAMES GURNEY, her servant

HUBERT, supporter of King John

EARL OF SALISBURY
EARL OF PEMBROKE
EARL OF ESSEX
LORD BIGOT
} *English nobles*

A CITIZEN of Angiers
PETER of Pomfret, a Prophet
AN ENGLISH HERALD
EXECUTIONERS

English MESSENGER, French MESSENGER, Sheriff, Lords, Soldiers, Attendants

The Life and Death of

KING JOHN

ACT 1

1.1 John, King of England, is told by a messenger from the King of France that the territories held by John should belong instead to John's nephew Arthur. When John refuses to be swayed by this message, he is threatened with war; John counters with a warning that he will attack France first. John then judges a quarrel between Robert and Philip Faulconbridge that concludes with Philip's decision to acknowledge the dead King Richard I as his natural father. Philip is knighted as Sir Richard Plantagenet and prepares to go with King John and the English army to France; Sir Richard's mother, Lady Faulconbridge, confesses to him that Richard I was indeed his father.

---

0 SD. **the Chatillion of France:** See longer note, page 211.

1. **would France:** i.e., does the king of **France** want

3. **In my behavior:** in my person; through me

4. **borrowed majesty:** For King John, Prince Arthur, and "**borrowed majesty,**" see Historical Background 1, page 231.

6. **embassy:** message brought by an ambassador

9. **Plantagenet:** This surname was applied to the royal line descended from Geoffrey of Anjou, John's grandfather and Arthur's great-grandfather. The name **Plantagenet** was Geoffrey of Anjou's nickname, alluding to his wearing a sprig of broom (Latin: *planta genista*) in his cap.

10. **territories:** lands under the dominion of a ruler (See longer note, page 211.)

(continued)

ACT 1

Scene 1

Enter King John, Queen Eleanor, Pembroke, Essex, and Salisbury, with the Chatillion of France.

KING JOHN
Now say, Chatillion, what would France with us?

CHATILLION
Thus, after greeting, speaks the King of France
In my behavior to the majesty,
The borrowed majesty, of England here.

QUEEN ELEANOR
A strange beginning: "borrowed majesty"!

KING JOHN
Silence, good mother. Hear the embassy.

CHATILLION
Philip of France, in right and true behalf
Of thy deceasèd brother Geoffrey's son,
Arthur Plantagenet, lays most lawful claim
To this fair island and the territories,
To Ireland, Poitiers, Anjou, Touraine, Maine,
Desiring thee to lay aside the sword
Which sways usurpingly these several titles,
And put the same into young Arthur's hand,
Thy nephew and right royal sovereign.

KING JOHN
What follows if we disallow of this?

11. **Poitiers, Anjou, Touraine, Maine:** regions on the Continent (now part of France) under John's dominion (Elizabethans used **Poitiers** to refer to the province of Poitou as well as to the city of Poitiers.) See map, page xii.

12. **sword: sword** of state, a symbol of authority

13. **sways usurpingly:** i.e., rules in the hand of a usurper; **several:** individual, separate

15. **right:** (1) very; (2) true, legitimate

16. **disallow of:** reject

17. **proud:** mighty, forceful; **control:** domination, command

19. **blood for blood:** Proverbial: "**Blood** will have **blood**."

20. **Controlment:** control (See note to line 17.)

22. **my embassy:** my power as ambassador; the message I bring you

24. **as lightning:** Proverbial: "as swift **as lightning.**"

25. **report:** (1) repeat your message; (2) resound (like **thunder** or like **cannon** [line 26])

27. **Be thou the trumpet of:** i.e., proclaim

28. **sullen:** gloomy, dark

29. **conduct:** escort (to guarantee him the privilege of safe-conduct)

32. **How that:** i.e., **that**

33. **France:** (1) the king of **France;** (2) the country of **France**

34. **party:** side, interest

35. **prevented:** anticipated; **made whole:** healed, repaired

36. **arguments of love:** i.e., friendly discussions; or, tokens or manifestations of friendship

(continued)

CHATILLION
The proud control of fierce and bloody war,
To enforce these rights so forcibly withheld.

KING JOHN
Here have we war for war and blood for blood,
Controlment for controlment: so answer France.

CHATILLION
Then take my king's defiance from my mouth,
The farthest limit of my embassy.

KING JOHN
Bear mine to him, and so depart in peace.
Be thou as lightning in the eyes of France,
For ere thou canst report, I will be there;
The thunder of my cannon shall be heard.
So, hence. Be thou the trumpet of our wrath
And sullen presage of your own decay.—
An honorable conduct let him have.
Pembroke, look to 't.—Farewell, Chatillion.

Chatillion and Pembroke exit.

QUEEN ELEANOR, ⌜*aside to King John*⌝
What now, my son! Have I not ever said
How that ambitious Constance would not cease
Till she had kindled France and all the world
Upon the right and party of her son?
This might have been prevented and made whole
With very easy arguments of love,
Which now the manage of two kingdoms must
With fearful bloody issue arbitrate.

KING JOHN, ⌜*aside to Queen Eleanor*⌝
Our strong possession and our right for us.

QUEEN ELEANOR, ⌜*aside to King John*⌝
Your strong possession much more than your right,
Or else it must go wrong with you and me—
So much my conscience whispers in your ear,
Which none but ⌜God⌝ and you and I shall hear.

37. **manage:** i.e., management, conduct (Originally, the term referred to the training and managing of horses.)

43. **God:** The Folio here reads "heauen." The text of *King John,* like many in the Folio, seems to have been censored before printing to eliminate the use of God's name. Where the meter and the context suggest that a censor has replaced "God" with "heaven," we have chosen to emend.

48. **abbeys . . . shall pay:** For John's relationship with the Roman Catholic Church, see Historical Background 2, page 232.

49. **charge:** expense (For our change of the Folio's "expeditious" to **"expedition's,"** see longer note, page 211.)

55. **Coeur de Lion:** i.e., Lion-heart, the name by which King Richard I, King John's elder brother, was known

56. **What:** i.e., who

59. **You came . . . mother:** Since the law of primogeniture makes the eldest legitimate son the legal heir, King John assumes that Philip's mother was not Faulconbridge's wife.

60. **certain:** i.e., certainly

63. **put you o'er:** refer **you**

64. **Of that . . . may:** Proverbial: "It is a wise child that knows his own father."

65. **Out on thee:** an interjection of reproach

67. **diffidence:** distrust, doubt

Enter a Sheriff, ⌜*who speaks aside to Essex.*⌝

ESSEX
My liege, here is the strangest controversy
Come from the country to be judged by you
That e'er I heard. Shall I produce the men?

KING JOHN Let them approach. ⌜*Sheriff exits.*⌝
Our abbeys and our priories shall pay
This ⌜expedition's⌝ charge.

Enter Robert Faulconbridge and Philip ⌜*Faulconbridge.*⌝

What men are you?

PHILIP FAULCONBRIDGE
Your faithful subject I, a gentleman,
Born in Northamptonshire, and eldest son,
As I suppose, to Robert Faulconbridge,
A soldier, by the honor-giving hand
Of Coeur de Lion knighted in the field.

KING JOHN, ⌜*to Robert Faulconbridge*⌝ What art thou?

ROBERT FAULCONBRIDGE
The son and heir to that same Faulconbridge.

KING JOHN
Is that the elder, and art thou the heir?
You came not of one mother then, it seems.

PHILIP FAULCONBRIDGE
Most certain of one mother, mighty king—
That is well known—and, as I think, one father.
But for the certain knowledge of that truth
I put you o'er to heaven and to my mother.
Of that I doubt, as all men's children may.

QUEEN ELEANOR
Out on thee, rude man! Thou dost shame thy
mother
And wound her honor with this diffidence.

PHILIP FAULCONBRIDGE
I, madam? No, I have no reason for it.
That is my brother's plea, and none of mine,

71. **fair:** fully

76. **once:** on one occasion; in short

77. **whe'er:** whether; **true:** legitimately

78. **upon . . . head:** i.e., to my mother's responsibility

80. **Fair fall:** i.e., may good fortune befall; **for me:** i.e., to generate **me**

83. **this son like him:** i.e., if **this son** (i.e., Robert Faulconbridge the younger) looks **like** his father, old Sir Robert

87. **trick:** characteristic expression

88. **affecteth him:** i.e., naturally resembles that of Coeur de Lion

90. **composition:** physique; physical constitution

93. **Sirrah:** a term of address to a boy or a male social inferior

94. **move:** provoke, impel, incite

95. **half-face:** thin or pinched face; imperfect or unfinished face; or a face in profile (on a coin)

96. **face:** with wordplay on the sense of "insolence" or "impudence"

97. **half-faced groat:** the small silver coin called a **groat** (worth less than four pence), which bore the monarch's face in profile

The which if he can prove, he pops me out
At least from fair five hundred pound a year.
Heaven guard my mother's honor and my land!

KING JOHN
A good blunt fellow.—Why, being younger born,
Doth he lay claim to thine inheritance?

PHILIP FAULCONBRIDGE
I know not why, except to get the land.
But once he slandered me with bastardy.
But whe'er I be as true begot or no,
That still I lay upon my mother's head.
But that I am as well begot, my liege—
Fair fall the bones that took the pains for me!—
Compare our faces and be judge yourself.
If old Sir Robert did beget us both
And were our father, and this son like him,
O, old Sir Robert, father, on my knee
I give heaven thanks I was not like to thee!

KING JOHN
Why, what a madcap hath heaven lent us here!

QUEEN ELEANOR, ⌜*aside to King John*⌝
He hath a trick of Coeur de Lion's face;
The accent of his tongue affecteth him.
Do you not read some tokens of my son
In the large composition of this man?

KING JOHN, ⌜*aside to Queen Eleanor*⌝
Mine eye hath well examinèd his parts
And finds them perfect Richard. ⌜*To Robert Faulconbridge*⌝ Sirrah, speak.
What doth move you to claim your brother's land?

PHILIP FAULCONBRIDGE
Because he hath a half-face, like my father.
With half that face would he have all my land—
A half-faced groat five hundred pound a year!

ROBERT FAULCONBRIDGE
My gracious liege, when that my father lived,
Your brother did employ my father much—

104. **touching:** pertaining or relating to

108. **truth is truth:** proverbial

111. **this . . . gentleman:** i.e., Philip **lusty:** merry; **got:** begotten, fathered

112. **his, he:** referring to Sir Robert Faulconbridge

113. **took . . . death:** perhaps, swore as deathbed testimony (i.e., swore by his chance at salvation); or, perhaps, staked his life

115. **An if:** i.e., if

116. **Full:** i.e., fully

121. **did play false:** i.e., was unfaithful to her husband; **fault:** offense; moral defect

122. **lies on the hazards of:** i.e., is a risk taken by

123. **how:** i.e., what; **my brother:** i.e., Richard I

124. **get:** beget, father

126. **sooth:** truth

King John.
From John Taylor, *A briefe remembrance of all the English monarchs* . . . (1618).

PHILIP FAULCONBRIDGE
Well, sir, by this you cannot get my land.
Your tale must be how he employed my mother.

ROBERT FAULCONBRIDGE
And once dispatched him in an embassy
To Germany, there with the Emperor
To treat of high affairs touching that time.
Th' advantage of his absence took the King
And in the meantime sojourned at my father's;
Where how he did prevail I shame to speak.
But truth is truth: large lengths of seas and shores
Between my father and my mother lay,
As I have heard my father speak himself,
When this same lusty gentleman was got.
Upon his deathbed he by will bequeathed
His lands to me, and took it on his death
That this my mother's son was none of his;
An if he were, he came into the world
Full fourteen weeks before the course of time.
Then, good my liege, let me have what is mine,
My father's land, as was my father's will.

KING JOHN
Sirrah, your brother is legitimate.
Your father's wife did after wedlock bear him,
An if she did play false, the fault was hers,
Which fault lies on the hazards of all husbands
That marry wives. Tell me, how if my brother,
Who as you say took pains to get this son,
Had of your father claimed this son for his?
In sooth, good friend, your father might have kept
This calf, bred from his cow, from all the world;
In sooth he might. Then if he were my brother's,
My brother might not claim him, nor your father,
Being none of his, refuse him. This concludes:
My mother's son did get your father's heir;
Your father's heir must have your father's land.

136. **will:** intention (There is probable wordplay on other meanings of the word, including "carnal desire" and "penis.")

137. **Whether:** i.e., which of the two; **hadst thou rather:** i.e., would you prefer

140. **thy presence:** (1) your noble appearance; (2) the space immediately around you

141 SP. **Bastard:** We follow the Folio in changing the speech prefix from "Philip" to "Bastard" at this point in the play. See longer note, page 212.

142. **And . . . him:** i.e., and I, **like him, had Sir Robert's** (**Robert's his** is a double possessive, meaning simply **Robert's.**)

143. **riding-rods:** switches used in horseback riding

145–47. **That in . . . goes:** a reference to the three-farthing coin, which bore a profile of Queen Elizabeth with a Tudor rose approximately behind her ear (See longer note, page 212.)

148. **to his shape, were heir:** i.e., if, in addition to looking like Sir Robert's son, I **were heir**

149. **Would . . . place:** i.e., if I am not telling the truth, may I never move from where I stand

150. **it every foot:** i.e., every foot of it; **this face:** i.e., the **face** I have

151. **Nob:** a diminutive form of "Robert" (with possible wordplay on "knob" as an insulting term for "head")

153. **Bequeath:** transfer, deliver

157. **dear:** expensive (because **your face** is not worth **five pence**)

160. **give . . . way:** leave the way clear for our social superiors

ROBERT FAULCONBRIDGE
Shall then my father's will be of no force
To dispossess that child which is not his?

PHILIP FAULCONBRIDGE
Of no more force to dispossess me, sir,
Than was his will to get me, as I think.

QUEEN ELEANOR
Whether hadst thou rather: be a Faulconbridge
And, like thy brother, to enjoy thy land,
Or the reputed son of Coeur de Lion,
Lord of thy presence, and no land besides?

BASTARD
Madam, an if my brother had my shape
And I had his, Sir Robert's his like him,
And if my legs were two such riding-rods,
My arms such eel-skins stuffed, my face so thin
That in mine ear I durst not stick a rose,
Lest men should say "Look where three-farthings
goes,"
And, to his shape, were heir to all this land,
Would I might never stir from off this place,
I would give it every foot to have this face.
⌜I⌝ would not be Sir Nob in any case.

QUEEN ELEANOR
I like thee well. Wilt thou forsake thy fortune,
Bequeath thy land to him, and follow me?
I am a soldier and now bound to France.

BASTARD
Brother, take you my land. I'll take my chance.
Your face hath got five hundred pound a year,
Yet sell your face for five pence and 'tis dear.—
Madam, I'll follow you unto the death.

QUEEN ELEANOR
Nay, I would have you go before me thither.

BASTARD
Our country manners give our betters way.

174–77. **by chance . . . night:** expressions that refer to the irregularity of the Bastard's birth (See longer note, page 212.) **What though:** i.e., but **what** does it matter

178. **have is have:** Proverbial: "[To] own is [to] own," referring here to the Bastard's status as the Queen's grandson. **catch:** acquire possession

179. **Near . . . shot:** i.e., no matter whether an archer stands **near** to or **far** from the target, the winning shot still deserves the praise **"well shot"**

"Richard, that robbed the lion of his heart." (2.1.3)
From John Rastell, *The pastyme of people* . . . [1529?].

KING JOHN What is thy name?

BASTARD
Philip, my liege, so is my name begun,
Philip, good old Sir Robert's wife's eldest son.

KING JOHN
From henceforth bear his name whose form thou
bearest.
Kneel thou down Philip, but rise more great.
⌈*Philip kneels. King John dubs him a knight, tapping him on the shoulder with his sword.*⌉
Arise Sir Richard and Plantagenet.

BASTARD, ⌈*rising, to Robert Faulconbridge*⌉
Brother by th' mother's side, give me your hand.
My father gave me honor, yours gave land.
Now blessèd be the hour, by night or day,
When I was got, Sir Robert was away!

QUEEN ELEANOR
The very spirit of Plantagenet!
I am thy grandam, Richard. Call me so.

BASTARD
Madam, by chance but not by truth. What though?
Something about, a little from the right,
In at the window, or else o'er the hatch.
Who dares not stir by day must walk by night,
And have is have, however men do catch.
Near or far off, well won is still well shot,
And I am I, howe'er I was begot.

KING JOHN, ⌈*to Robert Faulconbridge*⌉
Go, Faulconbridge, now hast thou thy desire.
A landless knight makes thee a landed squire.—
Come, madam,—and come, Richard. We must
speed
For France, for France, for it is more than need.

BASTARD
Brother, adieu, good fortune come to thee,

189. **many a many foot:** i.e., **many** feet (with repetition for emphasis)

190. **Joan:** in Shakespeare's day a generic name for a woman of the lower social order

191. **Good den:** good evening or good afternoon (Sir Richard imagines himself greeted by a social inferior.) **God-a-mercy:** God reward you (i.e., thank you; literally, God have mercy)

194. **'Tis too respective:** i.e., remembering people's names is too considerate

195. **your: Your** is sometimes not a personal pronoun. In this line, it is a dismissive colloquialism meaning "the **conversion** (and the **traveler**) that you know of." **conversion:** i.e., change of status

196. **toothpick:** a device widely associated with pretentious travelers; **my Worship's:** "Your Worship" was a title of honor for a person of note. **mess:** company of people eating together

199. **pickèd:** refined (with wordplay on **toothpick**)

201. **Question:** one of the characters in the imagined dialogue between the Bastard and a traveler

202. **absey-book:** (1) ABC book; (2) an introductory book to any subject, often in question-and-answer form, like a catechism (ABC books and catechisms were often bound as a single book for children's instruction.)

206. **would:** i.e., wants to ask

207. **Saving in . . . compliment:** except for ceremonious, formal, and polite conversation

209. **Pyrenean:** Pyrenees

210. **It draws toward supper:** i.e., the time of day nears evening

(continued)

For thou wast got i' th' way of honesty.
All but Bastard exit.
A foot of honor better than I was,
But many a many foot of land the worse.
Well, now can I make any Joan a lady.
"Good den, Sir Richard!" "God-a-mercy, fellow!"
An if his name be George, I'll call him "Peter,"
For new-made honor doth forget men's names;
'Tis too respective and too sociable
For your conversion. Now your traveler,
He and his toothpick at my Worship's mess,
And when my knightly stomach is sufficed,
Why then I suck my teeth and catechize
My pickèd man of countries: "My dear sir,"
Thus leaning on mine elbow I begin,
"I shall beseech you"—that is Question now,
And then comes Answer like an absey-book:
"O, sir," says Answer, "at your best command,
At your employment, at your service, sir."
"No, sir," says Question, "I, sweet sir, at yours."
And so, ere Answer knows what Question would,
Saving in dialogue of compliment
And talking of the Alps and Apennines,
The Pyrenean and the river Po,
It draws toward supper in conclusion so.
But this is worshipful society
And fits the mounting spirit like myself;
For he is but a bastard to the time
That doth not ⌜smack⌝ of observation,
And so am I whether I smack or no;
And not alone in habit and device,
Exterior form, outward accouterment,
But from the inward motion to deliver
Sweet, sweet, sweet poison for the age's tooth,
Which though I will not practice to deceive,

211. **worshipful:** honorable (by virtue of rank)

212. **mounting spirit: spirit** ascending to a higher level of rank, estimation, or power

213–22. **For he . . . rising:** See longer note, page 213.

213. **but a bastard to:** not a true child of; i.e., ill-suited to (with wordplay, in line 215, on his own status as an illegitimate son)

214. **observation:** the practice of observing ceremonious courtesy

216. **habit:** clothing; **device:** emblematic figure that appears on a knight's coat of arms

218. **motion:** desire, inclination

219. **Sweet . . . poison:** Proverbial: "Flattery is **sweet poison." tooth:** taste, liking

220. **practice:** habitually act; plot

221. **deceit:** i.e., being deceived

222. **it:** i.e., the **sweet poison** of deceitful flattery

224. **post:** messenger (as if riding a post-horse, the most rapid form of travel)

225. **blow a horn:** i.e., announce her arrival (with possible wordplay on the horns that were represented as growing from the forehead of a cuckold—i.e., a husband, like the late Sir Robert, whose wife had been unfaithful)

229. **holds in chase:** pursues as in hunting; **up and down:** (1) everywhere; (2) entirely

231. **Colbrand the Giant:** a legendary giant slain by the hero of the fourteenth-century romance *Guy of Warwick* (This is the first of a number of ironic allusions to literature that dot the Bastard's speeches in this scene.) See picture, page 104.

233. **unreverent:** irreverent

(continued)

Yet to avoid deceit I mean to learn,
For it shall strew the footsteps of my rising.

Enter Lady Faulconbridge and James Gurney.

But who comes in such haste in riding robes?
What woman post is this? Hath she no husband
That will take pains to blow a horn before her?
O me, 'tis my mother.—How now, good lady?
What brings you here to court so hastily?

LADY FAULCONBRIDGE
Where is that slave thy brother? Where is he
That holds in chase mine honor up and down?

BASTARD
My brother Robert, old Sir Robert's son?
Colbrand the Giant, that same mighty man?
Is it Sir Robert's son that you seek so?

LADY FAULCONBRIDGE
"Sir Robert's son"? Ay, thou unreverent boy,
Sir Robert's son. Why scorn'st thou at Sir Robert?
He is Sir Robert's son, and so art thou.

BASTARD
James Gurney, wilt thou give us leave awhile?

GURNEY
Good leave, good Philip.

BASTARD "Philip Sparrow," James.
There's toys abroad. Anon I'll tell thee more.

James ⌜Gurney⌝ exits.

Madam, I was not old Sir Robert's son.
Sir Robert might have eat his part in me
Upon Good Friday and ne'er broke his fast.
Sir Robert could do well—marry, to confess—
Could ⌜he⌝ get me. Sir Robert could not do it;
We know his handiwork. Therefore, good mother,
To whom am I beholding for these limbs?
Sir Robert never holp to make this leg.

236. **give us leave:** i.e., **leave us** alone

237. **Good leave:** a phrase indicating his willingness to **leave**

238. **Philip Sparrow:** The Bastard responds to Gurney's calling him "Philip" by scornfully alluding to the name as one used for pet sparrows. (See longer note, page 213, and picture, page 162.)

239. **toys:** (1) foolish tales; (2) fantastic tricks; (3) melodies in birds' songs (possibly alluding to **Philip Sparrow**); **Anon:** soon

241. **eat:** i.e., eaten (pronounced *et*)

242. **Good Friday:** The Catholic and the Anglican Church prescribed fasting from meat on Fridays.

243. **marry, to confess:** i.e., indeed, to tell the truth (originally **marry** was an oath on the name of the Virgin Mary)

244. **Could he get me:** i.e., if he could father me

246. **beholding:** beholden, obliged

247. **holp:** helped

249. **That:** i.e., who (referring to the Bastard)

251. **untoward:** indecent, indecorous

252. **Basilisco-like: Basilisco,** a character in Thomas Kyd's *Soliman and Perseda,* insists on being called a **knight.** The servant Piston in Kyd's play, like the Bastard's mother, instead uses the term **knave.**

253. **What:** an interjection used to introduce a question or an exclamation

256. **Legitimation:** legitimacy

258. **proper:** handsome

260. **As . . . devil:** The Bastard's language recalls that of the rites of baptism and confirmation during which the devil is explicitly renounced.

262. **suit:** wooing, petition

(continued)

LADY FAULCONBRIDGE

Hast thou conspirèd with thy brother too,
That for thine own gain shouldst defend mine
honor?
What means this scorn, thou most untoward knave?

BASTARD

Knight, knight, good mother, Basilisco-like.
What, I am dubbed! I have it on my shoulder.
But, mother, I am not Sir Robert's son.
I have disclaimed Sir Robert and my land.
Legitimation, name, and all is gone.
Then, good my mother, let me know my father—
Some proper man, I hope. Who was it, mother?

LADY FAULCONBRIDGE

Hast thou denied thyself a Faulconbridge?

BASTARD

As faithfully as I deny the devil.

LADY FAULCONBRIDGE

King Richard Coeur de Lion was thy father.
By long and vehement suit I was seduced
To make room for him in my husband's bed.
Heaven lay not my transgression to my charge!
⌜Thou⌝ art the issue of my dear offense,
Which was so strongly urged past my defense.

BASTARD

Now, by this light, were I to get again,
Madam, I would not wish a better father.
Some sins do bear their privilege on earth,
And so doth yours. Your fault was not your folly.
Needs must you lay your heart at his dispose,
Subjected tribute to commanding love,
Against whose fury and unmatchèd force
The aweless lion could not wage the fight,
Nor keep his princely heart from Richard's hand.
He that perforce robs lions of their hearts

264. **charge:** responsibility

265. **issue:** (1) result; (2) offspring; **dear:** (1) loving; (2) grievous, heavy

267. **to get:** i.e., to be fathered

269. **do . . . privilege:** (1) have immunity; (2) have their advantage

270. **fault:** transgression; **folly:** unwise action, wickedness

271. **Needs must you:** i.e., you had to; **dispose:** disposal

272. **Subjected tribute to:** a gift subject to the power and authority of

273–75. **Against . . . hand:** an allusion to the legend that when Richard the Lion-heart was in prison and a lion was sent to devour him, Richard reached into the lion's gaping mouth and tore out its heart (See picture, page 18.) **aweless:** fearless **his:** i.e., its

276. **perforce:** forcibly

279. **Who:** i.e., whoever

284. **says it was:** i.e., **says** that your saying "yea" to Richard **was a sin**

May easily win a woman's. Ay, my mother,
With all my heart I thank thee for my father.
Who lives and dares but say thou didst not well
When I was got, I'll send his soul to hell.
Come, lady, I will show thee to my kin,
And they shall say when Richard me begot,
If thou hadst said him nay, it had been sin.
Who says it was, he lies. I say 'twas not.

They exit.

The consequences of said actions could range to various extentions of the law

The Life and Death of

KING JOHN

ACT 2

2.1 King Philip of France and the Duke of Austria, on behalf of Arthur, begin to lay siege to the city of Angiers, property of the English monarch. John and his army arrive. Each king demands that the citizens of Angiers allow the "King of England" to enter, but the citizens ask for proof as to which (John or Arthur) is the true king. When the kings decide to join forces to destroy the city, the citizens propose that the kings instead become allies through a marriage of the French Dauphin Louis to John's niece Blanche. To further this proposed alliance, John gives up five Continental provinces and makes Arthur Duke of Brittany and Earl of Richmond, while Philip abandons Arthur's cause.

---

0 SD. **Angiers:** i.e., Angers, a city in the province of Anjou (See picture, page 36, and map, page xii.)

1 SP. **Dauphin:** See longer note, page 213.

2. **that great . . . blood:** your great ancestor (Richard I was Arthur's uncle. The words **forerunner** and **offspring** [line 13] confusingly suggest a father-son relationship.)

3. **that robbed . . . heart:** See note to 1.1.273–75 above, and picture, page 18.

4. **the holy . . . Palestine:** From 1095 to c. 1450 a series of wars—the Crusades—were fought by Christians to recover the Holy Sepulcher in Jerusalem from the Muslims. Richard I was one of the military leaders of the 3rd Crusade (c. 1189–92).

5. **By this . . . grave:** See longer note, page 215.

7. **importance:** urging

(continued)

⌜*ACT 2*⌝

Scene ⌜1⌝

Enter, before Angiers, ⌜*at one side, with Forces,*⌝ *Philip King of France, Louis* ⌜*the*⌝ *Dauphin, Constance, Arthur,* ⌜*and Attendants; at the other side, with Forces,*⌝ *Austria,* ⌜*wearing a lion's skin.*⌝

DAUPHIN

Before Angiers well met, brave Austria.—
Arthur, that great forerunner of thy blood,
Richard, that robbed the lion of his heart
And fought the holy wars in Palestine,
By this brave duke came early to his grave.
And, for amends to his posterity,
At our importance hither is he come
To spread his colors, boy, in thy behalf,
And to rebuke the usurpation
Of thy unnatural uncle, English John.
Embrace him, love him, give him welcome hither.

ARTHUR

God shall forgive you Coeur de Lion's death
The rather that you give his offspring life,
Shadowing their right under your wings of war.
I give you welcome with a powerless hand
But with a heart full of unstainèd love.
Welcome before the gates of Angiers, duke.

DAUPHIN

A noble boy. Who would not do thee right?

8. **spread his colors:** i.e., display the banner bearing his personal insignia, as a sign that he is prepared to do battle

9. **rebuke:** beat down; **usurpation:** For background on the charge that John was a usurper, see Historical Background 1, page 231.

13. **The rather that:** all the sooner because

14. **Shadowing:** sheltering, protecting (Compare Psalm 63.7: "under the shadow [i.e., shelter] of thy wings will I rejoice.")

23. **pale:** i.e., the chalk cliffs of Dover (The word **pale** means "whitish," as an adjective, and "fence" or "defensive barrier," as a noun.)

25. **coops:** confines for defensive purposes

26. **main:** ocean

27. **still:** always

27–28. **secure / And confident:** safe and sure (but both words also have the sense of "overconfident")

29. **that utmost corner of the West:** i.e., England, imaged here as lying at the outermost western **corner** of the world (See longer note, page 215.) **utmost:** uttermost, outermost

34. **more:** greater

37. **bent:** aimed, directed

39. **our chiefest men of discipline:** i.e., those most expert in military matters

40. **plots of best advantages:** i.e., sites that afford us the greatest superiority for combat

43. **But we will:** i.e., if **we** must in order to

44. **Stay:** wait; **embassy:** message

45. **unadvised:** rashly, thoughtlessly

49. **indirectly:** wrongfully

AUSTRIA, ⌜*to Arthur*⌝

Upon thy cheek lay I this zealous kiss
As seal to this indenture of my love:
That to my home I will no more return
Till Angiers and the right thou hast in France,
Together with that pale, that white-faced shore,
Whose foot spurns back the ocean's roaring tides
And coops from other lands her islanders,
Even till that England, hedged in with the main,
That water-wallèd bulwark, still secure
And confident from foreign purposes,
Even till that utmost corner of the West
Salute thee for her king. Till then, fair boy,
Will I not think of home, but follow arms.

CONSTANCE

O, take his mother's thanks, a widow's thanks,
Till your strong hand shall help to give him strength
To make a more requital to your love.

AUSTRIA

The peace of heaven is theirs that lift their swords
In such a just and charitable war.

KING PHILIP

Well, then, to work. Our cannon shall be bent
Against the brows of this resisting town.
Call for our chiefest men of discipline
To cull the plots of best advantages.
We'll lay before this town our royal bones,
Wade to the marketplace in Frenchmen's blood,
But we will make it subject to this boy.

CONSTANCE

Stay for an answer to your embassy,
Lest unadvised you stain your swords with blood.
My lord Chatillion may from England bring
That right in peace which here we urge in war,
And then we shall repent each drop of blood
That hot rash haste so indirectly shed.

52. **gentle:** noble

53. **coldly:** calmly, dispassionately

56. **England:** i.e., King John

58. **Whose . . . stayed:** i.e., the cessation of which I've been awaiting (Literally, "to stay upon a person's **leisure**" is to wait until he or she is unoccupied.)

60. **expedient:** direct (and speedy)

63. **Ate:** personification of discord

64. **niece:** i.e., granddaughter

66. **unsettled humors:** restless, turbulent individuals (See longer note, page 216.)

67. **inconsiderate:** thoughtless; **voluntaries:** volunteers

68. **spleens:** The spleen was then believed to be the seat of the passions—in this case, of violent ill-temper (and, possibly, courage). See picture of **dragon,** page 94.

70. **birthrights:** inheritances

71. **To make a hazard of:** i.e., to take a chance at

72. **braver:** (1) more splendid; (2) more courageous

73. **bottoms:** ships; **waft:** i.e., wafted

75. **scathe:** harm

77. **circumstance:** detailed description

79. **expedition:** (1) warlike enterprise; (2) speedy arrival

Enter Chatillion.

KING PHILIP

A wonder, lady! Lo, upon thy wish
Our messenger Chatillion is arrived.—
What England says say briefly, gentle lord.
We coldly pause for thee. Chatillion, speak.

CHATILLION

Then turn your forces from this paltry siege
And stir them up against a mightier task.
England, impatient of your just demands,
Hath put himself in arms. The adverse winds,
Whose leisure I have stayed, have given him time
To land his legions all as soon as I.
His marches are expedient to this town,
His forces strong, his soldiers confident.
With him along is come the Mother Queen,
An ⌜Ate⌝ stirring him to blood and strife;
With her her niece, the Lady Blanche of Spain;
With them a bastard of the King's deceased.
And all th' unsettled humors of the land—
Rash, inconsiderate, fiery voluntaries,
With ladies' faces and fierce dragons' spleens—
Have sold their fortunes at their native homes,
Bearing their birthrights proudly on their backs,
To make a hazard of new fortunes here.
In brief, a braver choice of dauntless spirits
Than now the English bottoms have waft o'er
Did never float upon the swelling tide
To do offense and scathe in Christendom.

Drum beats.

The interruption of their churlish drums
Cuts off more circumstance. They are at hand,
To parley or to fight, therefore prepare.

KING PHILIP

How much unlooked-for is this expedition.

82. **occasion:** necessity

85. **Our . . . own:** i.e., my taking possession of what is mine by right of my lineage **our own:** i.e., my kingdom (including large sections of France); also, my city (Angiers)

87. **Whiles:** i.e., while; **correct:** tame

89. **if that:** i.e., **if**

95. **underwrought:** sought to undermine; **his:** i.e., its (England's)

96. **sequence of posterity:** i.e., order of succession

97. **Outfacèd infant state:** i.e., arrogantly defied the boy king (Arthur)

97–98. **done a rape / Upon:** violently stolen (Attributing **maiden virtue** to the **crown** allows wordplay on **rape** as "sexual assault.")

101. **large:** i.e., complete form, full size

103. **draw:** enlarge; **brief:** abridgment, abstract

106. **this is Geoffrey's:** The reference here might be to Prince Arthur or to the crown that King John wears, or even to Angiers.

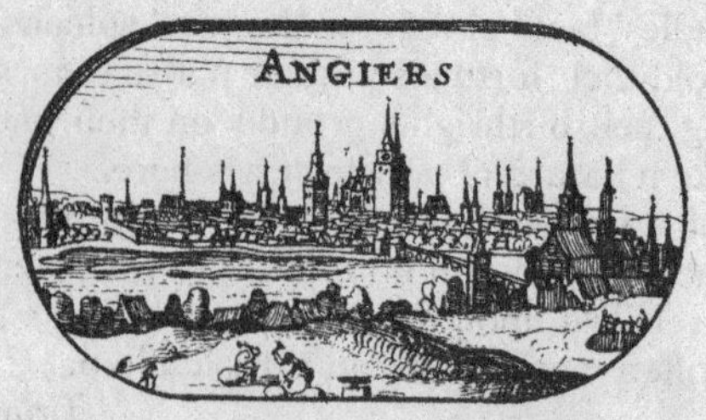

Angiers. (2.1, 3.4)
From John Speed, *A prospect of the most famous parts of the world . . .* (1631).

AUSTRIA

By how much unexpected, by so much
We must awake endeavor for defense,
For courage mounteth with occasion.
Let them be welcome, then. We are prepared.

Enter King ⌜John⌝ of England, Bastard, Queen ⌜Eleanor,⌝ Blanche, ⌜Salisbury,⌝ Pembroke, and others.

KING JOHN

Peace be to France, if France in peace permit
Our just and lineal entrance to our own.
If not, bleed France, and peace ascend to heaven,
Whiles we, God's wrathful agent, do correct
Their proud contempt that beats his peace to heaven.

KING PHILIP

Peace be to England, if that war return
From France to England, there to live in peace.
England we love, and for that England's sake
With burden of our armor here we sweat.
This toil of ours should be a work of thine;
But thou from loving England art so far
That thou hast underwrought his lawful king,
Cut off the sequence of posterity,
Outfacèd infant state, and done a rape
Upon the maiden virtue of the crown.
Look here upon thy brother Geoffrey's face.
⌜He points to Arthur.⌝
These eyes, these brows, were molded out of his;
This little abstract doth contain that large
Which died in Geoffrey, and the hand of time
Shall draw this brief into as huge a volume.
That Geoffrey was thy elder brother born,
And this his son. England was Geoffrey's right,
And this is Geoffrey's. In the name of God,
How comes it then that thou art called a king,

109. **owe:** own; **o'ermasterest:** hold in your possession

112. **articles:** accusations, charges

117. **whose:** i.e., God's; **impeach:** challenge

119. **Alack:** an exclamation of reprobation

120. **Excuse . . . down:** i.e., my excuse for usurping authority is that I am attacking usurpation

123. **Out:** an exclamation of indignant reproach

124. **check:** threaten to capture (as in chess when the queen places the opposing king in check); control

127. **Liker:** i.e., closer

128. **in manners . . . like:** i.e., who **in manners** are as similar

129. **dam:** mother (Proverbial: "The **devil** and his **dam.**")

131. **true begot:** legitimately fathered

132. **an if thou wert: if** you were

133. **blots:** slanders (Repeated in line 134 as **blot,** the word also has the sense of "efface, obliterate.")

Queen Eleanor.
From *Chronologie et sommaire des souuerains . . .* (1622).

When living blood doth in these temples beat
Which owe the crown that thou o'ermasterest?

KING JOHN

From whom hast thou this great commission,
  France,
To draw my answer from thy articles?

KING PHILIP

From that supernal judge that stirs good thoughts
In any ⌜breast⌝ of strong authority
To look into the blots and stains of right.
That judge hath made me guardian to this boy,
Under whose warrant I impeach thy wrong,
And by whose help I mean to chastise it.

KING JOHN

Alack, thou dost usurp authority.

KING PHILIP

Excuse it is to beat usurping down.

QUEEN ELEANOR

Who is it thou dost call usurper, France?

CONSTANCE

Let me make answer: thy usurping son.

QUEEN ELEANOR

Out, insolent! Thy bastard shall be king
That thou mayst be a queen and check the world.

CONSTANCE

My bed was ever to thy son as true
As thine was to thy husband, and this boy
Liker in feature to his father Geoffrey
Than thou and John, in manners being as like
As rain to water or devil to his dam.
My boy a bastard? By my soul, I think
His father never was so true begot.
It cannot be, an if thou wert his mother.

QUEEN ELEANOR, ⌜*to Arthur*⌝

There's a good mother, boy, that blots thy father.

136. **the crier:** perhaps, the town **crier;** or, perhaps, the minor courtroom official whose function it was to call for silence

138. **play:** act the part of

139. **An:** if; **hide:** referring, perhaps, to the lion's skin that was once Richard's, now possessed by Austria; or, perhaps, to Austria's own skin

140. **proverb:** "So hares may pull **dead lions by the beard."**

142. **smoke:** smack, beat; **skin-coat:** See note to **hide,** line 139.

144. **become:** suit, grace

146–47. **It lies . . . ass:** These lines play on two proverbs: "Hercules' shoe will not fit a little foot" and "An **ass** in a lion's skin." **sightly:** handsomely **him:** i.e., Austria **Alcides:** i.e., Hercules, the Greek mythological hero who killed the Nemean lion, whose pelt he then wore (See picture, page 54.)

149. **that:** i.e., **that** which

150. **cracker:** braggart (with wordplay on **crack** in line 149); **deafs:** deafens

152. **Louis:** pronounced throughout the play as "Lewis," as is signaled in its Folio spelling; **straight:** straightaway, immediately

153. **conference:** conversation

159. **Brittany:** Arthur inherited the province of Brittany from his father, Geoffrey; in the play, Arthur's title as duke is formally confirmed by John at 2.1.577. (See map, page xii.) **thee:** i.e., yourself

CONSTANCE
There's a good grandam, boy, that would blot thee.

AUSTRIA
Peace!

BASTARD Hear the crier!

AUSTRIA What the devil art thou?

BASTARD
One that will play the devil, sir, with you,
An he may catch your hide and you alone.
You are the hare of whom the proverb goes,
Whose valor plucks dead lions by the beard.
I'll smoke your skin-coat an I catch you right.
Sirrah, look to 't. I' faith, I will, i' faith!

threats from the newly knighted bastard

BLANCHE
O, well did he become that lion's robe
That did disrobe the lion of that robe.

BASTARD
It lies as sightly on the back of him
As great Alcides' shoes upon an ass.—
But, ass, I'll take that burden from your back
Or lay on that shall make your shoulders crack.

AUSTRIA
What cracker is this same that deafs our ears
With this abundance of superfluous breath?

common insults are still just as common

⌜KING PHILIP⌝
Louis, determine what we shall do straight.

DAUPHIN
Women and fools, break off your conference.—
King John, this is the very sum of all:
England and Ireland, ⌜Anjou,⌝ Touraine, Maine,
In right of Arthur do I claim of thee.
Wilt thou resign them and lay down thy arms?

KING JOHN
My life as soon! I do defy thee, France.—
Arthur of Brittany, yield thee to my hand,

John states that is most definitely not going anywhere

161. **coward:** i.e., cowardly

164, 165. **it:** i.e., its (baby talk for "your")

166. **it:** i.e., you; **fig:** perhaps with wordplay on **fig** as a contemptuous gesture made with the thumb

169. **would:** wish

170. **coil:** fuss

171. **shames him:** makes him ashamed; disgraces him

172. **whe'er:** whether

173. **wrongs:** wrongdoings

174. **shames:** injurious language

175. **Draws:** i.e., draw

177. **in nature of a fee:** i.e., as if paid to a lawyer to advocate his case

178. **beads:** i.e., tears (with wordplay on the **beads** for counting prayers)

183. **dominations:** dominions; **royalties:** the prerogatives and privileges of the sovereign

184. **eldest son's son:** i.e., eldest grandson

185. **Infortunate:** unfortunate

186–89. **Thy sins . . . womb:** Compare Exodus 20.5: "For I the Lord thy God . . . visit the sins of the fathers upon the children, unto the third and fourth generation." **visited:** punished **canon of the law:** rule of the church, the biblical decree alluded to in this passage (See longer note, page 217.)

And out of my dear love I'll give thee more
Than e'er the coward hand of France can win.
Submit thee, boy.

QUEEN ELEANOR Come to thy grandam, child.

CONSTANCE
Do, child, go to it grandam, child.
Give grandam kingdom, and it grandam will
Give it a plum, a cherry, and a fig.
There's a good grandam.

ARTHUR, ⌜*weeping*⌝ Good my mother, peace.
I would that I were low laid in my grave.
I am not worth this coil that's made for me.

QUEEN ELEANOR
His mother shames him so, poor boy, he weeps.

CONSTANCE
Now shame upon you whe'er she does or no!
His grandam's wrongs, and not his mother's shames,
Draws those heaven-moving pearls from his poor eyes,
Which heaven shall take in nature of a fee.
Ay, with these crystal beads heaven shall be bribed
To do him justice and revenge on you.

QUEEN ELEANOR
Thou monstrous slanderer of heaven and earth!

CONSTANCE
Thou monstrous injurer of heaven and earth,
Call not me slanderer. Thou and thine usurp
The dominations, royalties, and rights
Of this oppressèd boy. This is thy eldest son's son,
Infortunate in nothing but in thee.
Thy sins are visited in this poor child.
The canon of the law is laid on him,
Being but the second generation
Removèd from thy sin-conceiving womb.

190. **Bedlam:** lunatic (**Bedlam** was the Hospital of the Priory of St. Mary of Bethlehem, a London asylum for the insane.)

192–95. **he . . . her plague:** See longer note, page 217. **removèd issue:** i.e., second-generation descendant, grandson

195–96. **her sin . . . sin:** See longer note, page 217. **Her injury:** i.e., Eleanor's injuriousness **beadle to:** i.e., punisher of (A **beadle** was a parish constable, charged with punishing offenders, sometimes with a whip.)

199. **unadvisèd:** rash, heedless

200. **will:** Richard I's last **will** bequeathed the crown to John and revoked an earlier **will** that had named Prince Arthur as heir to Richard's throne. (In lines 201–2, Constance uses **will** in the sense of "willfulness.")

202. **A woman's will:** Proverbial: "Women will have their wills." **cankered:** spiteful; corrupt; malignant

204. **It ill beseems:** it is not fitting or appropriate to; **this presence:** i.e., the **presence** of royalty

204–5. **cry aim / To:** encourage (a term from archery contests, at which spectators encouraged contestants by crying **"Aim!"**)

206. **trumpet:** trumpeter

208. **admit:** acknowledge (with wordplay on **admit** as "allow to enter")

209. **warned:** summoned

210. **France:** i.e., the king of **France; England:** i.e., Prince Arthur, the rightful king of **England,** according to Philip

(continued)

KING JOHN
Bedlam, have done.
CONSTANCE I have but this to say,
That he is not only plaguèd for her sin,
But God hath made her sin and her the plague
On this removèd issue, plagued for her,
And with her plague; her sin his injury,
Her injury the beadle to her sin,
All punished in the person of this child
And all for her. A plague upon her!
QUEEN ELEANOR
Thou unadvisèd scold, I can produce
A will that bars the title of thy son.
CONSTANCE
Ay, who doubts that? A will—a wicked will,
A woman's will, a cankered grandam's will.
KING PHILIP
Peace, lady. Pause, or be more temperate.
It ill beseems this presence to cry aim
To these ill-tunèd repetitions.—
Some trumpet summon hither to the walls
These men of Angiers. Let us hear them speak
Whose title they admit, Arthur's or John's.
Trumpet sounds.

Enter ⌜*Citizens*⌝ *upon the walls.*

CITIZEN
Who is it that hath warned us to the walls?
KING PHILIP
'Tis France, for England.
KING JOHN England, for itself.
You men of Angiers, and my loving subjects—
KING PHILIP
You loving men of Angiers, Arthur's subjects,
Our trumpet called you to this gentle parle—

211. **England, for itself:** i.e., myself, the king of **England,** who am one with and who speaks **for** the kingdom **itself**

214. **parle:** parley, discussion under truce

215. **our, us:** i.e., my, me (the royal "we")

216. **advancèd:** raised

218. **endamagement:** injury, harm

224. **winking:** i.e., closed

226. **waist:** garment encircling the **waist**

227. **ordinance:** ordnance, artillery (See picture, page 48.)

228. **lime:** mortar or cement

229. **dishabited:** dislodged; **wide havoc made:** i.e., a **wide** breach would have been **made** and destruction (**havoc**) would have taken place

232. **painfully:** laboriously, with care and effort; **expedient:** speedy

235. **amazed:** bewildered, alarmed, terror-stricken

236. **bullets:** cannonballs

238. **smoke:** obscurity, fraudulence

239. **faithless:** perfidious or treacherous; **error:** false belief

240. **trust accordingly:** i.e., do not **trust**

241. **labored:** oppressed (with toil)

242. **Forwearied:** exhausted

243. **harborage:** shelter

244. **said:** finished speaking

KING JOHN
For our advantage. Therefore hear us first.
These flags of France that are advancèd here
Before the eye and prospect of your town,
Have hither marched to your endamagement.
The cannons have their bowels full of wrath,
And ready mounted are they to spit forth
Their iron indignation 'gainst your walls.
All preparation for a bloody siege
And merciless proceeding by these French
⌜Confronts your⌝ city's eyes, your winking gates,
And, but for our approach, those sleeping stones,
That as a waist doth girdle you about,
By the compulsion of their ordinance
By this time from their fixèd beds of lime
Had been dishabited, and wide havoc made
For bloody power to rush upon your peace.
But on the sight of us your lawful king,
Who painfully with much expedient march
Have brought a countercheck before your gates
To save unscratched your city's threatened cheeks,
Behold, the French, amazed, vouchsafe a parle.
And now, instead of bullets wrapped in fire
To make a shaking fever in your walls,
They shoot but calm words folded up in smoke
To make a faithless error in your ears,
Which trust accordingly, kind citizens,
And let us in. Your king, whose labored spirits
Forwearied in this action of swift speed,
Craves harborage within your city walls.

KING PHILIP
When I have said, make answer to us both.
⌜He takes Arthur by the hand.⌝
Lo, in this right hand, whose protection
Is most divinely vowed upon the right

247. **young Plantagenet:** i.e., Prince Arthur

250. **this downtrodden equity:** i.e., that which is right and has been **downtrodden**

257. **owes:** owns

259. **aspect:** accent on second syllable

262. **unvexed:** quiet; **retire:** retreat

264. **lusty:** vigorous, strong

267. **fondly pass:** i.e., foolishly disregard

268. **roundure:** rounded form

270. **discipline:** military skill

271. **rude:** rough

273. **In that behalf which:** i.e., on **behalf** of him (Arthur) for whom

279. **proves:** i.e., **proves** to be

"Our cannon shall be bent / Against . . . this resisting town." (2.1.37–38)
From [John Lydgate,] *The hystorye sege and dystruccyon of Troye* [1513].

Of him it holds, stands young Plantagenet,
Son to the elder brother of this man,
And king o'er him and all that he enjoys.
For this downtrodden equity we tread
In warlike march these greens before your town,
Being no further enemy to you
Than the constraint of hospitable zeal
In the relief of this oppressèd child
Religiously provokes. Be pleasèd then
To pay that duty which you truly owe
To him that owes it, namely, this young prince,
And then our arms, like to a muzzled bear
Save in aspect, hath all offense sealed up.
Our cannons' malice vainly shall be spent
Against th' invulnerable clouds of heaven,
And with a blessèd and unvexed retire,
With unhacked swords and helmets all unbruised,
We will bear home that lusty blood again
Which here we came to spout against your town,
And leave your children, wives, and you in peace.
But if you fondly pass our proffered offer,
'Tis not the roundure of your old-faced walls
Can hide you from our messengers of war,
Though all these English and their discipline
Were harbored in their rude circumference.
Then tell us, shall your city call us lord
In that behalf which we have challenged it?
Or shall we give the signal to our rage
And stalk in blood to our possession?

CITIZEN

In brief, we are the King of England's subjects.
For him, and in his right, we hold this town.

KING JOHN

Acknowledge then the King and let me in.

CITIZEN

That can we not. But he that proves the King,

281. **rammed up:** blocked, closed
284. **breed:** breeding, generation
285. **else:** others
287. **bloods:** men of spirit
289. **in his face:** i.e., against him
290. **compound:** agree
291. **for:** in the interest of
295. **trial of:** i.e., battle to determine
297. **Saint George:** legendary patron saint of England, famous for slaying a **dragon; swinged:** thrashed (See picture, page 52.)
297–99. **e'er since . . . door:** referring to the many Elizabethan taverns called "St. George and the Dragon" and to their signs depicting these figures
300. **fence:** defense; use of the sword
302. **lioness:** another mocking reference to Austria's display of Richard I's lion's skin (but also see longer note, page 218)
304. **monster:** (1) cuckold (often imaged with horns); (2) a beast that is both a lion and an ox

A cuckold. (2.1.304)
From *Bagford Ballads* (printed 1878).

To him will we prove loyal. Till that time
Have we rammed up our gates against the world.

KING JOHN
Doth not the crown of England prove the King?
And if not that, I bring you witnesses,
Twice fifteen thousand hearts of England's breed—

BASTARD Bastards and else.

KING JOHN
To verify our title with their lives.

KING PHILIP
As many and as wellborn bloods as those—

BASTARD Some bastards too.

KING PHILIP
Stand in his face to contradict his claim.

CITIZEN
Till you compound whose right is worthiest,
We for the worthiest hold the right from both.

KING JOHN
Then God forgive the sin of all those souls
That to their everlasting residence,
Before the dew of evening fall, shall fleet
In dreadful trial of our kingdom's king.

KING PHILIP
Amen, amen.—Mount, chevaliers! To arms!

BASTARD
Saint George, that swinged the dragon and e'er
since
Sits on 's horseback at mine hostess' door,
Teach us some fence! ⌜*To Austria.*⌝ Sirrah, were I at
home
At your den, sirrah, with your lioness,
I would set an ox head to your lion's hide
And make a monster of you.

AUSTRIA Peace! No more.

BASTARD
O, tremble, for you hear the lion roar.

308. **appointment:** equipment

309. **advantage:** the superior position; highest ground

311. **the rest:** i.e., our reserves

311 SD. **excursions:** soldiers moving across the stage as if against the enemy; **Trumpets:** trumpeters

314. **hand of France:** i.e., help of the king of **France**

321. **displayed:** unfurled (if **displayed** modifies **banners**), or spread out in an extended line (if **displayed** modifies **the French**)

326. **Commander:** controller, i.e., master; **malicious:** malignant, virulent (a metaphor that draws on medical terminology for disease)

328. **gilt:** gilded, i.e., smeared

330. **staff:** spear

"Saint George, that swinged the dragon." (2.1.297)
From [Jacobus de Voragine,] *Here begynneth the legende named in latyn legenda aurea* . . . [1493].

KING JOHN, ⌜*to his officers*⌝
Up higher to the plain, where we'll set forth
In best appointment all our regiments.

BASTARD
Speed, then, to take advantage of the field.

KING PHILIP, ⌜*to his officers*⌝
It shall be so, and at the other hill
Command the rest to stand. God and our right!

They exit. ⌜*Citizens remain, above.*

Here, after excursions, enter the Herald of France, with Trumpets, to the gates.

FRENCH HERALD
You men of Angiers, open wide your gates,
And let young Arthur, Duke of Brittany, in,
Who by the hand of France this day hath made
Much work for tears in many an English mother,
Whose sons lie scattered on the bleeding ground.
Many a widow's husband groveling lies
Coldly embracing the discolored earth,
And victory with little loss doth play
Upon the dancing banners of the French,
Who are at hand, triumphantly displayed,
To enter conquerors and to proclaim
Arthur of Brittany England's king and yours.

Enter English Herald, with Trumpet.

ENGLISH HERALD
Rejoice, you men of Angiers, ring your bells!
King John, your king and England's, doth approach,
Commander of this hot malicious day.
Their armors, that marched hence so silver bright,
Hither return all gilt with Frenchmen's blood.
There stuck no plume in any English crest
That is removèd by a staff of France.

333–35. **And like . . . foes:** an allusion to the practice of hunters who celebrate their kill by bathing their hands in their quarry's blood

337 SP. **Citizen:** See longer note, page 218.

338. **retire:** retreat

339–40. **whose equality . . . censurèd:** i.e., the **equality** of which is so exact that the **best eyes** among us can see no difference **censurèd:** judged

347 SD. **Powers:** armies; **several:** separate

349. **current of our right:** John images his **right** to the throne as a powerful river which has met the **impediment** (line 350) of the French army.

351. **his native:** i.e., its natural

358. **climate:** part of the sky

Hercules wearing the Nemean lion's skin. (2.1.146–47)
From Henry Peacham, *Minerua Britanna* . . . [1612].

Our colors do return in those same hands
That did display them when we first marched forth,
And like a jolly troop of huntsmen come
Our lusty English, all with purpled hands,
Dyed in the dying slaughter of their foes.
Open your gates, and give the victors way.

⌜CITIZEN⌝

Heralds, from off our towers we might behold,
From first to last the onset and retire
Of both your armies, whose equality
By our best eyes cannot be censurèd.
Blood hath bought blood, and blows have answered blows,
Strength matched with strength, and power confronted power.
Both are alike, and both alike we like.
One must prove greatest. While they weigh so even,
We hold our town for neither, yet for both.

Enter the two Kings with their Powers (⌜including the Bastard, Queen Eleanor, Blanche, and Salisbury; Austria, and Louis the Dauphin⌝), at several doors.

KING JOHN

France, hast thou yet more blood to cast away?
Say, shall the current of our right roam on,
Whose passage, vexed with thy impediment,
Shall leave his native channel and o'erswell
With course disturbed even thy confining shores,
Unless thou let his silver water keep
A peaceful progress to the ocean?

KING PHILIP

England, thou hast not saved one drop of blood
In this hot trial more than we of France,
Rather lost more. And by this hand I swear
That sways the earth this climate overlooks,

359. **just-borne arms:** (1) the **arms** that we have only now **borne** into battle; (2) the **arms** that we have **borne** in a **just** cause

360. **put thee down:** (1) crush you; (2) dethrone you

362. **royal number:** i.e., a king (a threat against John, and an assertion of Philip's determination to risk even his own life)

365. **towers:** soars

367. **chaps:** chops, jaws

369. **mousing:** tearing, biting

371. **fronts:** foreheads, faces; **amazèd:** bewildered

372. **havoc:** the war cry that meant "give no quarter" (i.e., seize or slaughter at will)

373. **potents:** potentates, powerful persons

374. **confusion:** destruction, overthrow; **part:** party, side

377. **yet:** now; **admit:** acknowledge (with wordplay on "allow to enter")

380. **us:** i.e., me (the royal "we")

381–83. **In us . . . presence:** i.e., know me for your king because, unlike Prince Arthur, I can speak and act for myself

386. **scruple:** i.e., doubt about what is the right thing to do

Before we will lay down our just-borne arms,
We'll put thee down, 'gainst whom these arms we bear,
Or add a royal number to the dead,
Gracing the scroll that tells of this war's loss
With slaughter coupled to the name of kings.

BASTARD, ⌜*aside*⌝
Ha, majesty! How high thy glory towers
When the rich blood of kings is set on fire!
O, now doth Death line his dead chaps with steel,
The swords of soldiers are his teeth, his fangs,
And now he feasts, mousing the flesh of men
In undetermined differences of kings.
Why stand these royal fronts amazèd thus?
Cry havoc, kings! Back to the stainèd field,
You equal potents, fiery-kindled spirits.
Then let confusion of one part confirm
The other's peace. Till then, blows, blood, and death!

KING JOHN
Whose party do the townsmen yet admit?

KING PHILIP
Speak, citizens, for England. Who's your king?

⌜CITIZEN⌝
The King of England, when we know the King.

KING PHILIP
Know him in us, that here hold up his right.

KING JOHN
In us, that are our own great deputy
And bear possession of our person here,
Lord of our presence, Angiers, and of you.

⌜CITIZEN⌝
A greater power than we denies all this,
And till it be undoubted, we do lock
Our former scruple in our strong-barred gates,

387. **fear:** i.e., apprehension about doing the wrong thing; **resolved:** allayed

388. **some certain king:** i.e., a legitimate ruler

389. **scroyles:** scoundrels, wretches

392. **industrious:** laborious

394. **mutines of Jerusalem:** a reference to an event in **Jerusalem** in 70 CE, when three warring factions banded together against Roman forces **mutines:** rebels (in this case, against Roman rule)

395. **conjointly bend:** together direct

396. **deeds of malice:** i.e., power to do harm

399. **soul-fearing:** soul-frightening; **brawled down:** driven or forced down by wrangling (Because **brawled** is associated in this line with **clamors,** there is also wordplay on *brawl* as "quarrel noisily.")

401. **play:** i.e., with the siege cannon; **these jades:** i.e., the people of Angiers (**Jades** were broken-down horses, but the word was also applied to fickle or worthless women, and may have that sense here.)

402. **unfencèd:** undefended, unprotected

403. **vulgar:** common

407–10. **Fortune . . . victory:** The image here is of the Goddess Fortuna who, following her whim, selects her current darling (**minion**) and grants him the **kiss** of **victory.** (See page 78.) **happy:** lucky

411. **states:** powers (i.e., kings)

412. **the policy:** statecraft; political cunning

416. **after fight:** afterward **fight** about

418. **peevish:** silly, foolish; obstinate

Kings of our fear, until our fears resolved
Be by some certain king purged and deposed.

BASTARD

By heaven, these scroyles of Angiers flout you, kings,
And stand securely on their battlements
As in a theater, whence they gape and point
At your industrious scenes and acts of death.
Your royal presences, be ruled by me:
Do like the mutines of Jerusalem,
Be friends awhile, and both conjointly bend
Your sharpest deeds of malice on this town.
By east and west let France and England mount
Their battering cannon chargèd to the mouths,
Till their soul-fearing clamors have brawled down
The flinty ribs of this contemptuous city.
I'd play incessantly upon these jades,
Even till unfencèd desolation
Leave them as naked as the vulgar air.
That done, dissever your united strengths
And part your mingled colors once again;
Turn face to face and bloody point to point.
Then in a moment Fortune shall cull forth
Out of one side her happy minion,
To whom in favor she shall give the day
And kiss him with a glorious victory.
How like you this wild counsel, mighty states?
Smacks it not something of the policy?

KING JOHN

Now by the sky that hangs above our heads,
I like it well. France, shall we knit our powers
And lay this Angiers even with the ground,
Then after fight who shall be king of it?

BASTARD, ⌜*to King Philip*⌝

An if thou hast the mettle of a king,
Being wronged as we are by this peevish town,

420. **saucy:** insolent, presumptuous

422. **pell-mell:** headlong, helter-skelter; in hand-to-hand combat

423. **Make work:** wreak havoc

429. **their drift:** i.e., its shower

430. **discipline:** military skill

433. **stay:** wait

434. **show you peace:** i.e., **show you** how to achieve **peace; fair-faced:** attractive

435. **Win you:** i.e., **show you** how to **win**

438. **Persever:** i.e., persevere (in your attack) **Persever** is accented on the second syllable.

439. **favor:** permission; **bent:** inclined

441. **near:** closely related (often emended by editors to "niece," since John was Blanche's uncle); **England:** the king of **England**

443. **lusty:** desirous

446. **purer than in Blanche:** perhaps playing on the French meaning of *blanche* as "white"

447. **match of birth:** i.e., dynastic marriage

Turn thou the mouth of thy artillery,
As we will ours, against these saucy walls,
And when that we have dashed them to the ground,
Why, then, defy each other and pell-mell
Make work upon ourselves, for heaven or hell.

KING PHILIP
Let it be so. Say, where will you assault?

KING JOHN
We from the west will send destruction
Into this city's bosom.

AUSTRIA I from the north.

KING PHILIP Our thunder from the south
Shall rain their drift of bullets on this town.

BASTARD, ⌜*aside*⌝
O, prudent discipline! From north to south,
Austria and France shoot in each other's mouth.
I'll stir them to it.—Come, away, away!

⌜CITIZEN⌝
Hear us, great kings. Vouchsafe awhile to stay,
And I shall show you peace and fair-faced league,
Win you this city without stroke or wound,
Rescue those breathing lives to die in beds
That here come sacrifices for the field.
Persever not, but hear me, mighty kings.

KING JOHN
Speak on with favor. We are bent to hear.

⌜CITIZEN⌝
That daughter there of Spain, the Lady Blanche,
Is near to England. Look upon the years
Of Louis the Dauphin and that lovely maid.
If lusty love should go in quest of beauty,
Where should he find it fairer than in Blanche?
If zealous love should go in search of virtue,
Where should he find it purer than in Blanche?
If love ambitious sought a match of birth,

448. **bound:** confine, contain

448–49. **Lady Blanche:** i.e., Lady Blanche's **veins**

452–58. **If . . . in him:** These lines play with the idea that the only way in which the Lady Blanche and the Dauphin lack completeness and perfection is in not being each other; their union will complete the perfection of both. **wants:** lacks **want:** lack

463. **princes:** The term **prince** could refer to either sex.

464. **battery:** bombardment

465. **match: union** in marriage of the Dauphin and Lady Blanche (but with wordplay on the **match** used to fire the **powder** [line 466] in a cannon)

466. **spleen:** eagerness

469. **The sea . . . deaf:** Proverbial: "As **deaf** as the **sea.**" (See picture, page 132.)

470. **Lions more confident:** Proverbial: "As bold as a lion."

470–71. **mountains . . . motion:** Proverbial: "A mountain might be sooner moved" and "As firm as a rock."

472. **peremptory:** absolutely determined (accented on first and third syllables)

474. **stay:** obstacle, hindrance; or, means of reconciliation

476. **mouth:** i.e., that of the Citizen (but with wordplay on the **mouth** of a cannon that also **spits forth death** [line 477])

Whose veins bound richer blood than Lady Blanche?
Such as she is, in beauty, virtue, birth,
Is the young Dauphin every way complete.
If not complete of, say he is not she,
And she again wants nothing, to name want,
If want it be not that she is not he.
He is the half part of a blessèd man,
Left to be finishèd by such as she,
And she a fair divided excellence,
Whose fullness of perfection lies in him.
O, two such silver currents when they join
Do glorify the banks that bound them in,
And two such shores to two such streams made one,
Two such controlling bounds shall you be, kings,
To these two princes, if you marry them.
This union shall do more than battery can
To our fast-closèd gates, for at this match,
With swifter spleen than powder can enforce,
The mouth of passage shall we fling wide ope
And give you entrance. But without this match,
The sea enragèd is not half so deaf,
Lions more confident, mountains and rocks
More free from motion, no, not Death himself
In mortal fury half so peremptory
As we to keep this city.

⌜*King Philip and Louis the Dauphin walk aside and talk.*⌝

BASTARD, ⌜*aside*⌝ Here's a stay
That shakes the rotten carcass of old Death
Out of his rags! Here's a large mouth indeed
That spits forth death and mountains, rocks and seas;
Talks as familiarly of roaring lions
As maids of thirteen do of puppy dogs.

483. **bounce:** explosion

484. **bastinado:** beating

487. **Zounds:** i.e., by God's wounds (a strong oath); **bethumped:** soundly thumped

489. **list:** listen; **conjunction:** i.e., proposal to unite the Dauphin and Lady Blanche

492. **unsured:** precarious, uncertain, insecure; **assurance:** i.e., hold on the title

493. **yon green boy:** i.e., Prince Arthur **green:** (1) youthful; (2) not yet ripe

498. **capable of:** open to

500. **remorse:** compassion

503. **treaty:** request

504. **forward:** prompt, eager

507. **read "I love":** a reference to the use of *amo* (**"I love"**) as a paradigm in the standard Latin grammars used in grammar schools in Shakespeare's day

508. **queen:** i.e., queen's

510. **this side the sea:** i.e., **this side** of the English Channel, in what we now call France

What cannoneer begot this lusty blood?
He speaks plain cannon fire, and smoke, and bounce.
He gives the bastinado with his tongue.
Our ears are cudgeled. Not a word of his
But buffets better than a fist of France.
Zounds, I was never so bethumped with words
Since I first called my brother's father Dad.

QUEEN ELEANOR, ⌜*aside to King John*⌝
Son, list to this conjunction; make this match.
Give with our niece a dowry large enough,
For by this knot thou shalt so surely tie
Thy now unsured assurance to the crown
That yon green boy shall have no sun to ripe
The bloom that promiseth a mighty fruit.
I see a yielding in the looks of France.
Mark how they whisper. Urge them while their souls
Are capable of this ambition,
Lest zeal, now melted by the windy breath
Of soft petitions, pity, and remorse,
Cool and congeal again to what it was.

⌜CITIZEN⌝
Why answer not the double majesties
This friendly treaty of our threatened town?

KING PHILIP
Speak England first, that hath been forward first
To speak unto this city. What say you?

KING JOHN
If that the Dauphin there, thy princely son,
Can in this book of beauty read "I love,"
Her dowry shall weigh equal with a queen.
For ⌜Anjou⌝ and fair Touraine, Maine, Poitiers,
And all that we upon this side the sea—
Except this city now by us besieged—

512. **liable:** subject; belonging

514. **promotions:** advancements in rank

516. **Holds hand:** matches, is equal to

520. **shadow:** reflection (See longer note, page 218.)

521. **shadow:** insubstantial image (In the following line, the word takes its normal meaning of a dark figure cast on a surface by an object in sunlight.)

524. **infixèd:** fastened, fixed

525. **Drawn:** traced, delineated; **table:** flat surface on which a picture is painted

526–32. **Drawn . . . he:** The punishment for a common **traitor** was to be **hanged,** cut down while still breathing, then disemboweled (**drawn**), and cut into four pieces (**quartered**). The lines play on other meanings of **drawn, hanged** ("suspended"), and **quartered** ("lodged") **love's traitor:** i.e., a **traitor** in love (not a **traitor** to love)

533. **will:** wish

534. **aught:** anything whatsoever

536. **translate . . . will:** i.e., carry it over to **my will** (from **my uncle's will** [line 533])

537. **properly:** accurately

538. **enforce it:** urge it, press it home

Find liable to our crown and dignity,
Shall gild her bridal bed and make her rich
In titles, honors, and promotions,
As she in beauty, education, blood,
Holds hand with any princess of the world.

KING PHILIP
What sayst thou, boy? Look in the lady's face.

DAUPHIN
I do, my lord, and in her eye I find
A wonder or a wondrous miracle,
The shadow of myself formed in her eye,
Which, being but the shadow of your son,
Becomes a sun and makes your son a shadow.
I do protest I never loved myself
Till now infixèd I beheld myself
Drawn in the flattering table of her eye.
⌜He⌝ whispers with Blanche.

BASTARD, *⌜aside⌝*
"Drawn in the flattering table of her eye"?
Hanged in the frowning wrinkle of her brow
And quartered in her heart! He doth espy
Himself love's traitor. This is pity now,
That hanged and drawn and quartered there should be
In such a love so vile a lout as he.

BLANCHE, *⌜aside to Dauphin⌝*
My uncle's will in this respect is mine.
If he see aught in you that makes him like,
That anything he sees which moves his liking
I can with ease translate it to my will.
Or if you will, to speak more properly,
I will enforce it eas'ly to my love.
Further I will not flatter you, my lord,
That all I see in you is worthy love,
Than this: that nothing do I see in you,

542. **churlish:** grudging, stingy

547. **still:** always (as also in line 548)

552. **Volquessen:** i.e., Vexin, a small but valuable region near Paris (See map, page xii.)

555. **marks:** a mark was a coin worth about thirteen shillings

556. **withal:** therewith

557. **daughter:** i.e., future daughter-in-law

558. **likes us:** pleases me; **close:** join

560. **assured:** betrothed, engaged (In the previous line, the word has its standard meaning.)

563. **presently:** immediately

568. **who:** whoever

"Philip of France." (1.1.7)
From Jean de Serres, *A generall historie of France . . .* (1611).

Though churlish thoughts themselves should be your judge,
That I can find should merit any hate.

KING JOHN
What say these young ones? What say you, my niece?

BLANCHE
That she is bound in honor still to do
What you in wisdom still vouchsafe to say.

KING JOHN
Speak then, Prince Dauphin. Can you love this lady?

DAUPHIN
Nay, ask me if I can refrain from love,
For I do love her most unfeignedly.

KING JOHN
Then do I give Volquessen, Touraine, Maine,
Poitiers and Anjou, these five provinces
With her to thee, and this addition more:
Full thirty thousand marks of English coin.—
Philip of France, if thou be pleased withal,
Command thy son and daughter to join hands.

KING PHILIP
It likes us well.—Young princes, close your hands.

AUSTRIA
And your lips too, for I am well assured
That I did so when I was first assured.

⌜*Dauphin and Blanche join hands and kiss.*⌝

KING PHILIP
Now, citizens of Angiers, ope your gates.
Let in that amity which you have made,
For at Saint Mary's Chapel presently
The rites of marriage shall be solemnized.—
Is not the Lady Constance in this troop?
I know she is not, for this match made up
Her presence would have interrupted much.
Where is she and her son? Tell me, who knows.

569. **passionate:** sorrowful, grieved

578. **Richmond:** Lordship of this municipal center in Yorkshire was highly valued and was normally held by the royal family.

581. **solemnity:** celebration (of the Dauphin and Lady Blanche's wedding)

583. **measure:** vessel (used for measuring); **will:** desire

585. **exclamation:** loud reproach

586. **suffer:** allow

587. **pomp:** splendid celebration

588. **composition:** compromise, agreement

590. **departed with:** given away, given up

593. **rounded:** whispered (to)

594. **With:** i.e., by

595. **broker:** middleman, agent; pimp; **still:** always; **breaks . . . faith:** i.e., beats promise-keeping over the head (To **break the pate** is to cut the scalp.)

596. **break-vow:** oath-breaker; **wins of:** gets the better of

598. **Who:** i.e., **maids**

599. **the word "maid":** i.e., her virginity; **cheats:** i.e., **Commodity cheats**

DAUPHIN
She is sad and passionate at your Highness' tent.
KING PHILIP
And by my faith, this league that we have made
Will give her sadness very little cure.—
Brother of England, how may we content
This widow lady? In her right we came,
Which we, God knows, have turned another way
To our own vantage.
KING JOHN We will heal up all,
For we'll create young Arthur Duke of Brittany
And Earl of Richmond, and this rich, fair town
We make him lord of.—Call the Lady Constance.
Some speedy messenger bid her repair
To our solemnity. ⌜*Salisbury exits.*⌝ I trust we shall,
If not fill up the measure of her will,
Yet in some measure satisfy her so
That we shall stop her exclamation.
Go we as well as haste will suffer us
To this unlooked-for, unpreparèd pomp.
⌜*All but the Bastard*⌝ *exit.*
BASTARD
Mad world, mad kings, mad composition!
John, to stop Arthur's title in the whole,
Hath willingly departed with a part;
And France, whose armor conscience buckled on,
Whom zeal and charity brought to the field
As God's own soldier, rounded in the ear
With that same purpose-changer, that sly devil,
That broker that still breaks the pate of faith,
That daily break-vow, he that wins of all,
Of kings, of beggars, old men, young men, maids—
Who having no external thing to lose
But the word "maid," cheats the poor maid of that—

601. **smooth-faced:** i.e., ingratiating; **Commodity:** self-interest

602. **the bias:** In lawn bowling, **the bias** is the lead inserted in one side of the ball that causes the ball to move in a curved, rather than a straight, path. (See picture, page 120.)

603. **who of itself:** i.e., which in **itself; peisèd well:** well-balanced, in equilibrium

604. **run even:** i.e., move rapidly in a straight line

605. **advantage:** opportunity to benefit oneself; **vile-drawing bias:** impetus toward what is morally debased or depraved

606. **sway of motion:** i.e., force affecting **motion**

607. **take head from:** throw off all control of; **indifferency:** impartiality, equity, and fairness

610. **all-changing word:** i.e., **word** that changes everything

611. **Clapped . . . eye:** wordplay on **eye** as the hole in which the lead is placed in a bowling ball **Clapped:** placed **outward:** as opposed to the inward **eye** of conscience

616. **But for:** i.e., only; **he:** i.e., Commodity

617. **clutch:** close or clench (in a gesture of refusal of what is offered)

618. **angels:** gold coins worth about ten shillings in Shakespeare's day and stamped with the figure of Michael the archangel (See picture, page 106.) **salute:** kiss

619. **unattempted yet:** against which no attempt has **yet** been made

That smooth-faced gentleman, tickling Commodity,
Commodity, the bias of the world—
The world, who of itself is peisèd well,
Made to run even upon even ground,
Till this advantage, this vile-drawing bias,
This sway of motion, this Commodity,
Makes it take head from all indifferency,
From all direction, purpose, course, intent.
And this same bias, this Commodity,
This bawd, this broker, this all-changing word,
Clapped on the outward eye of fickle France,
Hath drawn him from his own determined aid,
From a resolved and honorable war
To a most base and vile-concluded peace.
And why rail I on this Commodity?
But for because he hath not wooed me yet.
Not that I have the power to clutch my hand
When his fair angels would salute my palm,
But for my hand, as unattempted yet,
Like a poor beggar raileth on the rich.
Well, whiles I am a beggar, I will rail
And say there is no sin but to be rich;
And being rich, my virtue then shall be
To say there is no vice but beggary.
Since kings break faith upon Commodity,
Gain, be my lord, for I will worship thee!

He exits.

The Life and Death of

KING JOHN

ACT 3

3.1 The league between John and Philip is attacked first by Constance, who accuses Philip of treacherously betraying Arthur's cause, and then by Pandulph, legate from Pope Innocent. Pandulph excommunicates John when John refuses to obey the Pope; Pandulph then threatens Philip with excommunication if he does not turn against John. When Philip obeys Pandulph, John prepares for war.

---

5. **misspoke:** spoken wrongly or improperly

9. **breath of a common man:** in contrast to a **king's oath** (line 11) (Salisbury is in fact an earl, not a commoner.)

12. **frighting:** frightening

13. **capable of:** susceptible to

17. **though thou now:** i.e., even if you were **now** to

18. **cannot:** i.e., would not be able to; **take a truce:** make peace

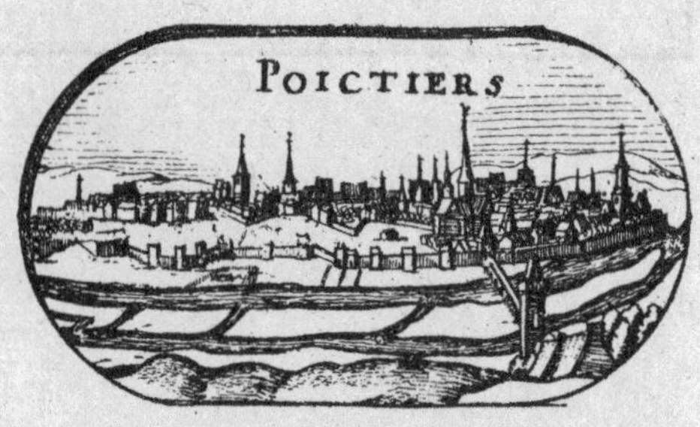

Poitiers. (1.1.11; 2.1.553)
From John Speed, *A prospect of the most famous parts of the world* . . . (1631).

ACT ⌜3⌝

⌜Scene 1⌝

Enter Constance, Arthur, and Salisbury.

CONSTANCE, ⌜*to Salisbury*⌝
Gone to be married? Gone to swear a peace?
False blood to false blood joined? Gone to be friends?
Shall Louis have Blanche and Blanche those provinces?
It is not so. Thou hast misspoke, misheard.
Be well advised; tell o'er thy tale again.
It cannot be; thou dost but say 'tis so.
I trust I may not trust thee, for thy word
Is but the vain breath of a common man.
Believe me, I do not believe thee, man.
I have a king's oath to the contrary.
Thou shalt be punished for thus frighting me,
For I am sick and capable of fears,
Oppressed with wrongs and therefore full of fears,
A widow, husbandless, subject to fears,
A woman naturally born to fears.
And though thou now confess thou didst but jest,
With my vexed spirits I cannot take a truce,
But they will quake and tremble all this day.
What dost thou mean by shaking of thy head?
Why dost thou look so sadly on my son?
What means that hand upon that breast of thine?

23. **lamentable rheum:** i.e., tears **lamentable:** doleful, mournful (accent on first syllable)

24. **his:** i.e., its

38. **Fellow:** a contemptuous and insulting term of familiar address when applied, as it is here, to someone not greatly inferior in rank

41. **spoke:** i.e., spoken

44. **content:** calm

46. **sland'rous:** a source of shame and disgrace

47. **blots:** blemishes, disfigurements; **sightless:** unsightly; **stains:** blotches, sores

48. **swart:** swarthy; **prodigious:** unnatural, monstrous

Fortune, "her humorous ladyship." (3.1.125)
From *Fortunes tennis-ball: a warning . . .* (1640).

Why holds thine eye that lamentable rheum,
Like a proud river peering o'er his bounds?
Be these sad signs confirmers of thy words?
Then speak again—not all thy former tale,
But this one word, whether thy tale be true.

SALISBURY

As true as I believe you think them false
That give you cause to prove my saying true.

CONSTANCE

O, if thou teach me to believe this sorrow,
Teach thou this sorrow how to make me die,
And let belief and life encounter so
As doth the fury of two desperate men
Which in the very meeting fall and die.
Louis marry Blanche?—O, boy, then where art thou?—
France friend with England? What becomes of me?
Fellow, be gone. I cannot brook thy sight.
This news hath made thee a most ugly man.

SALISBURY

What other harm have I, good lady, done
But spoke the harm that is by others done?

CONSTANCE

Which harm within itself so heinous is
As it makes harmful all that speak of it.

ARTHUR

I do beseech you, madam, be content.

CONSTANCE

If thou that bidd'st me be content wert grim,
Ugly, and sland'rous to thy mother's womb,
Full of unpleasing blots and sightless stains,
Lame, foolish, crooked, swart, prodigious,
Patched with foul moles and eye-offending marks,
I would not care; I then would be content,
For then I should not love thee; no, nor thou

54. **Nature and Fortune:** The gifts of these two "goddesses" were frequently contrasted. "**Fortune** reigns in gifts of the world" (to quote Rosalind in *As You Like It*), while **Nature** is responsible for the gifts one is born with. (See note to 2.1.407–10.)

56. **half-blown:** i.e., just opened (as opposed to full-blown)

58. **Sh' adulterates:** i.e., she commits adultery

60. **respect of sovereignty:** i.e., **respect** for his own **sovereignty** and yours

61. **bawd:** go-between, pimp; **theirs:** i.e., the majesties of **Fortune and King John** (line 62)

63. **strumpet Fortune:** Proverbial: "**Fortune** is a **strumpet.**" (See picture, page 98.)

65. **Envenom him with words:** i.e., speak of **him with** bitter **words**

67. **underbear:** endure

72. **his:** i.e., its; **stoop:** bow to superior authority (Constance may sit down at this point, as we indicate, or she could choose to sit at almost any point in the speech through line 76.)

73. **state:** (1) condition; (2) throne (said ironically, since her seat is on the ground)

77 SD. **hand in hand:** See longer note, page 219.

78. **daughter:** i.e., daughter-in-law

Become thy great birth, nor deserve a crown.
But thou art fair, and at thy birth, dear boy,
Nature and Fortune joined to make thee great.
Of Nature's gifts thou mayst with lilies boast,
And with the half-blown rose. But Fortune, O,
She is corrupted, changed, and won from thee;
Sh' adulterates hourly with thine Uncle John,
And with her golden hand hath plucked on France
To tread down fair respect of sovereignty,
And made his majesty the bawd to theirs.
France is a bawd to Fortune and King John,
That strumpet Fortune, that usurping John.—
Tell me, thou fellow, is not France forsworn?
Envenom him with words, or get thee gone
And leave those woes alone which I alone
Am bound to underbear.

SALISBURY Pardon me, madam,
I may not go without you to the Kings.

CONSTANCE
Thou mayst, thou shalt, I will not go with thee.
I will instruct my sorrows to be proud,
For grief is proud and makes his owner stoop.
⌜*She sits down.*⌝
To me and to the state of my great grief
Let kings assemble, for my grief's so great
That no supporter but the huge firm earth
Can hold it up. Here I and sorrows sit.
Here is my throne; bid kings come bow to it.

Enter King John, ⌜*hand in hand with King Philip of*⌝ *France,* ⌜*Louis the*⌝ *Dauphin, Blanche,* ⌜*Queen*⌝ *Eleanor,* ⌜*Bastard,*⌝ *Austria,* ⌜*and Attendants.*⌝

KING PHILIP, ⌜*to Blanche*⌝
'Tis true, fair daughter, and this blessèd day
Ever in France shall be kept festival.

81. **Stays:** halts; **his:** i.e., its (Compare Joshua 10.13–14: "The sun stayed in the midst of heaven and did not hasten to go down for about a whole day.")

81–83. **plays the alchemist . . . gold:** See Shakespeare's sonnet 33, where the sun kisses "with golden face the meadows green, / Gilding pale streams with heav'nly alchemy." **meager:** poor

88. **golden letters:** i.e., red **letters** (reserved in calendars of this period for noteworthy days)

89. **high tides:** important festivals

90. **turn . . . week:** Compare Job 3.3, 6: "Let the day perish. . . . Let it not be joined unto the days of the year, nor let it come into the count of the months."

92. **stand still:** remain

93. **burdens . . . fall:** i.e., babies not be born

94. **prodigiously be crossed:** i.e., be thwarted by the birth of an abnormal child

95. **But on this day:** i.e., **on** any **day but this** one

97. **ill:** unfortunate; evil

101. **pawned:** pledged

102. **counterfeit:** spurious imitation; likeness

103. **touched and tried:** i.e., rubbed against a touchstone to test its genuineness (See picture, page 146.) **tried:** tested

105. **in arms:** armed, furnished with weapons

106. **in arms:** arm in arm (with King John)

108. **painted peace: Peace** is personified here as a woman whose only attractiveness arises from her use of cosmetics.

109. **our:** Constance and Prince Arthur's; **made up:** composed, completed

To solemnize this day the glorious sun
Stays in his course and plays the alchemist,
Turning with splendor of his precious eye
The meager cloddy earth to glittering gold.
The yearly course that brings this day about
Shall never see it but a holy day.

CONSTANCE, ⌜*rising*⌝
A wicked day, and not a holy day!
What hath this day deserved? What hath it done
That it in golden letters should be set
Among the high tides in the calendar?
Nay, rather turn this day out of the week,
This day of shame, oppression, perjury.
Or if it must stand still, let wives with child
Pray that their burdens may not fall this day,
Lest that their hopes prodigiously be crossed.
But on this day let seamen fear no wrack;
No bargains break that are not this day made;
This day, all things begun come to ill end,
Yea, faith itself to hollow falsehood change!

KING PHILIP
By heaven, lady, you shall have no cause
To curse the fair proceedings of this day.
Have I not pawned to you my majesty?

CONSTANCE
You have beguiled me with a counterfeit
Resembling majesty, which, being touched and tried,
Proves valueless. You are forsworn, forsworn.
You came in arms to spill mine enemies' blood,
But now in arms you strengthen it with yours.
The grappling vigor and rough frown of war
Is cold in amity and painted peace,
And our oppression hath made up this league.
Arm, arm, you heavens, against these perjured
kings!

112. **A widow . . . God:** Compare Isaiah 54.4–5: "Thou . . . shalt not remember the reproach of thy widowhood any more. For he that made thee is thine husband (whose Name is the Lord of hosts)." **A widow cries:** i.e., it is **a widow** who **cries**

119. **O Limoges:** For the play's combining of **Limoges** and **Austria,** see longer note to 2.1.5.

120. **That bloody spoil:** i.e., the lion's skin taken from Richard the Lion-heart **spoil:** possession of a defeated enemy stripped by the victor

125. **humorous:** capricious (See picture, page 78.) **by:** nearby

126. **safety:** i.e., how to keep safe (**upon the stronger side** [line 123])

127. **sooth'st up greatness:** flatter the powerful

128. **ramping:** *To ramp* is to rage with violent gestures, to act in a threatening manner.

129. **Upon my party:** in my cause

133. **fall over:** go over

135. **calfskin:** "Calf" was a term for a meek, inoffensive person. **recreant:** cowardly; forsworn, perjured

140. **We:** i.e., I (the royal "we"); **forget thyself:** behave improperly

A widow cries; be husband to me, ⌜God!⌝
Let not the hours of this ungodly day
Wear out the days in peace, but ere sunset
Set armèd discord 'twixt these perjured kings.
Hear me, O, hear me!

AUSTRIA
Lady Constance, peace.

CONSTANCE
War, war, no peace! Peace is to me a war.
O Limoges, O Austria, thou dost shame
That bloody spoil. Thou slave, thou wretch, thou coward,
Thou little valiant, great in villainy,
Thou ever strong upon the stronger side,
Thou Fortune's champion, that dost never fight
But when her humorous ladyship is by
To teach thee safety. Thou art perjured too,
And sooth'st up greatness. What a fool art thou,
A ramping fool, to brag and stamp and swear
Upon my party. Thou cold-blooded slave,
Hast thou not spoke like thunder on my side?
Been sworn my soldier, bidding me depend
Upon thy stars, thy fortune, and thy strength?
And dost thou now fall over to my foes?
Thou wear a lion's hide! Doff it for shame,
And hang a calfskin on those recreant limbs.

AUSTRIA
O, that a man should speak those words to me!

BASTARD
"And hang a calfskin on those recreant limbs."

AUSTRIA
Thou dar'st not say so, villain, for thy life!

BASTARD
"And hang a calfskin on those recreant limbs."

KING JOHN
We like not this. Thou dost forget thyself.

144. **Milan:** accent on first syllable

145. **Innocent:** i.e., Innocent III (pope 1198–1216, and thus pope throughout King John's reign) See below.

148. **spurn:** display scornful opposition; **force perforce:** by **force**

149. **Stephen Langton:** the Englishman appointed **Archbishop of Canterbury** by the pope (in opposition to John's wishes) See the "Homily" in Historical Background 3, page 234.

153. **earthy:** worldly (in contrast to **sacred** [line 154])

154. **task:** force (to answer)

157. **charge me to:** command me to (give)

160. **toll:** collect tax

165–66. **all reverence set apart / To him:** i.e., putting aside all respect due him because of his office

166. **usurped authority:** See Historical Background 2, page 232.

169. **led:** i.e., misled

Pope Innocent III. (3.1.145, 152)
From *Chronologie et sommaire des souuerains* . . . (1622).

Enter Pandulph.

KING PHILIP

Here comes the holy legate of the Pope.

PANDULPH

Hail, you anointed deputies of heaven!
To thee, King John, my holy errand is.
I, Pandulph, of fair Milan cardinal
And from Pope Innocent the legate here,
Do in his name religiously demand
Why thou against the Church, our holy mother,
So willfully dost spurn, and force perforce
Keep Stephen Langton, chosen Archbishop
Of Canterbury, from that Holy See.
This, in our foresaid Holy Father 's name,
Pope Innocent, I do demand of thee.

The said attack most likely won't do much but it will show where they stand

KING JOHN

What earthy name to interrogatories
Can ⌜task⌝ the free breath of a sacred king?
Thou canst not, cardinal, devise a name
So slight, unworthy, and ridiculous
To charge me to an answer, as the Pope.
Tell him this tale, and from the mouth of England
Add thus much more, that no Italian priest
Shall tithe or toll in our dominions;
But as we under ⌜God⌝ are supreme head,
So, under Him, that great supremacy
Where we do reign we will alone uphold
Without th' assistance of a mortal hand.
So tell the Pope, all reverence set apart
To him and his usurped authority.

King Phillip might've realized that its just easier to side with John

KING PHILIP

Brother of England, you blaspheme in this.

KING JOHN

Though you and all the kings of Christendom
Are led so grossly by this meddling priest,

theres more risk in siding with someone who isnt even king

170. **the curse:** i.e., excommunication; **that money may buy out:** i.e., from which one may ransom oneself by payment

171–73. **And by . . . himself:** These lines allude to the practice of selling indulgences, i.e., remission of punishment for sins of which one has been absolved.

171. **by the merit:** i.e., through the "good works" (wordplay in which the Catholic position—that salvation can be achieved by **merit** instead of only through faith—is mocked through equating **merit** with **vile gold**)

172–73. **of a man . . . himself:** i.e., from a **man** who damns **himself** by selling pardons

175. **juggling:** cheating, deceptive; **revenue:** accent on second syllable; **cherish:** foster

176. **do me oppose:** i.e., **oppose** myself

181. **an heretic:** i.e., in this case, King John

187. **room, Rome:** These two words may have sounded alike in Shakespeare's day.

188–89. **Amen . . . keen curses:** "A Commination against Sinners" in the Church of England's official prayer book called for the congregation to say **"Amen"** to each of a series of **curses** recited by the priest. Constance suggests a reversal of clerical and lay roles. **keen:** fierce, stinging

189. **without my wrong:** i.e., without making reference to the **wrong** done to me by King John; or, without being motivated by suffering that **wrong**

193. **bar:** stop; **wrong:** i.e., her cursing King John without any legal warrant to do so

196. **wrong:** injustice (to me and Prince Arthur)

198. **a curse:** i.e., excommunication

199. **the hand:** See longer note to line 77 SD.

Dreading the curse that money may buy out,
And by the merit of vile gold, dross, dust,
Purchase corrupted pardon of a man
Who in that sale sells pardon from himself,
Though you and all the rest, so grossly led,
This juggling witchcraft with revenue cherish,
Yet I alone, alone do me oppose
Against the Pope, and count his friends my foes.

PANDULPH

Then, by the lawful power that I have,
Thou shalt stand cursed and excommunicate;
And blessèd shall he be that doth revolt
From his allegiance to an heretic;
And meritorious shall that hand be called,
Canonizèd and worshiped as a saint,
That takes away by any secret course
Thy hateful life.

CONSTANCE O, lawful let it be
That I have room with Rome to curse awhile!
Good father cardinal, cry thou "Amen"
To my keen curses, for without my wrong
There is no tongue hath power to curse him right.

PANDULPH

There's law and warrant, lady, for my curse.

CONSTANCE

And for mine, too. When law can do no right,
Let it be lawful that law bar no wrong.
Law cannot give my child his kingdom here,
For he that holds his kingdom holds the law.
Therefore, since law itself is perfect wrong,
How can the law forbid my tongue to curse?

PANDULPH

Philip of France, on peril of a curse,
Let go the hand of that arch-heretic,
And raise the power of France upon his head
Unless he do submit himself to Rome.

Money could give power, but only the throne gives loyalty

Constance's next course of action is what?

Finding a new country to side with?

These two are likely to be the only ones involved

207. **pocket up:** meekly endure (The Bastard's speech at line 209 gives **pocket up** its literal meaning.)

211. **as the Cardinal:** i.e., **as the Cardinal** says

212. **Bethink you:** take thought

218. **untrimmèd bride:** unadorned **bride;** or, perhaps, a **bride** with her hair unadorned by clasps and therefore hanging down to her shoulders in the style of a virgin

221. **need:** i.e., **need** to obtain aid in procuring England's throne for Arthur

222. **faith:** i.e., Philip's promise to aid Arthur, which, if he kept it, would eliminate Constance's **need**

223. **infer:** introduce, imply

"Lady Blanche of Spain." (2.1.64)
From *Chronologie et sommaire des souuerains . . .* (1622).

QUEEN ELEANOR
Look'st thou pale, France? Do not let go thy hand.

CONSTANCE
Look to that, devil, lest that France repent
And by disjoining hands, hell lose a soul.

AUSTRIA
King Philip, listen to the Cardinal.

BASTARD
And hang a calfskin on his recreant limbs.

AUSTRIA
Well, ruffian, I must pocket up these wrongs,
Because—

BASTARD Your breeches best may carry them.

KING JOHN
Philip, what sayst thou to the Cardinal?

CONSTANCE
What should he say, but as the Cardinal?

DAUPHIN
Bethink you, father, for the difference
Is purchase of a heavy curse from Rome,
Or the light loss of England for a friend.
Forgo the easier.

BLANCHE That's the curse of Rome.

CONSTANCE
O Louis, stand fast! The devil tempts thee here
In likeness of a new untrimmèd bride.

BLANCHE
The Lady Constance speaks not from her faith,
But from her need.

CONSTANCE, ⌜*to King Philip*⌝
O, if thou grant my need,
Which only lives but by the death of faith,
That need must needs infer this principle:
That faith would live again by death of need.
O, then tread down my need, and faith mounts up;
Keep my need up, and faith is trodden down.

227. **moved:** perturbed, angered

228. **removed:** separated (with wordplay on **moved**, line 227)

231. **perplexed:** full of doubt

234. **make . . . yours:** i.e., put yourself in my place

235. **bestow:** acquit

240. **latest:** most recent

243. **even:** just; **but new:** i.e., immediately

245. **clap . . . peace:** i.e., (1) clasp hands to formalize this peace agreement between kings; (2) hastily put together this royal agreement

246. **overstained:** covered with stains

247. **pencil:** paintbrush

251. **seizure:** grasp; **regreet:** reciprocal salutation

252. **fast and loose:** a cheating game involving seemingly tight (i.e., **fast**) knots that are actually **loose; jest with heaven:** Proverbial: "It is ill jesting with gods."

253. **unconstant:** inconstant

Peace. (2.1.84–90)
From Gilles Corrozet, *Hecatongraphie* . . . (1543).

KING JOHN
The King is moved, and answers not to this.

CONSTANCE, ⌜*to King Philip*⌝
O, be removed from him, and answer well!

AUSTRIA
Do so, King Philip. Hang no more in doubt.

BASTARD
Hang nothing but a calfskin, most sweet lout.

KING PHILIP
I am perplexed and know not what to say.

PANDULPH
What canst thou say but will perplex thee more
If thou stand excommunicate and cursed?

KING PHILIP
Good reverend father, make my person yours,
And tell me how you would bestow yourself.
This royal hand and mine are newly knit,
And the conjunction of our inward souls
Married, in league, coupled, and linked together
With all religious strength of sacred vows.
The latest breath that gave the sound of words
Was deep-sworn faith, peace, amity, true love
Between our kingdoms and our royal selves;
And even before this truce, but new before,
No longer than we well could wash our hands
To clap this royal bargain up of peace,
⌜God⌝ knows they were besmeared and overstained
With slaughter's pencil, where revenge did paint
The fearful difference of incensèd kings.
And shall these hands, so lately purged of blood,
So newly joined in love, so strong in both,
Unyoke this seizure and this kind regreet?
Play fast and loose with faith? So jest with heaven?
Make such unconstant children of ourselves
As now again to snatch our palm from palm,

267. **revolting:** rebelling
268. **mayst hold:** i.e., may sooner **hold**
269. **chafèd:** raging, furious; **mortal:** deadly
272. **faith:** i.e., sworn agreement
273–308. **So mak'st . . . weight:** See longer note, page 219.
284. **act:** acting, performance
285. **indirect:** devious, deceitful; oblique
286. **indirection:** deceit; **direct:** straightforward, morally upright

A "fierce dragon." (2.1.68)
From Ulisse Aldrovandi, . . . *Serpentum, et draconum historiae libri duo* . . . [1639].

Unswear faith sworn, and on the marriage bed
Of smiling peace to march a bloody host
And make a riot on the gentle brow
Of true sincerity? O holy sir,
My reverend father, let it not be so!
Out of your grace, devise, ordain, impose
Some gentle order, and then we shall be blest
To do your pleasure and continue friends.

PANDULPH

All form is formless, order orderless,
Save what is opposite to England's love.
Therefore to arms! Be champion of our Church,
Or let the Church, our mother, breathe her curse,
A mother's curse, on her revolting son.
France, thou mayst hold a serpent by the tongue,
A ⌜chafèd⌝ lion by the mortal paw,
A fasting tiger safer by the tooth,
Than keep in peace that hand which thou dost hold.

KING PHILIP

I may disjoin my hand, but not my faith.

PANDULPH

So mak'st thou faith an enemy to faith,
And like a civil war sett'st oath to oath,
Thy tongue against thy tongue. O, let thy vow
First made to ⌜God,⌝ first be to ⌜God⌝ performed,
That is, to be the champion of our Church!
What since thou swor'st is sworn against thyself
And may not be performèd by thyself,
For that which thou hast sworn to do amiss
Is not amiss when it is truly done;
And being not done where doing tends to ill,
The truth is then most done not doing it.
The better act of purposes mistook
Is to mistake again; though indirect,
Yet indirection thereby grows direct,

287–88. **as fire . . . new-burned:** Proverbial: "One **fire** drives out another." These lines also may refer to an old belief that burns could be alleviated with heat.

303. **suggestions:** temptations

304. **which better part:** i.e., **thy constant and thy nobler parts** (line 302)

305. **vouchsafe:** deign to accept

308. **black:** deadly

310. **Will 't not be:** i.e., **will** you never **be** quiet?

314. **the blood . . . marrièd:** i.e., King John, my blood relative

317. **be measures to our pomp:** i.e., provide the music for our wedding celebration

"Death . . . in mortal fury." (2.1.471–72)
From *Imagines mortis* . . . (1557).

And falsehood falsehood cures, as fire cools fire
Within the scorchèd veins of one new-burned.
It is religion that doth make vows kept,
But thou hast sworn against religion
By what thou swear'st against the thing thou
  swear'st,
And mak'st an oath the surety for thy truth
Against an oath. The truth thou art unsure
To swear swears only not to be forsworn,
Else what a mockery should it be to swear?
But thou dost swear only to be forsworn,
And most forsworn to keep what thou dost swear.
Therefore thy later vows against thy first
Is in thyself rebellion to thyself.
And better conquest never canst thou make
Than arm thy constant and thy nobler parts
Against these giddy loose suggestions,
Upon which better part our prayers come in,
If thou vouchsafe them. But if not, then know
The peril of our curses light on thee
So heavy as thou shalt not shake them off,
But in despair die under their black weight.

AUSTRIA
Rebellion, flat rebellion!

BASTARD
                                        Will 't not be?
Will not a calfskin stop that mouth of thine?

DAUPHIN
Father, to arms!

BLANCHE
                        Upon thy wedding day?
Against the blood that thou hast marrièd?
What, shall our feast be kept with slaughtered men?
Shall braying trumpets and loud churlish drums,
Clamors of hell, be measures to our pomp?
                                        ⌜*She kneels.*⌝
O husband, hear me! Ay, alack, how new
Is "husband" in my mouth! Even for that name,

325. **doom:** irrevocable destiny

326. **Forethought:** premeditated

331. **cold:** deliberate, unimpassioned

332. **profound respects:** great considerations

333. **denounce:** proclaim, publicly announce

334. **fall from:** forsake, renounce my connection with

339. **bald:** Proverbial: "Take **Time** (occasion) by the forelock, for she is **bald** behind." **sexton:** parish official responsible for ringing the church bell, setting the church clock, and digging graves

339, 340. **Time, rue:** perhaps with wordplay on *thyme* and *rue* as the names of herbs

342. **withal:** i.e., with

"That strumpet Fortune." (3.1.63)
From George Wither, *A collection of emblemes . . .* (1635).

Which till this time my tongue did ne'er pronounce,
Upon my knee I beg, go not to arms
Against mine uncle.

CONSTANCE, ⌜*kneeling*⌝
O, upon my knee
Made hard with kneeling, I do pray to thee,
Thou virtuous Dauphin, alter not the doom
Forethought by heaven!

BLANCHE, ⌜*to Dauphin*⌝
Now shall I see thy love. What motive may
Be stronger with thee than the name of wife?

CONSTANCE
That which upholdeth him that thee upholds,
His honor.—O, thine honor, Louis, thine honor!

DAUPHIN, ⌜*to King Philip*⌝
I muse your Majesty doth seem so cold,
When such profound respects do pull you on.

PANDULPH
I will denounce a curse upon his head.

KING PHILIP, ⌜*dropping King John's hand*⌝
Thou shalt not need.—England, I will fall from
thee.

CONSTANCE, ⌜*rising*⌝
O, fair return of banished majesty!

QUEEN ELEANOR
O, foul revolt of French inconstancy!

KING JOHN
France, thou shalt rue this hour within this hour.

BASTARD
Old Time the clock-setter, that bald sexton Time,
Is it as he will? Well, then, France shall rue.

BLANCHE, ⌜*rising*⌝
The sun's o'ercast with blood. Fair day, adieu.
Which is the side that I must go withal?
I am with both, each army hath a hand,

348. **Father:** i.e., father-in-law

354. **Cousin:** kinsman; **puissance:** army (**Puissance** is here pronounced as a three-syllable word.)

3.2 The Bastard, having killed the Duke of Austria, reports that he has rescued Queen Eleanor. Arthur, captured by John, is turned over to Hubert's care.

---

0 SD. **Alarums:** trumpet signaling a call to arms; **excursions:** sorties

3. **mischief:** calamity, harm, evil

4, 5. **Philip:** a reversion to the Bastard's original name, changed to *Richard* when he was knighted

4. **breathes:** catches his breath, pauses, rests

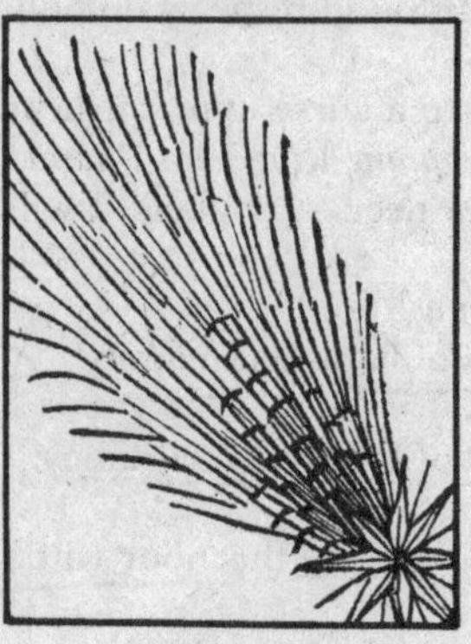

A "natural exhalation in the sky." (3.4.156)
From Hartmann Schedel, *Liber chronicorum* [1493].

And in their rage, I having hold of both,
They whirl asunder and dismember me.
Husband, I cannot pray that thou mayst win.—
Uncle, I needs must pray that thou mayst lose.—
Father, I may not wish the fortune thine.—
Grandam, I will not wish thy wishes thrive.
Whoever wins, on that side shall I lose.
Assurèd loss before the match be played.

DAUPHIN
Lady, with me, with me thy fortune lies.

BLANCHE
There where my fortune lives, there my life dies.

KING JOHN, ⌜*to Bastard*⌝
Cousin, go draw our puissance together.

⌜*Bastard exits.*⌝

France, I am burned up with inflaming wrath,
A rage whose heat hath this condition,
That nothing can allay, nothing but blood—
The blood, and dearest-valued blood, of France.

KING PHILIP
Thy rage shall burn thee up, and thou shalt turn
To ashes ere our blood shall quench that fire.
Look to thyself. Thou art in jeopardy.

KING JOHN
No more than he that threats.—To arms let's hie!

They exit.

Scene 2

Alarums, excursions.
Enter Bastard with Austria's head.

BASTARD
Now, by my life, this day grows wondrous hot.
Some airy devil hovers in the sky
And pours down mischief. Austria's head lie there,
While Philip breathes.

5. **make up:** advance in a certain direction (in this case toward John's **tent** [line 6])

10–11. **pains, labor:** with wordplay on **labor pains**

3.3 John prepares to leave for England with his forces. He tells Hubert that Arthur must die. Hubert promises to kill Arthur.

---

0 SD. **retreat:** trumpet signals for a **retreat**

2. **So:** thus; **Cousin:** kinsman

4. **dear:** affectionate, loving

8. **hoarding abbots:** For King John and the Roman Catholic Church, see Historical Background 2, page 232. **angels:** gold coins (with wordplay on "spiritual beings") See note to 2.1.618 and picture, page 106.

11. **his:** its

12. **Bell, book, and candle:** Proverbial: "To curse with **bell, book, and candle.**" The "curse" was excommunication.

13. **becks:** beckons

Enter ⌜King⌝ John, Arthur, Hubert.

KING JOHN

Hubert, keep this boy.—Philip, make up.
My mother is assailed in our tent
And ta'en, I fear.

BASTARD My lord, I rescued her.
Her Highness is in safety, fear you not.
But on, my liege, for very little pains
Will bring this labor to an happy end.

⌜They⌝ exit.

⌜Scene 3⌝

Alarums, excursions, retreat.
Enter ⌜King⌝ John, ⌜Queen⌝ Eleanor, Arthur, Bastard, Hubert, Lords.

KING JOHN, ⌜*to Queen Eleanor*⌝

So shall it be. Your Grace shall stay behind
So strongly guarded. ⌜*To Arthur.*⌝ Cousin, look not sad.
Thy grandam loves thee, and thy uncle will
As dear be to thee as thy father was.

ARTHUR

O, this will make my mother die with grief!

KING JOHN, ⌜*to Bastard*⌝

Cousin, away for England! Haste before,
And ere our coming see thou shake the bags
Of hoarding abbots; imprisoned angels
Set at liberty. The fat ribs of peace
Must by the hungry now be fed upon.
Use our commission in his utmost force.

BASTARD

Bell, book, and candle shall not drive me back
When gold and silver becks me to come on.
I leave your Highness.—Grandam, I will pray,

18. **Coz:** cousin, i.e., kinsman

24. **advantage:** interest, profit

25. **voluntary oath:** vow (of allegiance) freely offered

30. **respect:** regard, esteem

31. **bounden:** obliged

38. **wanton:** frivolous; **gauds:** pranks, tricks; toys

39. **give me audience:** i.e., pay attention to **me**

40. **his:** its; **brazen:** brass

41. **Sound on:** continue to resound; **race:** course

43. **possessèd with:** possessing (with possible wordplay on "**possessed** by" in the sense of demonic possession)

Guy fights to free all Englands feares,
With Colbrond, Gyant Dane:

Guy of Warwick fights "Colbrand the Giant." (1.1.231)
From [Samuel Rowlands,] *The famous historie* . . . [1609].

If ever I remember to be holy,
For your fair safety. So I kiss your hand.

QUEEN ELEANOR
Farewell, gentle cousin.

KING JOHN Coz, farewell. ⌜*Bastard exits.*⌝

QUEEN ELEANOR, ⌜*to Arthur*⌝
Come hither, little kinsman. Hark, a word.
⌜*They walk aside.*⌝

KING JOHN
Come hither, Hubert. ⌜*He takes Hubert aside.*⌝
O, my gentle Hubert,
We owe thee much. Within this wall of flesh
There is a soul counts thee her creditor,
And with advantage means to pay thy love.
And, my good friend, thy voluntary oath
Lives in this bosom dearly cherishèd.
Give me thy hand. I had a thing to say,
But I will fit it with some better tune.
By heaven, Hubert, I am almost ashamed
To say what good respect I have of thee.

HUBERT
I am much bounden to your Majesty.

KING JOHN
Good friend, thou hast no cause to say so yet,
But thou shalt have. And, creep time ne'er so slow,
Yet it shall come for me to do thee good.
I had a thing to say—but let it go.
The sun is in the heaven, and the proud day,
Attended with the pleasures of the world,
Is all too wanton and too full of gauds
To give me audience. If the midnight bell
Did with his iron tongue and brazen mouth
Sound on into the drowsy race of night;
If this same were a churchyard where we stand,
And thou possessèd with a thousand wrongs;

44–45. **melancholy . . . thick:** For **melancholy** as a substance that affects the **blood,** see longer note, page 220.

46. **else:** otherwise; **tickling:** tingling

47. **idiot:** professional jester or fool

49. **passion:** mood

52. **conceit:** imagination; thought

54. **brooded:** brooding, like a bird watching a nest of eggs (Many editors emend to "broad-eyed.")

67. **keeper:** (1) jailer; (2) guardian

An "angel." (2.1.618; 3.3.8)
From Henry William Henfrey, *A guide to the study of English coins . . .* (1885).

Or if that surly spirit, melancholy,
Had baked thy blood and made it heavy, thick,
Which else runs tickling up and down the veins,
Making that idiot, laughter, keep men's eyes
And strain their cheeks to idle merriment,
A passion hateful to my purposes;
Or if that thou couldst see me without eyes,
Hear me without thine ears, and make reply
Without a tongue, using conceit alone,
Without eyes, ears, and harmful sound of words;
Then, in despite of brooded watchful day,
I would into thy bosom pour my thoughts.
But, ah, I will not. Yet I love thee well,
And by my troth I think thou lov'st me well.

HUBERT
So well that what you bid me undertake,
Though that my death were adjunct to my act,
By heaven, I would do it.

KING JOHN Do not I know thou wouldst?
Good Hubert, Hubert, Hubert, throw thine eye
On yon young boy. I'll tell thee what, my friend,
He is a very serpent in my way,
And wheresoe'er this foot of mine doth tread,
He lies before me. Dost thou understand me?
Thou art his keeper.

HUBERT And I'll keep him so
That he shall not offend your Majesty.

KING JOHN
Death.

HUBERT My lord?

KING JOHN A grave.

HUBERT He shall not live.

KING JOHN Enough.
I could be merry now. Hubert, I love thee.
Well, I'll not say what I intend for thee.

79. **powers:** armed forces

82. **man:** personal servant

83. **Calais:** seaport on the English Channel (Pronunciation is suggested by the Folio spelling, "Callice.") See picture, page 110, and map, page xii.

3.4 John's victories and his capture of Arthur lead the French to despair and Constance to wild grief. Pandulph, predicting Arthur's death and the hatred of John that will inevitably ensue, encourages the Dauphin to invade England and claim the throne as Blanche's husband.

1–3. **So . . . fellowship:** See longer note, page 220. **flood:** ocean, sea **convicted:** vanquished **sail:** i.e., ships

5. **run so ill:** ended up being so unfortunate (with wordplay on **go** as "walk")

9. **O'erbearing interruption:** overwhelming or crushing obstruction; **spite:** in **spite**

11. **advice:** wisdom, deliberation, design

13. **want example:** lack precedent

14. **kindred:** similar

16. **So:** i.e., if; **pattern of:** precedent for

16 SD. **hair unbound:** an expression of grief

Remember. ⌜*He turns to Queen Eleanor.*⌝ Madam, fare
you well.
I'll send those powers o'er to your Majesty.

QUEEN ELEANOR My blessing go with thee.

KING JOHN, ⌜*to Arthur*⌝ For England, cousin, go.
Hubert shall be your man, attend on you
With all true duty.—On toward Calais, ho!

They exit.

Scene ⌜4⌝

Enter ⌜King Philip of⌝ France, ⌜Louis the⌝ Dauphin, Pandulph, Attendants.

KING PHILIP
So, by a roaring tempest on the flood,
A whole armada of convicted sail
Is scattered and disjoined from fellowship.

PANDULPH
Courage and comfort. All shall yet go well.

KING PHILIP
What can go well when we have run so ill?
Are we not beaten? Is not Angiers lost?
Arthur ta'en prisoner? Divers dear friends slain?
And bloody England into England gone,
O'erbearing interruption, spite of France?

DAUPHIN
What he hath won, that hath he fortified.
So hot a speed, with such advice disposed,
Such temperate order in so fierce a cause,
Doth want example. Who hath read or heard
Of any kindred action like to this?

KING PHILIP
Well could I bear that England had this praise,
So we could find some pattern of our shame.

Enter Constance, ⌜with her hair unbound.⌝

17–19. **A grave . . . breath:** Proverbial: "The body is the prison of the **soul.**"

21. **issue:** outcome (perhaps with wordplay on "offspring")

23. **defy:** reject, despise

26. **odoriferous:** sweet, fragrant

30. **in thy vaulty brows:** i.e., beneath your **brows** that are arched like vaults (See picture, page 112.)

31. **thy household worms:** i.e., the **worms** that are your retinue

32. **gap of breath:** i.e., mouth; **fulsome:** foul, loathsome; **dust:** decayed remains of dead bodies

33. **carrion:** rotten; skeleton-like

35. **buss:** kiss; **Misery's love:** i.e., that which misery loves

40. **a passion:** an outburst

41. **fell anatomy:** dreadful skeleton

43. **a modern:** an ordinary

45. **belie:** misrepresent

Calais. (3.3.83)
From John Speed, *A prospect of the most famous parts of the world . . .* (1631).

Look who comes here! A grave unto a soul,
Holding th' eternal spirit against her will
In the vile prison of afflicted breath.—
I prithee, lady, go away with me.

CONSTANCE

Lo, now, now see the issue of your peace!

KING PHILIP

Patience, good lady. Comfort, gentle Constance.

CONSTANCE

No, I defy all counsel, all redress,
But that which ends all counsel, true redress.
Death, death, O amiable, lovely death,
Thou odoriferous stench, sound rottenness,
Arise forth from the couch of lasting night,
Thou hate and terror to prosperity,
And I will kiss thy detestable bones
And put my eyeballs in thy vaulty brows,
And ring these fingers with thy household worms,
And stop this gap of breath with fulsome dust,
And be a carrion monster like thyself.
Come, grin on me, and I will think thou smil'st,
And buss thee as thy wife. Misery's love,
O, come to me!

KING PHILIP O fair affliction, peace!

CONSTANCE

No, no, I will not, having breath to cry.
O, that my tongue were in the thunder's mouth!
Then with a passion would I shake the world
And rouse from sleep that fell anatomy
Which cannot hear a lady's feeble voice,
Which scorns a modern invocation.

PANDULPH

Lady, you utter madness and not sorrow.

CONSTANCE

Thou art ⌜not⌝ holy to belie me so.
I am not mad. This hair I tear is mine;

49. **would:** wish
50. **like:** likely; **forget myself:** lose consciousness
53. **canonized:** accent on second syllable
54. **sensible:** aware
56. **delivered of:** freed from
59. **babe of clouts:** rag doll **clouts:** clothes, rags
61. **different plague:** distinctive affliction
64. **silver drop:** i.e., tear
65. **wiry friends:** i.e., hairs
66. **sociable:** companionable
71. **wherefore:** why
75. **envy at:** begrudge

Death's "vaulty brows." (3.4.30)
From Geoffrey Whitney, *A choice of emblemes* . . . (1586).

My name is Constance; I was Geoffrey's wife;
Young Arthur is my son, and he is lost.
I am not mad; I would to heaven I were,
For then 'tis like I should forget myself.
O, if I could, what grief should I forget!
Preach some philosophy to make me mad,
And thou shalt be canonized, cardinal.
For, being not mad but sensible of grief,
My reasonable part produces reason
How I may be delivered of these woes,
And teaches me to kill or hang myself.
If I were mad, I should forget my son,
Or madly think a babe of clouts were he.
I am not mad. Too well, too well I feel
The different plague of each calamity.

KING PHILIP
Bind up those tresses.—O, what love I note
In the fair multitude of those her hairs;
Where but by chance a silver drop hath fall'n,
Even to that drop ten thousand wiry ⌜friends⌝
Do glue themselves in sociable grief,
Like true, inseparable, faithful loves,
Sticking together in calamity.

CONSTANCE
To England, if you will.

KING PHILIP
Bind up your hairs.

CONSTANCE
Yes, that I will. And wherefore will I do it?
I tore them from their bonds and cried aloud
"O, that these hands could so redeem my son,
As they have given these hairs their liberty!"
But now I envy at their liberty,
And will again commit them to their bonds,
Because my poor child is a prisoner.

⌜She binds up her hair.⌝

81. **Cain:** the firstborn son of Adam and Eve (Genesis 4.1)

82. **To . . . suspire:** i.e., until the birth of the child born yesterday **suspire:** breathe

83. **gracious:** graceful, attractive

84. **canker:** the cankerworm (See picture, page 124.)

85. **native:** natural

87. **an ague's fit:** the shaking caused by chills and fever

92. **heinous:** severe

95. **room:** empty space

98. **Remembers:** reminds; **parts:** qualities

99. **Stuffs out:** i.e., fills up; **his form:** i.e., its **form**

103. **form:** coiffure (orderly arrangement of her hair)

104. **wit:** mind

An image of despair. (3.4.57; 4.3.133)
From Jean François Senault, *The use of passions . . .* (1649).

And father cardinal, I have heard you say
That we shall see and know our friends in heaven.
If that be true, I shall see my boy again;
For since the birth of Cain, the first male child,
To him that did but yesterday suspire,
There was not such a gracious creature born.
But now will canker sorrow eat my bud
And chase the native beauty from his cheek,
And he will look as hollow as a ghost,
As dim and meager as an ague's fit,
And so he'll die; and, rising so again,
When I shall meet him in the court of heaven
I shall not know him. Therefore never, never
Must I behold my pretty Arthur more.

PANDULPH

You hold too heinous a respect of grief.

CONSTANCE

He talks to me that never had a son.

KING PHILIP

You are as fond of grief as of your child.

CONSTANCE

Grief fills the room up of my absent child,
Lies in his bed, walks up and down with me,
Puts on his pretty looks, repeats his words,
Remembers me of all his gracious parts,
Stuffs out his vacant garments with his form;
Then, have I reason to be fond of grief?
Fare you well. Had you such a loss as I,
I could give better comfort than you do.

⌜*She unbinds her hair.*⌝

I will not keep this form upon my head
When there is such disorder in my wit.
O Lord! My boy, my Arthur, my fair son,
My life, my joy, my food, my all the world,
My widow-comfort and my sorrows' cure! *She exits.*

108. **outrage:** violence (that she may do against herself)

116. **repair:** restoration (of health)

117. **fit:** attack of illness

118. **show:** appear

119. **this day:** i.e., **this day**'s battle (In the Dauphin's reply, **days** has its usual meaning.)

131. **dust:** i.e., speck of **dust; rub:** obstacle (In the game of bowls, a **rub** is any obstruction that hinders or deflects the course of the bowl.)

133. **mark:** pay attention

135. **infant's:** noble youth's (As a legal term, *infant* refers to anyone under twenty-one years of age.)

"And so he'll die; and, rising so again. . . ." (3.4.88)
From Thomas Fisher's etching of the wall painting of Doomsday in the Guild Chapel at Stratford-upon-Avon, 1807.

KING PHILIP
I fear some outrage, and I'll follow her.
He exits, ⌜*with Attendants.*⌝

DAUPHIN
There's nothing in this world can make me joy.
Life is as tedious as a twice-told tale,
Vexing the dull ear of a drowsy man;
And bitter shame hath spoiled the sweet ⌜world's⌝
taste,
That it yields naught but shame and bitterness.

PANDULPH
Before the curing of a strong disease,
Even in the instant of repair and health,
The fit is strongest. Evils that take leave
On their departure most of all show evil.
What have you lost by losing of this day?

DAUPHIN
All days of glory, joy, and happiness.

PANDULPH
If you had won it, certainly you had.
No, no. When Fortune means to men most good,
She looks upon them with a threat'ning eye.
'Tis strange to think how much King John hath lost
In this which he accounts so clearly won.
Are not you grieved that Arthur is his prisoner?

DAUPHIN
As heartily as he is glad he hath him.

PANDULPH
Your mind is all as youthful as your blood.
Now hear me speak with a prophetic spirit.
For even the breath of what I mean to speak
Shall blow each dust, each straw, each little rub,
Out of the path which shall directly lead
Thy foot to England's throne. And therefore mark:
John hath seized Arthur, and it cannot be
That, whiles warm life plays in that infant's veins,

136. **misplaced:** occupying the wrong place; usurping; **entertain:** maintain, preserve

138. **unruly:** disorderly, violent

139. **boisterously:** violently

141. **Makes nice of no:** i.e., shows no scruple about using any; **stay him up:** support himself

142. **That:** i.e., so **that**

148. **green:** inexperienced

149. **lays you plots:** i.e., devises plans for **you** to exploit

152. **This act:** i.e., the murder of Arthur (predicted at line 142); **borne:** carried out (although, perhaps, with wordplay on *born*)

154. **none . . . advantage:** i.e., no opportunity, no matter how **small**

155. **check:** stop; **reign:** power; period on the throne

156. **exhalation:** i.e., luminous appearance (See picture, page 100.)

157. **No . . . nature:** i.e., nothing in the range of natural events; **distempered:** inclement, stormy

158. **customèd:** customary

159. **his:** i.e., its

161. **Abortives:** i.e., monstrous, unnatural events

162. **denouncing:** portending

164. **hold . . . prisonment:** i.e., regard himself as secure as long as Arthur is imprisoned

The misplaced John should entertain an hour,
One minute, nay, one quiet breath of rest.
A scepter snatched with an unruly hand
Must be as boisterously maintained as gained.
And he that stands upon a slipp'ry place
Makes nice of no vile hold to stay him up.
That John may stand, then Arthur needs must fall.
So be it, for it cannot be but so.

DAUPHIN

But what shall I gain by young Arthur's fall?

PANDULPH

You, in the right of Lady Blanche your wife,
May then make all the claim that Arthur did.

DAUPHIN

And lose it, life and all, as Arthur did.

PANDULPH

How green you are and fresh in this old world!
John lays you plots. The times conspire with you,
For he that steeps his safety in true blood
Shall find but bloody safety, and untrue.
This act so evilly borne shall cool the hearts
Of all his people and freeze up their zeal,
That none so small advantage shall step forth
To check his reign but they will cherish it.
No natural exhalation in the sky,
No scope of nature, no distempered day,
No common wind, no customèd event,
But they will pluck away his natural cause
And call them meteors, prodigies, and signs,
Abortives, presages, and tongues of heaven,
Plainly denouncing vengeance upon John.

DAUPHIN

Maybe he will not touch young Arthur's life,
But hold himself safe in his prisonment.

PANDULPH

O, sir, when he shall hear of your approach,

169. **unacquainted:** strange

170. **pick strong matter of:** i.e., find **strong** reasons for **matter:** reasons, grounds (with wordplay on the meanings "pus, corruption")

172. **hurly:** uproar, tumult; **all on foot:** fully in motion

173. **better:** i.e., even **better; breeds:** comes into being

177. **call:** decoy bird

178. **train:** entice, attract

179–80. **as a little snow . . . mountain:** Proverb: "Like a snowball, that rolling becomes bigger."

184. **whet on:** urge on

185. **makes:** i.e., make

Lawn bowling. (2.1.602–9; 3.4.131)
From *Le centre de l'amour . . .* [1650?].

If that young Arthur be not gone already,
Even at that news he dies; and then the hearts
Of all his people shall revolt from him
And kiss the lips of unacquainted change,
And pick strong matter of revolt and wrath
Out of the bloody fingers' ends of John.
Methinks I see this hurly all on foot;
And, O, what better matter breeds for you
Than I have named! The bastard Faulconbridge
Is now in England ransacking the Church,
Offending charity. If but a dozen French
Were there in arms, they would be as a call
To train ten thousand English to their side,
Or as a little snow, tumbled about,
Anon becomes a mountain. O noble dauphin,
Go with me to the King. 'Tis wonderful
What may be wrought out of their discontent,
Now that their souls are topful of offense.
For England, go. I will whet on the King.

DAUPHIN

Strong reasons makes strange actions. Let us go.
If you say ay, the King will not say no.

They exit.

The Life and Death of

KING JOHN

ACT 4

4.1 Hubert prepares to put out Arthur's eyes with hot irons. Arthur begs him to show mercy. Hubert plans to tell John that Arthur is dead.

---

1. **Heat me:** i.e., **heat; look:** make sure, take care

4. **which:** i.e., whom

6. **bear out:** back up, corroborate

7. **Uncleanly scruples fear not you:** i.e., do not be frightened by doubts about the immorality of what is to be done **Uncleanly:** morally or spiritually impure

8. **have to say:** must speak

9. **Good morrow:** i.e., **good** morning

11–12. **As little . . . may be:** i.e., I am as inconsequential a **prince** as it is possible to be, despite my right to an even greater **title**

12. **sad:** serious; sorrowful

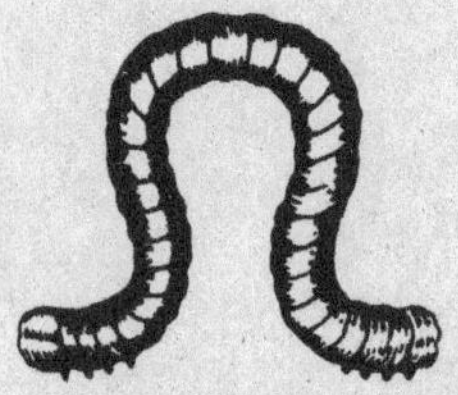

A cankerworm. (3.4.84)
From John Johnstone, [*Opera aliquot*] [1650–62].

ACT 4

Scene 1

Enter Hubert and Executioners, ⌜*with irons and rope.*⌝

HUBERT

Heat me these irons hot, and look thou stand
Within the arras. When I strike my foot
Upon the bosom of the ground, rush forth
And bind the boy which you shall find with me
Fast to the chair. Be heedful. Hence, and watch.

EXECUTIONER

I hope your warrant will bear out the deed.

HUBERT

Uncleanly scruples fear not you. Look to 't.

⌜*Executioners exit.*⌝

Young lad, come forth. I have to say with you.

Enter Arthur.

ARTHUR

Good morrow, Hubert.

HUBERT

Good morrow, little prince.

ARTHUR

As little prince, having so great a title
To be more prince, as may be. You are sad.

HUBERT

Indeed, I have been merrier.

ARTHUR

Mercy on me!

17. **as sad as night:** The word **sad** meant "dark" as well as "mournful."

18. **wantonness:** caprice, whim; **By my christendom:** as I am a Christian

19. **So:** i.e., if

21. **doubt:** fear

22. **practices:** plots

26. **so:** provided that

29. **dispatch:** be quick; be done with it

31. **In sooth, I would:** truly, I wish

32. **watch with:** stay awake in order to tend to

36. **rheum:** i.e., tears

37. **Turning . . . door:** i.e., dismissing or banishing pitiless **torture**

38. **brief:** expeditious

40. **fair writ:** legibly written

"So I were out of prison and kept sheep." (4.1.19)
From *Hortus sanitatis* . . . (1536).

Methinks nobody should be sad but I.
Yet I remember, when I was in France,
Young gentlemen would be as sad as night
Only for wantonness. By my christendom,
So I were out of prison and kept sheep,
I should be as merry as the day is long.
And so I would be here but that I doubt
My uncle practices more harm to me.
He is afraid of me, and I of him.
Is it my fault that I was Geoffrey's son?
No, indeed, is 't not. And I would to heaven
I were your son, so you would love me, Hubert.

HUBERT, ⌜*aside*⌝

If I talk to him, with his innocent prate
He will awake my mercy, which lies dead.
Therefore I will be sudden and dispatch.

ARTHUR

Are you sick, Hubert? You look pale today.
In sooth, I would you were a little sick
That I might sit all night and watch with you.
I warrant I love you more than you do me.

HUBERT, ⌜*aside*⌝

His words do take possession of my bosom.

⌜*He shows Arthur a paper.*

Read here, young Arthur. (⌜*Aside.*⌝) How now,
foolish rheum?
Turning dispiteous torture out of door?
I must be brief lest resolution drop
Out at mine eyes in tender womanish tears.—
Can you not read it? Is it not fair writ?

ARTHUR

Too fairly, Hubert, for so foul effect.
Must you with hot irons burn out both mine eyes?

HUBERT

Young boy, I must.

47. **knit:** bound; **handkercher:** handkerchief

48. **wrought it me:** i.e., embroidered **it** for **me**

49. **ask it you again:** i.e., **ask you** to give **it** back

51. **watchful:** vigilant (but with wordplay on *watch,* meaning both "timepiece" and "stay awake to tend the sick")

52. **Still and anon:** faithfully from time to time; **heavy:** sluggish; distressful

54. **grief:** pain; sickness

55. **love:** act of kindness

56. **lien:** lain

58. **sick service:** i.e., **service** when you were **sick**

59. **crafty:** self-serving

61. **ill:** injuriously; wickedly

67. **Iron Age:** The last and most morally degraded of the four ages (the Golden, Silver, Bronze, and **Iron**), the **Iron Age** is characterized by fraud, violence, and greed. (See Ovid, *Metamorphoses* 1.89–150.) See picture, page 130.

68. **heat:** i.e., heated

71. **matter:** substance (i.e., tears)

73. **But for containing:** i.e., just because it contained

75. **angel:** divine messenger

ARTHUR And will you?

HUBERT And I will.

ARTHUR

Have you the heart? When your head did but ache,
I knit my handkercher about your brows—
The best I had, a princess wrought it me—
And I did never ask it you again;
And with my hand at midnight held your head,
And like the watchful minutes to the hour
Still and anon cheered up the heavy time,
Saying "What lack you?" and "Where lies your grief?"
Or "What good love may I perform for you?"
Many a poor man's son would have lien still
And ne'er have spoke a loving word to you;
But you at your sick service had a prince.
Nay, you may think my love was crafty love,
And call it cunning. Do, an if you will.
If heaven be pleased that you must use me ill,
Why then you must. Will you put out mine eyes—
These eyes that never did nor never shall
So much as frown on you?

HUBERT I have sworn to do it.
And with hot irons must I burn them out.

ARTHUR

Ah, none but in this Iron Age would do it.
The iron of itself, though heat red-hot,
Approaching near these eyes, would drink my tears
And quench this fiery indignation
Even in the matter of mine innocence;
Nay, after that, consume away in rust
But for containing fire to harm mine eye.
Are you more stubborn-hard than hammered iron?
An if an angel should have come to me
And told me Hubert should put out mine eyes,

81–82. **out / Even with:** i.e., blinded just by

84. **boist'rous-rough:** violent

90. **angerly:** angrily

94. **from:** away **from,** absent **from**

95. **chid away:** driven away by complaining against

96. **stern:** merciless, cruel

The Iron Age:

Contayning the Rape of *Hellen*: The siege of *Troy*: The Combate betwixt *Hector* and *Aiax*: *Hector* and *Troilus* slayne by *Achilles*: *Achilles* slaine by *Paris*: *Aiax* and *Vlisses* contend for the Armour of *Achilles*: The Death of *Aiax*, &c.

Writen by THOMAS HEYWOOD.

Aut prodesse solent audi Delectare.

Printed at *London* by *Nicholas Okes*, 1632.

A seventeenth-century image of the Iron Age. (4.1.67)
From Thomas Heywood, *The Iron Age* (1632).

I would not have believed him. No tongue but
Hubert's.

HUBERT ⌜*stamps his foot and calls*⌝ Come forth.

⌜*Enter Executioners with ropes, a heated iron, and a brazier of burning coals.*⌝

Do as I bid you do.

ARTHUR

O, save me, Hubert, save me! My eyes are out
Even with the fierce looks of these bloody men.

HUBERT

Give me the iron, I say, and bind him here.

⌜*He takes the iron.*⌝

ARTHUR

Alas, what need you be so boist'rous-rough?
I will not struggle; I will stand stone-still.
For ⌜God's⌝ sake, Hubert, let me not be bound!
Nay, hear me, Hubert! Drive these men away,
And I will sit as quiet as a lamb.
I will not stir nor wince nor speak a word
Nor look upon the iron angerly.
Thrust but these men away, and I'll forgive you,
Whatever torment you do put me to.

HUBERT, ⌜*to Executioners*⌝

Go stand within. Let me alone with him.

EXECUTIONER

I am best pleased to be from such a deed.

⌜*Executioners exit.*⌝

ARTHUR

Alas, I then have chid away my friend!
He hath a stern look but a gentle heart.
Let him come back, that his compassion may
Give life to yours.

HUBERT Come, boy, prepare yourself.

ARTHUR

Is there no remedy?

103. **dust:** speck of **dust**

105. **boisterous:** painfully rough

108. **Go to:** an expression of impatience

109–10. **the utterance . . . eyes:** i.e., the **pleading** by a pair of **tongues** would not be adequate to the need of preserving two **eyes**

113. **So:** provided

119–20. **Being . . . extremes:** i.e., because it was created to provide **comfort** and is being used in the cause of extreme and unjust violence

120. **See else yourself:** i.e., **see** for **yourself** if it is otherwise

122, 123. **his:** i.e., its

126. **shame of:** i.e., **shame** at

127. **sparkle in:** throw out sparks into

"The sea enragèd." (2.1.469)
From Lodovico Dolce, *Imprese nobili* . . . (1583).

HUBERT None but to lose your eyes.

ARTHUR
O ⌜God,⌝ that there were but a mote in yours,
A grain, a dust, a gnat, a wandering hair,
Any annoyance in that precious sense.
Then, feeling what small things are boisterous there,
Your vile intent must needs seem horrible.

HUBERT
Is this your promise? Go to, hold your tongue.

ARTHUR
Hubert, the utterance of a brace of tongues
Must needs want pleading for a pair of eyes.
Let me not hold my tongue. Let me not, Hubert,
Or, Hubert, if you will, cut out my tongue,
So I may keep mine eyes. O, spare mine eyes,
Though to no use but still to look on you.
⌜*He seizes the iron.*⌝
Lo, by my troth, the instrument is cold,
And would not harm me.

HUBERT, ⌜*taking back the iron*⌝
I can heat it, boy.

ARTHUR
No, in good sooth. The fire is dead with grief,
Being create for comfort, to be used
In undeserved extremes. See else yourself.
There is no malice in this burning coal.
The breath of heaven hath blown his spirit out
And strewed repentant ashes on his head.

HUBERT
But with my breath I can revive it, boy.

ARTHUR
An if you do, you will but make it blush
And glow with shame of your proceedings, Hubert.
Nay, it perchance will sparkle in your eyes,

129. **Snatch:** snap; **tar him on:** incite the dog (to fight)

130. **should:** i.e., could

131. **office:** function

133. **Creatures of note:** i.e., objects notable or famous

135. **owes:** i.e., owns

141. **but:** i.e., **but** that

142. **doggèd:** doglike

143. **doubtless:** free of fears

145. **offend:** harm

147. **closely:** secretly, covertly

4.2 The nobles express their disapproval of John's second coronation and urge that he set Arthur free. When Hubert brings word that Arthur is dead, the nobles turn against John and go in search of Arthur's body. A messenger tells John that the French, under the Dauphin, have landed in England and that Eleanor and Constance have both died. After sending the Bastard to try to bring the nobles back, John attacks Hubert for having killed Arthur. When Hubert discloses that Arthur is unharmed, John sends the happy news to the nobles.

---

1. **we:** i.e., I (the royal "we")
3. **but:** except

And, like a dog that is compelled to fight,
Snatch at his master that doth tar him on.
All things that you should use to do me wrong
Deny their office. Only you do lack
That mercy which fierce fire and iron extends,
Creatures of note for mercy-lacking uses.

HUBERT

Well, see to live. I will not touch thine eye
For all the treasure that thine uncle owes.
Yet am I sworn, and I did purpose, boy,
With this same very iron to burn them out.

ARTHUR

O, now you look like Hubert. All this while
You were disguisèd.

HUBERT

Peace. No more. Adieu.
Your uncle must not know but you are dead.
I'll fill these doggèd spies with false reports.
And, pretty child, sleep doubtless and secure
That Hubert, for the wealth of all the world,
Will not offend thee.

ARTHUR

O heaven! I thank you, Hubert.

HUBERT

Silence. No more. Go closely in with me.
Much danger do I undergo for thee.

They exit.

Scene 2

Enter ⌜King⌝ John, Pembroke, Salisbury, and other Lords. ⌜King John ascends the throne.⌝

KING JOHN

Here once again we sit, once ⌜again⌝ crowned
And looked upon, I hope, with cheerful eyes.

PEMBROKE

This "once again," but that your Highness pleased,

4. **once superfluous:** i.e., one time too many (In the speeches of Pembroke and Salisbury that follow, their criticism of King John is made indirect through the use of elaborate and challenging figures of speech.)

6. **faiths:** allegiances

7. **expectation:** anticipation

9. **to be . . . pomp:** i.e., to take possession (of your crown and kingdom) by way of a second coronation **pomp:** splendid display (but also, specious show)

10. **guard:** (1) ornament (with borders or trim); (2) protect, defend

19. **troublesome:** causing annoyance, bothersome

20. **urgèd:** pressed upon the attention

21. **antique:** ancient; **well-noted:** well-known, familiar

23. **a shifted wind:** i.e., **a wind** that changes direction (This nautical metaphor continues in line 24 with **course** and with **fetch about,** meaning "take a roundabout course, tack, or change direction.")

25. **frights:** frightens; **consideration:** reflection, but also regard (for John) among people

29. **confound:** defeat, overthrow; **covetousness:** inordinate desire

32. **breach:** hole or tear

Was once superfluous. You were crownèd before,
And that high royalty was ne'er plucked off,
The faiths of men ne'er stainèd with revolt;
Fresh expectation troubled not the land
With any longed-for change or better state.

SALISBURY

Therefore, to be possessed with double pomp,
To guard a title that was rich before,
To gild refinèd gold, to paint the lily,
To throw a perfume on the violet,
To smooth the ice or add another hue
Unto the rainbow, or with taper-light
To seek the beauteous eye of heaven to garnish,
Is wasteful and ridiculous excess.

PEMBROKE

But that your royal pleasure must be done,
This act is as an ancient tale new told,
And, in the last repeating, troublesome,
Being urgèd at a time unseasonable.

SALISBURY

In this the antique and well-noted face
Of plain old form is much disfigurèd,
And like a shifted wind unto a sail,
It makes the course of thoughts to fetch about,
Startles and frights consideration,
Makes sound opinion sick and truth suspected
For putting on so new a fashioned robe.

PEMBROKE

When workmen strive to do better than well,
They do confound their skill in covetousness,
And oftentimes excusing of a fault
Doth make the fault the worse by th' excuse,
As patches set upon a little breach
Discredit more in hiding of the fault
Than did the fault before it was so patched.

36. **breathed:** made known, communicated
38. **overbear:** repress, overrule
39. **would:** desire
40. **make a stand:** halt; **will:** wishes, desires
41. **reasons of:** i.e., **reasons** for; **double:** i.e., second
44. **endue:** supply
49. **sound:** utter, proclaim (with wordplay on "measure the depth of")
51. **Your safety:** i.e., in the interest of **your** security
52. **Bend . . . studies:** i.e., direct their concern most assiduously
53. **enfranchisement:** release from imprisonment; **restraint:** confinement
56. **what . . . have:** perhaps, **what you have** seized or wrested, punning on **rest;** or, perhaps, **what you** quietly possess (**Rest** also meant "arrest.")
57. **Why then:** i.e., **why** is it, **then,** that
61. **exercise:** practice for the sake of training or improvement, whether physical, mental, or spiritual
63. **grace occasions:** confer dignity on pretexts or excuses (for discontent); **suit:** request
65. **for our goods:** i.e., **for our** own benefit
66. **whereupon:** as to, concerning which; **weal:** well-being, welfare

SALISBURY
To this effect, before you were new-crowned,
We breathed our counsel; but it pleased your Highness
To overbear it, and we are all well pleased,
Since all and every part of what we would
Doth make a stand at what your Highness will.

KING JOHN
Some reasons of this double coronation
I have possessed you with, and think them strong;
And more, more strong, ⌜when⌝ lesser is my fear,
I shall endue you with. Meantime, but ask
What you would have reformed that is not well,
And well shall you perceive how willingly
I will both hear and grant you your requests.

PEMBROKE
Then I, as one that am the tongue of these
To sound the purposes of all their hearts,
Both for myself and them, but chief of all
Your safety, for the which myself and them
Bend their best studies, heartily request
Th' enfranchisement of Arthur, whose restraint
Doth move the murmuring lips of discontent
To break into this dangerous argument:
If what in rest you have in right you hold,
Why then your fears, which, as they say, attend
The steps of wrong, should move you to mew up
Your tender kinsman and to choke his days
With barbarous ignorance and deny his youth
The rich advantage of good exercise.
That the time's enemies may not have this
To grace occasions, let it be our suit
That you have bid us ask, his liberty,
Which for our goods we do no further ask
Than whereupon our weal, on you depending,
Counts it your weal he have his liberty.

69 SD. **Enter Hubert:** See longer note, page 220.

71. **man should:** i.e., **man** who is to

74. **close aspect:** secretive look

80. **heralds:** Since **heralds** dressed in red, they can represent the blood coming into and leaving King John's face. **battles set:** battalions (or armies) marshaled for battle

81. **passion:** vehement feeling; **ripe:** at a head (like a boil ready to **break** or burst)

86. **suit:** request

87. **is deceased tonight:** died last night

91. **answered:** atoned or made amends for

92. **bend . . . brows:** i.e., frown

"Here once again we sit, once again crowned." (4.2.1)
From Raphael Holinshed, *The Chronicles of England* (1577).

KING JOHN
Let it be so. I do commit his youth
To your direction.

Enter Hubert.

Hubert, what news with you?
⌜*King John and Hubert talk aside.*⌝

PEMBROKE
This is the man should do the bloody deed.
He showed his warrant to a friend of mine.
The image of a wicked heinous fault
Lives in his eye. That close aspect of his
⌜Doth⌝ show the mood of a much troubled breast,
And I do fearfully believe 'tis done
What we so feared he had a charge to do.

SALISBURY
The color of the King doth come and go
Between his purpose and his conscience,
Like heralds 'twixt two dreadful battles set.
His passion is so ripe it needs must break.

PEMBROKE
And when it breaks, I fear will issue thence
The foul corruption of a sweet child's death.

KING JOHN, ⌜*coming forward with Hubert*⌝
We cannot hold mortality's strong hand.—
Good lords, although my will to give is living,
The suit which you demand is gone and dead.
He tells us Arthur is deceased tonight.

SALISBURY
Indeed, we feared his sickness was past cure.

PEMBROKE
Indeed, we heard how near his death he was
Before the child himself felt he was sick.
This must be answered either here or hence.

KING JOHN
Why do you bend such solemn brows on me?

93. **shears of destiny:** These **shears** are borne by Atropos, the one of the three Fates who cuts the thread of life. (See picture, page 144.)

94. **commandment on:** control over

95. **apparent:** evident, obvious

96. **grossly:** plainly, obviously; **offer:** inflict

97. **So . . . game:** i.e., may your intrigue bring you to the same end **game:** scheme, intrigue

100. **forcèd:** enforced

101. **owed:** owned

103. **this will break out:** The state of the kingdom is compared to an eruption on the skin ready to **break** and spill its corruption.

104. **doubt:** fear, anticipate with apprehension

108. **fearful:** (1) frightened; (2) frightening

112. **From . . . England:** i.e., **all goes from France to England** (The messenger's response implies a literal use of the words **goes all,** used figuratively in King John's line 111.) **power:** army

113. **any foreign preparation:** i.e., for the purpose of invading a **foreign** country

115. **copy:** example

117. **comes:** i.e., come

Think you I bear the shears of destiny?
Have I commandment on the pulse of life?

SALISBURY

It is apparent foul play, and 'tis shame
That greatness should so grossly offer it.
So thrive it in your game, and so farewell.

PEMBROKE

Stay yet, Lord Salisbury. I'll go with thee
And find th' inheritance of this poor child,
His little kingdom of a forcèd grave.
That blood which owed the breadth of all this isle,
Three foot of it doth hold. Bad world the while!
This must not be thus borne; this will break out
To all our sorrows, and ere long, I doubt.

⌜Pembroke, Salisbury, and other Lords⌝ exit.

KING JOHN

They burn in indignation. I repent.
There is no sure foundation set on blood,
No certain life achieved by others' death.

Enter Messenger.

A fearful eye thou hast. Where is that blood
That I have seen inhabit in those cheeks?
So foul a sky clears not without a storm.
Pour down thy weather: how goes all in France?

MESSENGER

From France to England. Never such a power
For any foreign preparation
Was levied in the body of a land.
The copy of your speed is learned by them,
For when you should be told they do prepare,
The tidings comes that they are all arrived.

KING JOHN

O, where hath our intelligence been drunk?
Where hath it slept? Where is my mother's care,

120. **drawn:** brought together, assembled

128. **occasion:** course of events or circumstances

129. **league:** covenant; **pleased:** appeased

131. **estate:** government; property, fortune

132. **conduct:** command; **powers:** armies

135. **giddy:** dizzy

136 SD. **Pomfret:** i.e., Pontefract, a town in northern England

140. **afeard:** afraid

142. **amazed:** stunned, alarmed, perplexed

143. **tide:** i.e., of **ill news**

144. **Aloft:** on the top of, above; **flood:** ocean, sea (continuing the metaphor of **tide** from line 143); **give audience:** listen

146. **sped:** succeeded

The three Fates. (4.2.93)
From Vincenzo Cartari, *Imagines deorum* . . . (1581).

That such an army could be drawn in France
And she not hear of it?

MESSENGER My liege, her ear
Is stopped with dust. The first of April died
Your noble mother. And as I hear, my lord,
The Lady Constance in a frenzy died
Three days before. But this from rumor's tongue
I idly heard. If true or false, I know not.

KING JOHN, ⌜*aside*⌝
Withhold thy speed, dreadful occasion!
O, make a league with me till I have pleased
My discontented peers. What? Mother dead?
How wildly then walks my estate in France!—
Under whose conduct came those powers of France
That thou for truth giv'st out are landed here?

MESSENGER
Under the Dauphin.

KING JOHN Thou hast made me giddy
With these ill tidings.

Enter Bastard and Peter of Pomfret.

⌜*To Bastard.*⌝ Now, what says the world
To your proceedings? Do not seek to stuff
My head with more ill news, for it is full.

BASTARD
But if you be afeard to hear the worst,
Then let the worst, unheard, fall on your head.

KING JOHN
Bear with me, cousin, for I was amazed
Under the tide, but now I breathe again
Aloft the flood and can give audience
To any tongue, speak it of what it will.

BASTARD
How I have sped among the clergymen
The sums I have collected shall express.

149. **fantasied:** whimsical, full of suppositions, notions, and changeful moods

150. **with rumors:** i.e., by **rumors**

155. **sung:** *Sing* could also mean "declare in verse." **rude:** inelegant; **rhymes:** verses

156. **Ascension Day:** the feast day, forty days after Easter Sunday, celebrating Christ's ascent into heaven

157. **deliver up:** surrender

158. **wherefore:** why

159. **Foreknowing:** knowing beforehand; **fall out:** happen

163. **safety:** confinement

165. **gentle:** noble; **cousin:** kinsman

171. **is killed tonight:** i.e., was **killed** last night

172. **suggestion:** prompting

174. **companies:** i.e., company

178. **the better foot before:** i.e., as fast as you can

A coin being "touched" against a touchstone. (3.1.102–4)
From George Wither, *A collection of emblemes . . .* (1635).

But as I traveled hither through the land,
I find the people strangely fantasied,
Possessed with rumors, full of idle dreams,
Not knowing what they fear, but full of fear.
And here's a prophet that I brought with me
From forth the streets of Pomfret, whom I found
With many hundreds treading on his heels,
To whom he sung in rude harsh-sounding rhymes
That ere the next Ascension Day at noon,
Your Highness should deliver up your crown.

KING JOHN, ⌜*to Peter*⌝
Thou idle dreamer, wherefore didst thou so?

PETER
Foreknowing that the truth will fall out so.

KING JOHN
Hubert, away with him! Imprison him.
And on that day at noon, whereon he says
I shall yield up my crown, let him be hanged.
Deliver him to safety and return,
For I must use thee. ⌜*Hubert and Peter exit.*⌝
O my gentle cousin,
Hear'st thou the news abroad, who are arrived?

BASTARD
The French, my lord. Men's mouths are full of it.
Besides, I met Lord Bigot and Lord Salisbury
With eyes as red as new-enkindled fire,
And others more, going to seek the grave
Of Arthur, whom they say is killed tonight
On your suggestion.

KING JOHN Gentle kinsman, go
And thrust thyself into their companies.
I have a way to win their loves again.
Bring them before me.

BASTARD I will seek them out.

KING JOHN
Nay, but make haste, the better foot before!

179. **subject enemies:** i.e., **enemies** who are my subjects

180. **affright:** terrify

181. **pomp:** display, show

182. **Mercury:** in mythology, the messenger-god, usually pictured with wings on his sandals (See below.)

185. **Spoke:** i.e., spoken; **sprightful:** lively, spirited (with wordplay on **spirit** in line 184)

188. **betwixt:** between

196–97. **Old men . . . dangerously:** See Pandulph's prediction regarding **prodigies and signs** among King John's subjects (3.4.156–62).

200. **whisper one another:** i.e., **whisper** to **one another**

202. **fearful action:** i.e., gestures indicative of fear

Mercury. (4.2.182)
From Innocenzio Ringhieri, *Cento giuochi liberali . . .* (1580).

O, let me have no subject enemies
When adverse foreigners affright my towns
With dreadful pomp of stout invasion.
Be Mercury, set feathers to thy heels,
And fly like thought from them to me again.

BASTARD
The spirit of the time shall teach me speed.

He exits.

KING JOHN
Spoke like a sprightful noble gentleman.
⌜*To Messenger.*⌝ Go after him, for he perhaps shall need
Some messenger betwixt me and the peers,
And be thou he.

MESSENGER With all my heart, my liege.

⌜*Messenger exits.*⌝

KING JOHN My mother dead!

Enter Hubert.

HUBERT
My lord, they say five moons were seen tonight—
Four fixèd, and the fifth did whirl about
The other four in wondrous motion.

KING JOHN
Five moons!

HUBERT Old men and beldams in the streets
Do prophesy upon it dangerously.
Young Arthur's death is common in their mouths,
And when they talk of him, they shake their heads
And whisper one another in the ear,
And he that speaks doth grip the hearer's wrist,
Whilst he that hears makes fearful action
With wrinkled brows, with nods, with rolling eyes.
I saw a smith stand with his hammer, thus,
The whilst his iron did on the anvil cool,

207. **measure:** tape **measure** or rule

209. **contrary:** i.e., the wrong

210. **a many:** i.e., many a

211. **embattlèd:** drawn up in battle array; **ranked:** arranged in ranks; **Kent:** a region in southeast England on the English Channel (See map, page xii.)

212. **artificer:** artisan, craftsman (accent on second syllable)

214. **possess me with:** cause me to feel

218. **No had:** i.e., had I not; **provoke:** incite, urge

220. **their humors:** i.e., the **kings'** whims

221. **To break . . . life:** i.e., kill **bloody house of life:** i.e., body, which both houses the blood and is made **bloody** by violence

222. **on the winking of:** i.e., from the connivance of, or, from the disregard of wrongdoing by

223. **To understand a law:** i.e., to interpret an order or command

225. **humor:** whim; **advised respect:** deliberately

226. **hand:** signature

227. **accompt:** reckoning, judgment; **twixt:** between

229. **us:** perhaps, me (the royal "we"); or, perhaps, you (Hubert) and me (John)

230. **ill:** evil

231. **Make:** i.e., makes; **ill:** badly; wickedly; unskillfully; **by:** nearby

232–33. **A fellow . . . shame:** In these lines, Hubert is figured as an official document created by **nature. Quoted:** written down **signed:** confirmed with a signature

235. **abhorred:** horrifying, loathsome; **aspect:** face (accent on second syllable)

With open mouth swallowing a tailor's news,
Who with his shears and measure in his hand,
Standing on slippers which his nimble haste
Had falsely thrust upon contrary feet,
Told of a many thousand warlike French
That were embattlèd and ranked in Kent.
Another lean, unwashed artificer
Cuts off his tale and talks of Arthur's death.

KING JOHN

Why seek'st thou to possess me with these fears?
Why urgest thou so oft young Arthur's death?
Thy hand hath murdered him. I had a mighty cause
To wish him dead, but thou hadst none to kill him.

HUBERT

No had, my lord! Why, did you not provoke me?

KING JOHN

It is the curse of kings to be attended
By slaves that take their humors for a warrant
To break within the bloody house of life,
And on the winking of authority
To understand a law, to know the meaning
Of dangerous majesty, when perchance it frowns
More upon humor than advised respect.

HUBERT, ⌜*showing a paper*⌝

Here is your hand and seal for what I did.

KING JOHN

O, when the last accompt twixt heaven and earth
Is to be made, then shall this hand and seal
Witness against us to damnation!
How oft the sight of means to do ill deeds
Make deeds ill done! Hadst not thou been by,
A fellow by the hand of nature marked,
Quoted, and signed to do a deed of shame,
This murder had not come into my mind.
But taking note of thy abhorred aspect,

237. **liable:** suitable; **danger:** harm, mischief

238. **broke . . . death:** i.e., mentioned **Arthur's death** to you

240. **conscience:** i.e., matter of **conscience**

242. **made a pause:** hesitated

243. **spake:** spoke; **darkly:** in an obscure, vague way

244. **doubt:** uncertainty, hesitation; fear

251. **stop:** hesitation, holding back

252. **rude:** violent

255. **state:** power, government; **braved:** challenged

257. **in the body . . . land:** i.e., within my own body (It is conventional in this period to equate the body of a king with the land he rules.)

258. **confine:** region

260. **my cousin's:** i.e., Prince Arthur's

261. **you:** i.e., yourself

267. **motion:** prompting, impulse

268. **nature in my form:** perhaps, "my nature by judging it only in terms of my outward appearance"

Finding thee fit for bloody villainy,
Apt, liable to be employed in danger,
I faintly broke with thee of Arthur's death;
And thou, to be endearèd to a king,
Made it no conscience to destroy a prince.

HUBERT My lord—

KING JOHN

Hadst thou but shook thy head or made a pause
When I spake darkly what I purposèd,
Or turned an eye of doubt upon my face,
As bid me tell my tale in express words,
Deep shame had struck me dumb, made me break off,
And those thy fears might have wrought fears in me.
But thou didst understand me by my signs
And didst in signs again parley with sin,
Yea, without stop didst let thy heart consent
And consequently thy rude hand to act
The deed which both our tongues held vile to name.
Out of my sight, and never see me more.
My nobles leave me, and my state is braved,
Even at my gates, with ranks of foreign powers.
Nay, in the body of this fleshly land,
This kingdom, this confine of blood and breath,
Hostility and civil tumult reigns
Between my conscience and my cousin's death.

HUBERT

Arm you against your other enemies.
I'll make a peace between your soul and you.
Young Arthur is alive. This hand of mine
Is yet a maiden and an innocent hand,
Not painted with the crimson spots of blood.
Within this bosom never entered yet
The dreadful motion of a murderous thought,
And you have slandered nature in my form,

269. **rude:** inelegant, rugged

275. **comment:** criticism; **that . . . made:** i.e., **that I made** in the course of my outburst (**passion**)

276. **feature:** i.e., appearance

277. **imaginary:** imaginative; **eyes of blood:** i.e., **eyes** blinded through passion

279. **closet:** private chamber

281. **conjure:** entreat

4.3 Arthur dies as he attempts to leap from the prison wall. The Bastard reaches the nobles, on their way to meet with the Dauphin, just as they discover Arthur's body and vow revenge for his death. When Hubert enters, they turn on him as a murderer. The Bastard takes Hubert's part, and the nobles proceed to their meeting with the Dauphin. Hubert convinces the Bastard of his own innocence, and the Bastard, predicting disaster, returns to King John.

---

4. **This shipboy's semblance:** i.e., my appearance as a boy who serves on board ship

7. **shifts:** means

11. **meet him:** It is suggested at line 16, and finally confirmed at line 119, that this meeting is with Louis, the Dauphin. **St. Edmundsbury:** a town, also known as Bury St. Edmunds, in east central England

Which, howsoever rude exteriorly,
Is yet the cover of a fairer mind
Than to be butcher of an innocent child.

KING JOHN
Doth Arthur live? O, haste thee to the peers,
Throw this report on their incensèd rage,
And make them tame to their obedience.
Forgive the comment that my passion made
Upon thy feature, for my rage was blind,
And foul imaginary eyes of blood
Presented thee more hideous than thou art.
O, answer not, but to my closet bring
The angry lords with all expedient haste.
I conjure thee but slowly; run more fast.

They exit.

Scene 3

Enter Arthur on the walls, ⌜*dressed as a shipboy.*⌝

ARTHUR
The wall is high, and yet will I leap down.
Good ground, be pitiful and hurt me not.
There's few or none do know me. If they did,
This shipboy's semblance hath disguised me quite.
I am afraid, and yet I'll venture it.
If I get down and do not break my limbs,
I'll find a thousand shifts to get away.
As good to die and go as die and stay.

⌜*He jumps.*⌝

O me, my uncle's spirit is in these stones.
Heaven take my soul, and England keep my bones.

⌜*He*⌝ *dies.*

Enter Pembroke, Salisbury ⌜*with a letter,*⌝ *and Bigot.*

SALISBURY
Lords, I will meet him at Saint Edmundsbury;

12. **It is our safety:** i.e., in this course lies **our safety**

13. **gentle:** noble; courteous

16. **private:** perhaps, **private** communication

20. **or ere:** before

21. **distempered:** vexed

22. **straight:** straightaway, immediately

24. **line:** (1) act as a lining for; (2) strengthen, fortify; **bestainèd:** stained

25. **attend:** wait upon, serve

29. **griefs:** sorrows; wrongs; **reason:** speak

30. **reason:** rationality

31. **reason:** common sense

32. **his:** i.e., its

33. **to hurt his master:** Proverbial: "Anger punishes itself." **his:** i.e., its

Holding a deer "in chase." (1.1.229)
From [George Turberville,] *The noble art of venerie or hunting* . . . (1611).

It is our safety, and we must embrace
This gentle offer of the perilous time.

PEMBROKE
Who brought that letter from the Cardinal?

SALISBURY
The Count Melun, a noble lord of France,
Whose private with me of the Dauphin's love
Is much more general than these lines import.

BIGOT
Tomorrow morning let us meet him, then.

SALISBURY
Or rather then set forward, for 'twill be
Two long days' journey, lords, or ere we meet.

Enter Bastard.

BASTARD
Once more today well met, distempered lords.
The King by me requests your presence straight.

SALISBURY
The King hath dispossessed himself of us.
We will not line his thin bestainèd cloak
With our pure honors, nor attend the foot
That leaves the print of blood where'er it walks.
Return, and tell him so. We know the worst.

BASTARD
Whate'er you think, good words I think were best.

SALISBURY
Our griefs and not our manners reason now.

BASTARD
But there is little reason in your grief.
Therefore 'twere reason you had manners now.

PEMBROKE
Sir, sir, impatience hath his privilege.

BASTARD
'Tis true, to hurt his master, no man's else.

35. **What:** i.e., who

38. **himself:** i.e., itself

41. **Found:** i.e., murder **found**

43. **Or have . . . heard:** i.e., **have you** either **read or heard**

45. **That:** i.e., **that** which

46. **such another:** i.e., one like it

47. **the crest:** the topmost part on a coat of **arms** (line 48) As the line continues, **the crest** is represented as doubled, with a **crest** set above a **crest.**

50. **wall-eyed:** glaring; **staring:** wild

51. **remorse:** pity

53. **sole:** unique

55. **times:** i.e., **times** to come

56. **but:** only

57. **Exampled by:** justified by the precedent of

59. **graceless:** wicked, merciless; **heavy:** violent

SALISBURY
This is the prison.
⌜*He sees Arthur's body.*⌝
What is he lies here?

PEMBROKE
O Death, made proud with pure and princely beauty!
The earth had not a hole to hide this deed.

SALISBURY
Murder, as hating what himself hath done,
Doth lay it open to urge on revenge.

BIGOT
Or when he doomed this beauty to a grave,
Found it too precious-princely for a grave.

SALISBURY, ⌜*to Bastard*⌝
Sir Richard, what think you? You have beheld.
Or have you read or heard, or could you think,
Or do you almost think, although you see,
That you do see? Could thought, without this object,
Form such another? This is the very top,
The height, the crest, or crest unto the crest,
Of murder's arms. This is the bloodiest shame,
The wildest savagery, the vilest stroke
That ever wall-eyed wrath or staring rage
Presented to the tears of soft remorse.

PEMBROKE
All murders past do stand excused in this.
And this, so sole and so unmatchable,
Shall give a holiness, a purity,
To the yet unbegotten sin of times
And prove a deadly bloodshed but a jest,
Exampled by this heinous spectacle.

BASTARD
It is a damnèd and a bloody work,
The graceless action of a heavy hand,
If that it be the work of any hand.

62. **light:** i.e., knowledge in advance

64. **practice:** scheme, plot

72. **set a glory to this hand:** i.e., made my **hand** renowned

73. **worship:** honor

78. **Avaunt:** be gone

81. **bright:** shiny (and therefore unused); **up:** away

"A smith . . . with his hammer." (4.2.204–5)
From Hartmann Schopper, *Panoplia omnium illiberalium* . . . (1568).

SALISBURY

If that it be the work of any hand?
We had a kind of light what would ensue.
It is the shameful work of Hubert's hand,
The practice and the purpose of the King,
From whose obedience I forbid my soul,
Kneeling before this ruin of sweet life ⌜*He kneels.*⌝
And breathing to his breathless excellence
The incense of a vow, a holy vow:
Never to taste the pleasures of the world,
Never to be infected with delight,
Nor conversant with ease and idleness,
Till I have set a glory to this hand
By giving it the worship of revenge.

PEMBROKE, BIGOT, ⌜*kneeling*⌝

Our souls religiously confirm thy words.
⌜*They rise.*⌝

Enter Hubert.

HUBERT

Lords, I am hot with haste in seeking you.
Arthur doth live; the King hath sent for you.

SALISBURY

O, he is bold and blushes not at death!—
Avaunt, thou hateful villain, get thee gone!

HUBERT

I am no villain.

SALISBURY, ⌜*drawing his sword*⌝ Must I rob the law?

BASTARD

Your sword is bright, sir. Put it up again.

SALISBURY

Not till I sheathe it in a murderer's skin.

HUBERT

Stand back, Lord Salisbury, stand back, I say.
By heaven, I think my sword's as sharp as yours.
⌜*He puts his hand on his sword.*⌝

87. **marking of:** i.e., paying attention only to

89. **Out:** an exclamation of indignant reproach; **brave a nobleman:** i.e., challenge **a nobleman** to a duel (something a commoner was forbidden to do)

93. **Do . . . so:** i.e., by making me kill you

94. **Yet:** as **yet; Whose . . . soe'er:** i.e., whoever

95. **Who:** i.e., whoever; **lies:** The accusation of lying demands a challenge (if the accuser is of high enough rank) or an attack (as here, when the accuser is a commoner).

98. **Stand by:** i.e., **stand** aside; **gall:** wound; **Faulconbridge:** the Bastard's name before he was knighted as Sir Richard Plantagenet

101. **spleen:** wrath, anger

102. **betime:** in good time (i.e., immediately)

103. **toasting-iron:** a contemptuous term for a sword

111. **date:** term

Here after folovvetth a
Litle boke of Philip Spa-
row compiled by ma-
ster. Skelton Poet
Laureate.

Pla ce bo
Who is there who
Di le xi,
Dame Margery
Fa re my my
Wherfore and why why
For the soule of philip sparow
That was late slaine at Carow
Amonge the Nunnes blake

For

First page of *A little boke of Philip Sparrow. . . .* (1.1.238)
From [John Skelton,] [*Pithy pleasaunt and profitable workes . . .*]
[1568].

I would not have you, lord, forget yourself,
Nor tempt the danger of my true defense,
Lest I, by marking of your rage, forget
Your worth, your greatness, and nobility.

BIGOT
Out, dunghill! Dar'st thou brave a nobleman?

HUBERT
Not for my life. But yet I dare defend
My innocent life against an emperor.

SALISBURY
Thou art a murderer.

HUBERT
Do not prove me so.
Yet I am none. Whose tongue soe'er speaks false,
Not truly speaks. Who speaks not truly, lies.

PEMBROKE, ⌜*drawing his sword*⌝
Cut him to pieces.

BASTARD, ⌜*drawing his sword*⌝ Keep the peace, I say.

SALISBURY
Stand by, or I shall gall you, Faulconbridge.

BASTARD
Thou wert better gall the devil, Salisbury.
If thou but frown on me, or stir thy foot,
Or teach thy hasty spleen to do me shame,
I'll strike thee dead. Put up thy sword betime,
Or I'll so maul you and your toasting-iron
That you shall think the devil is come from hell.

BIGOT
What wilt thou do, renownèd Faulconbridge?
Second a villain and a murderer?

HUBERT
Lord Bigot, I am none.

BIGOT
Who killed this prince?

HUBERT
'Tis not an hour since I left him well.
I honored him, I loved him, and will weep
My date of life out for his sweet life's loss.
⌜*He weeps.*⌝

113. **rheum:** i.e., tears

114. **traded:** skilled, experienced

117. **savors:** odors

118. **stifled with:** choked by

119. **Bury:** i.e., Bury St. Edmunds

128. **Lucifer:** i.e., Satan (who, as **Lucifer,** was the leader of the angels expelled from heaven and thrown into **hell** [line 129])

133. **but:** only

134. **want'st a cord:** lack a rope with which to hang yourself

140. **stifle such a villain up:** drown **such a villain**

141. **grievously:** strongly

An eagle's aerie. (5.2.150)
From Joachim Camerarius, *Symbolorum et emblematum* . . . (1605).

SALISBURY
Trust not those cunning waters of his eyes,
For villainy is not without such rheum,
And he, long traded in it, makes it seem
Like rivers of remorse and innocency.
Away with me, all you whose souls abhor
Th' uncleanly savors of a slaughterhouse,
For I am stifled with this smell of sin.

BIGOT
Away, toward Bury, to the Dauphin there.

PEMBROKE
There, tell the King, he may inquire us out.
Lords exit.

BASTARD
Here's a good world! Knew you of this fair work?
Beyond the infinite and boundless reach
Of mercy, if thou didst this deed of death,
Art thou damned, Hubert.

HUBERT Do but hear me, sir.

BASTARD Ha! I'll tell thee what.
Thou'rt damned as black—nay, nothing is so black—
Thou art more deep damned than Prince Lucifer.
There is not yet so ugly a fiend of hell
As thou shalt be, if thou didst kill this child.

HUBERT
Upon my soul—

BASTARD If thou didst but consent
To this most cruel act, do but despair,
And if thou want'st a cord, the smallest thread
That ever spider twisted from her womb
Will serve to strangle thee; a rush will be a beam
To hang thee on. Or wouldst thou drown thyself,
Put but a little water in a spoon
And it shall be as all the ocean,
Enough to stifle such a villain up.
I do suspect thee very grievously.

144. **embounded:** contained; **clay:** body

145. **want:** lack

148. **amazed:** bewildered

150. **easy:** i.e., easily; **England:** i.e., Prince Arthur (The Bastard's use of this term characterizes Arthur as rightful king of **England**.)

151. **morsel:** fragment

154. **scamble:** struggle; **part:** i.e., tear apart

155. **unowed:** unowned (i.e., not rightfully owned); **state:** sphere of supreme political power

157. **doggèd:** doglike; **bristle . . . crest:** i.e., angrily raise its hackles

159. **powers from home:** armies from abroad; **discontents:** i.e., those who are discontented

160. **Meet . . . line:** agree, unite

162. **wrested pomp:** splendor or magnificence taken by force

163. **cincture:** belt

164. **Hold out:** bear, endure; keep out

166. **businesses:** matters, tasks; **brief:** rife, abundantly; **in hand:** in process

HUBERT
If I in act, consent, or sin of thought
Be guilty of the stealing that sweet breath
Which was embounded in this beauteous clay,
Let hell want pains enough to torture me.
I left him well.
BASTARD Go, bear him in thine arms.
I am amazed, methinks, and lose my way
Among the thorns and dangers of this world.
⌜*Hubert takes up Arthur's body.*⌝
How easy dost thou take all England up!
From forth this morsel of dead royalty,
The life, the right, and truth of all this realm
Is fled to heaven, and England now is left
To tug and scamble and to part by th' teeth
The unowed interest of proud-swelling state.
Now for the bare-picked bone of majesty
Doth doggèd war bristle his angry crest
And snarleth in the gentle eyes of peace.
Now powers from home and discontents at home
Meet in one line, and vast confusion waits,
As doth a raven on a sick-fall'n beast,
The imminent decay of wrested pomp.
Now happy he whose cloak and cincture can
Hold out this tempest. Bear away that child,
And follow me with speed. I'll to the King.
A thousand businesses are brief in hand,
And heaven itself doth frown upon the land.
⌜*They*⌝ *exit,* ⌜*with Hubert carrying Arthur's body.*⌝

The Life and Death of

KING JOHN

ACT 5

5.1 King John submits his royal power to the Pope in exchange for Pandulph's intercession against the French forces. The Bastard reports the successes of the French army, the death of Arthur, and the revolt of the nobles, and urges John to fight the French rather than seek peace through Pandulph. King John gives the Bastard the authority to deal with the French as he chooses.

---

2. **circle of my glory:** i.e., **my** crown

4. **holding of:** deriving your title to the kingship from

7. **his Holiness:** i.e., the pope

8. **'fore:** i.e., before

9. **counties:** (1) shires; (2) counts, nobles

10–12. **Our people . . . foreign royalty:** For Elizabethan attitudes to King John's rebellious subjects, see Historical Background 3, page 233. **stranger:** foreign

13. **mistempered:** badly mixed (In this and the following lines, John compares his discontented kingdom to a human body suffering from an imbalance of [liquid] humors. See longer note to 2.1.66, on **humors.**)

14. **Rests . . . qualified:** i.e., can be controlled by you alone

16. **present med'cine:** i.e., medicine immediately; or, fast-acting medicine

19. **Upon:** following

ACT ⌜*5*⌝

Scene 1

Enter King John and Pandulph ⌜*with the crown, and their*⌝ *Attendants.*

KING JOHN
Thus have I yielded up into your hand
The circle of my glory.
PANDULPH, ⌜*handing John the crown*⌝ Take again
From this my hand, as holding of the Pope,
Your sovereign greatness and authority.
KING JOHN
Now keep your holy word. Go meet the French,
And from his Holiness use all your power
To stop their marches 'fore we are inflamed.
Our discontented counties do revolt,
Our people quarrel with obedience,
Swearing allegiance and the love of soul
To stranger blood, to foreign royalty.
This inundation of mistempered humor
Rests by you only to be qualified.
Then pause not, for the present time's so sick
That present med'cine must be ministered,
Or overthrow incurable ensues.
PANDULPH
It was my breath that blew this tempest up,
Upon your stubborn usage of the Pope;

20. **convertite:** person converted to a religious life, or to a proper course of action

22. **make fair weather:** be conciliatory (but also continuing the **tempest** metaphor begun in line 18)

28. **give off:** relinquish

32. **Dover Castle:** a **castle** from Roman or Saxon times that stood on the cliff above **Dover,** just across from Calais (For Calais, see map, page xii.)

36. **amazement:** bewilderment, distraction; **hurries:** drives with impetuosity and without deliberation

37. **little:** i.e., small; **doubtful:** (1) fearful; (2) uncertain

41. **casket: jewel** box

44. **aught:** anything whatever

45. **wherefore:** why

Mars, the Roman god of war. (5.1.55)
From Vincenzo Cartari, *Le imagini de i dei de gli antichi* . . . (1587).

But since you are a gentle convertite,
My tongue shall hush again this storm of war
And make fair weather in your blust'ring land.
On this Ascension Day, remember well:
Upon your oath of service to the Pope,
Go I to make the French lay down their arms.

He exits, ⌜with Attendants.

KING JOHN

Is this Ascension Day? Did not the prophet
Say that before Ascension Day at noon
My crown I should give off? Even so I have.
I did suppose it should be on constraint,
But, ⌜God⌝ be thanked, it is but voluntary.

Enter Bastard.

BASTARD

All Kent hath yielded. Nothing there holds out
But Dover Castle. London hath received
Like a kind host the Dauphin and his powers.
Your nobles will not hear you, but are gone
To offer service to your enemy;
And wild amazement hurries up and down
The little number of your doubtful friends.

KING JOHN

Would not my lords return to me again
After they heard young Arthur was alive?

BASTARD

They found him dead and cast into the streets,
An empty casket where the jewel of life
By some damned hand was robbed and ta'en away.

KING JOHN

That villain Hubert told me he did live!

BASTARD

So, on my soul, he did, for aught he knew.
But wherefore do you droop? Why look you sad?
Be great in act, as you have been in thought.

55. **god of war:** probably an allusion to Mars, the Roman **god of war** (See page 172.)

56. **become:** grace, adorn

58. **the lion in his den:** i.e., the king of England in his own castle (The **lion** is traditionally associated with the monarch, and is also the heraldic symbol of England. See below.)

59. **fright:** frighten

61. **displeasure:** trouble

64. **happy:** favorable

68. **upon the footing:** (1) on the occasion of the entering (i.e., invasion by a foreign power); (2) **upon the** surface (where we stand)

70. **Insinuation:** ingratiation; **base:** cowardly

71. **arms invasive:** i.e., invading forces

72. **cockered:** pampered; **silken:** effeminate; **wanton:** spoiled child; lewd person; **brave:** defy (with wordplay on "make a splendid show")

73. **flesh:** initiate or inure to bloodshed

74. **idly:** (1) vainly; (2) frivolously, carelessly

79. **ordering:** direction, management

The monarch as lion. (5.1.58)
From John Speed, *The theatre of the empire of Great Britaine . . .* (1627 [i.e., 1631]).

Let not the world see fear and sad distrust
Govern the motion of a kingly eye.
Be stirring as the time; be fire with fire;
Threaten the threat'ner, and outface the brow
Of bragging horror. So shall inferior eyes,
That borrow their behaviors from the great,
Grow great by your example and put on
The dauntless spirit of resolution.
Away, and glister like the god of war
When he intendeth to become the field.
Show boldness and aspiring confidence.
What, shall they seek the lion in his den
And fright him there? And make him tremble there?
O, let it not be said! Forage, and run
To meet displeasure farther from the doors,
And grapple with him ere he come so nigh.

KING JOHN
The legate of the Pope hath been with me,
And I have made a happy peace with him,
And he hath promised to dismiss the powers
Led by the Dauphin.

BASTARD O inglorious league!
Shall we upon the footing of our land
Send fair-play orders and make compromise,
Insinuation, parley, and base truce
To arms invasive? Shall a beardless boy,
A cockered silken wanton, brave our fields
And flesh his spirit in a warlike soil,
Mocking the air with colors idly spread,
And find no check? Let us, my liege, to arms!
Perchance the Cardinal cannot make your peace;
Or if he do, let it at least be said
They saw we had a purpose of defense.

KING JOHN
Have thou the ordering of this present time.

82. **prouder:** more valiant; mightier

5.2 The rebellious English nobles swear to support the Dauphin in his attack on England. Pandulph tells the Dauphin to take his army back to France, since John has submitted to the Pope, but the Dauphin refuses. The Bastard is pleased that the Dauphin wants war, and announces that John is close by with his army.

---

1. **this:** the agreement between the French invaders and their English supporters

3. **precedent:** original (from which the copy is to be made)

4. **fair order written down:** (1) advantageous arrangement **written down;** or (2) arrangement neatly inscribed

6. **wherefore:** why; **took the Sacrament:** i.e., confirmed our oaths by receiving Communion

7. **faiths:** obligations, promises

10. **unurged faith:** pledge that has not been thrust or pressed upon us

13. **plaster:** paste-like curative application, dressing; **contemned:** despised, despicable

14. **inveterate canker:** chronic spreading sore

18–19. **honorable rescue . . . Salisbury:** These lines play with the two opposing meanings of **"cries out upon."** The **honorable rescue** (of England from King John) "appeals to" Salisbury's **name,** while the **defense** (of England against foreign invasion) "exclaims against" his **name.**

(continued)

BASTARD
Away, then, with good courage! (⌜*Aside*⌝) Yet I know
Our party may well meet a prouder foe.
They exit.

Scene 2

Enter, in arms, ⌜*Louis the*⌝ *Dauphin, Salisbury, Melun, Pembroke, Bigot,* ⌜*and French and English*⌝ *Soldiers.*

DAUPHIN, ⌜*handing a paper to Melun*⌝
My Lord Melun, let this be copied out,
And keep it safe for our remembrance.
Return the precedent to these lords again,
That having our fair order written down,
Both they and we, perusing o'er these notes,
May know wherefore we took the Sacrament,
And keep our faiths firm and inviolable.

SALISBURY
Upon our sides it never shall be broken.
And, noble dauphin, albeit we swear
A voluntary zeal and unurged faith
To your proceedings, yet believe me, prince,
I am not glad that such a sore of time
Should seek a plaster by contemned revolt
And heal the inveterate canker of one wound
By making many. O, it grieves my soul
That I must draw this metal from my side
To be a widow-maker! O, and there
Where honorable rescue and defense
Cries out upon the name of Salisbury!
But such is the infection of the time
That for the health and physic of our right,
We cannot deal but with the very hand
Of stern injustice and confusèd wrong.

21. **physic:** medicinal cure

22. **deal:** act; **but:** except

23. **stern:** cruel

26. **Was:** i.e., were

27. **step . . . stranger:** i.e., march in the army of a foreigner

28. **her:** i.e., England's

30. **spot:** (1) place; (2) stain; **enforcèd cause:** i.e., **cause** that I am forced to join

31. **grace:** gratify

32. **unacquainted:** i.e., foreign

33. **that:** i.e., if only; **remove:** move off to somewhere else (England is imagined as a ship sailing the oceans.)

34. **That Neptune's . . . about:** i.e., if only the sea, which embraces you (Neptune was the Roman god of the sea. See picture, page 182.)

36. **grapple:** fasten (as if with grappling irons)

42. **earthquake:** In this period an **earthquake** was thought to be produced by the rush of winds within the earth.

44. **brave:** excellent, worthy

51. **Startles mine eyes:** causes my **eyes** to start; **amazed:** lost in wonder and astonishment

52. **vaulty:** vaultlike

56. **Commend:** commit, deliver (over)

And is 't not pity, O my grievèd friends,
That we, the sons and children of this isle,
Was born to see so sad an hour as this,
Wherein we step after a stranger, march
Upon her gentle bosom, and fill up
Her enemies' ranks? I must withdraw and weep
Upon the spot of this enforcèd cause,
To grace the gentry of a land remote,
And follow unacquainted colors here.
What, here? O nation, that thou couldst remove,
That Neptune's arms, who clippeth thee about,
Would bear thee from the knowledge of thyself
And ⌜grapple⌝ thee unto a pagan shore,
Where these two Christian armies might combine
The blood of malice in a vein of league,
And not to spend it so unneighborly. ⌜*He weeps.*⌝

DAUPHIN

A noble temper dost thou show in this,
And great affections wrestling in thy bosom
Doth make an earthquake of nobility.
O, what a noble combat hast ⌜thou⌝ fought
Between compulsion and a brave respect!
Let me wipe off this honorable dew
That silverly doth progress on thy cheeks.
My heart hath melted at a lady's tears,
Being an ordinary inundation,
But this effusion of such manly drops,
This shower, blown up by tempest of the soul,
Startles mine eyes and makes me more amazed
Than had I seen the vaulty top of heaven
Figured quite o'er with burning meteors.
Lift up thy brow, renownèd Salisbury,
And with a great heart heave away this storm.
Commend these waters to those baby eyes
That never saw the giant world enraged,
Nor met with fortune other than at feasts

59. **gossiping:** merrymaking

62. **nobles:** with possible wordplay on the sense of "gold coins" following **the purse of rich prosperity**

64. **And even . . . spake:** Proverbial: "There spoke an **angel,**" meaning "That was an inspired suggestion." (Since an **angel** was also a gold coin, the Dauphin's "inspired suggestion" may be his promise of wealth to English supporters.)

67. **set:** put (as a signature); affix (as a seal)

71. **is come in:** has yielded

73. **metropolis:** seat of the chief bishop

74. **wind up:** furl (and put away)

76. **fostered . . . hand:** i.e., raised by **hand** (and therefore, reputedly, tame)

78. **show:** appearance

79. **back:** withdraw, go **back**

80. **propertied:** made a tool of

81. **a secondary at control:** i.e., a subordinate acting under a superior's **control**

90. **interest:** i.e., my title

Full warm of blood, of mirth, of gossiping.
Come, come; for thou shalt thrust thy hand as deep
Into the purse of rich prosperity
As Louis himself.—So, nobles, shall you all,
That knit your sinews to the strength of mine.
And even there, methinks, an angel spake.

Enter Pandulph.

Look where the holy legate comes apace
To give us warrant from the hand of ⌜God,⌝
And on our actions set the name of right
With holy breath.

PANDULPH Hail, noble prince of France.
The next is this: King John hath reconciled
Himself to Rome; his spirit is come in
That so stood out against the holy Church,
The great metropolis and See of Rome.
Therefore thy threat'ning colors now wind up,
And tame the savage spirit of wild war
That, like a lion fostered up at hand,
It may lie gently at the foot of peace
And be no further harmful than in show.

DAUPHIN
Your Grace shall pardon me; I will not back.
I am too high-born to be propertied,
To be a secondary at control,
Or useful servingman and instrument
To any sovereign state throughout the world.
Your breath first kindled the dead coal of wars
Between this chastised kingdom and myself
And brought in matter that should feed this fire;
And now 'tis far too huge to be blown out
With that same weak wind which enkindled it.
You taught me how to know the face of right,
Acquainted me with interest to this land,
Yea, thrust this enterprise into my heart.

94. **by the honor . . . bed:** i.e., by virtue of my marriage to the Lady Blanche

97. **Because that:** i.e., **because**

98. **penny:** i.e., of the cost of my expedition

100. **underprop:** support, maintain

101. **undergo:** bear, sustain; **charge:** expense

102. **to my claim are liable:** i.e., are subject to my demand for military service

105. **Vive le Roi:** French for "long live the king!" (This phrase and the word **banked** may be expressions from games of **cards** [line 106].)

107. **crown:** with wordplay on a coin worth five shillings, such as might be wagered in a card game

108. **give o'er:** surrender; **yielded set:** i.e., the round in **the game** that has already been conceded

114. **drew:** assembled; **head of war:** armed force

116. **outlook:** stare down, overcome by looking

118. **lusty:** vigorous

Neptune. (5.2.34)
From Johann Basilius Herold, *Heydenweldt* . . . [1554].

And come you now to tell me John hath made
His peace with Rome? What is that peace to me?
I, by the honor of my marriage bed,
After young Arthur claim this land for mine.
And now it is half conquered, must I back
Because that John hath made his peace with Rome?
Am I Rome's slave? What penny hath Rome borne?
What men provided? What munition sent
To underprop this action? Is 't not I
That undergo this charge? Who else but I,
And such as to my claim are liable,
Sweat in this business and maintain this war?
Have I not heard these islanders shout out
"Vive le Roi" as I have banked their towns?
Have I not here the best cards for the game
To win this easy match played for a crown?
And shall I now give o'er the yielded set?
No, no, on my soul, it never shall be said.

PANDULPH

You look but on the outside of this work.

DAUPHIN

Outside or inside, I will not return
Till my attempt so much be glorified
As to my ample hope was promised
Before I drew this gallant head of war
And culled these fiery spirits from the world
To outlook conquest and to win renown
Even in the jaws of danger and of death.

⌜*A trumpet sounds.*⌝

What lusty trumpet thus doth summon us?

Enter Bastard.

BASTARD

According to the fair play of the world,
Let me have audience. I am sent to speak,
My holy lord of Milan, from the King.

123–24. **I do . . . tongue:** i.e., I will be able to determine the liberty and authority with which I am permitted to speak

125. **willful-opposite:** obstinately hostile

126. **temporize:** conform; come to terms

131. **reason:** i.e., there is good **reason; he should:** i.e., that **he should** be

133. **harnessed masque:** i.e., play performed in armor **masque:** a lavish entertainment at court in which masked and costumed nobility dance and perform; **unadvisèd:** imprudent, heedless

134. **unheard:** unheard-of, unknown, new; **sauciness:** insolent presumption

139. **take the hatch:** i.e., throw yourself over the lower half of a divided door (in order to save yourself in however undignified a way)

141. **litter . . . planks:** straw and rushes on the floors of your stables

143. **hug with:** lie close to, cuddle

144. **vaults:** burial chambers; drains, sewers; caves; **thrill:** be moved by strong emotion (i.e., fear)

145. **crying . . . crow:** possibly, crowing of the rooster (The rooster or cock was already associated with France in the sixteenth century.)

147. **feebled:** enfeebled

148. **chambers:** provinces, cities

150. **towers:** soars (See picture of **aerie,** page 164.)

151. **souse:** swoop upon

152. **ingrate:** ungrateful; **revolts:** rebels

153–54. **Neroes . . . mother:** Nero, a first-century CE emperor of Rome, was infamous for monstrous self-indulgence and atrocities. While he had his **mother** murdered, he did not rip open her **womb.**

I come to learn how you have dealt for him,
And, as you answer, I do know the scope
And warrant limited unto my tongue.

PANDULPH

The Dauphin is too willful-opposite
And will not temporize with my entreaties.
He flatly says he'll not lay down his arms.

BASTARD

By all the blood that ever fury breathed,
The youth says well! Now hear our English king,
For thus his royalty doth speak in me:
He is prepared—and reason too he should.
This apish and unmannerly approach,
This harnessed masque and unadvisèd revel,
This unheard sauciness and boyish troops,
The King doth smile at, and is well prepared
To whip this dwarfish war, these pigmy arms,
From out the circle of his territories.
That hand which had the strength, even at your door
To cudgel you and make you take the hatch,
To dive like buckets in concealèd wells,
To crouch in litter of your stable planks,
To lie like pawns locked up in chests and trunks,
To hug with swine, to seek sweet safety out
In vaults and prisons, and to thrill and shake
Even at the crying of your nation's crow,
Thinking this voice an armèd Englishman—
Shall that victorious hand be feebled here
That in your chambers gave you chastisement?
No! Know the gallant monarch is in arms,
And like an eagle o'er his aerie towers
To souse annoyance that comes near his nest.—
And you degenerate, you ingrate revolts,
You bloody Neroes, ripping up the womb
Of your dear mother England, blush for shame!
For your own ladies and pale-visaged maids

156. **Amazons:** an ancient legendary nation of women warriors

157. **armèd:** i.e., steel-plated (See below.)

159. **inclination:** dispositions

160. **brave:** bravado; boastful, threatening behavior; **turn thy face:** i.e., go away

161. **We:** i.e., I (the royal **"we"**); **outscold us:** outdo me in scolding

166. **attend:** listen

168. **interest:** title

172. **braced:** stretched (referring to the drum's skin)

175. **welkin's:** sky's, heaven's

176. **deep-mouthed:** deep-voiced

178. **sport:** amusement, diversion

180. **bare-ribbed:** skeletal (See picture, page 190.) **office:** function

182. **find:** (1) discover; (2) suffer

183. **doubt:** fear

An "armèd" gauntlet. (5.2.157)
From Louis de Gaya, *Traité des armes* . . . (1678).

Like Amazons come tripping after drums,
Their thimbles into armèd gauntlets change,
Their needles to lances, and their gentle hearts
To fierce and bloody inclination.

DAUPHIN
There end thy brave and turn thy face in peace.
We grant thou canst outscold us. Fare thee well.
We hold our time too precious to be spent
With such a brabbler.

PANDULPH Give me leave to speak.

BASTARD
No, I will speak.

DAUPHIN We will attend to neither.
Strike up the drums, and let the tongue of war
Plead for our interest and our being here.

BASTARD
Indeed, your drums being beaten will cry out,
And so shall you, being beaten. Do but start
An echo with the clamor of thy drum,
And even at hand a drum is ready braced
That shall reverberate all as loud as thine.
Sound but another, and another shall,
As loud as thine, rattle the welkin's ear
And mock the deep-mouthed thunder. For at hand,
Not trusting to this halting legate here,
Whom he hath used rather for sport than need,
Is warlike John, and in his forehead sits
A bare-ribbed Death, whose office is this day
To feast upon whole thousands of the French.

DAUPHIN
Strike up our drums to find this danger out.

BASTARD
And thou shalt find it, dauphin, do not doubt.

They exit.

5.3 King John, sick with a fever, is instructed by the Bastard to leave the battle. John receives the good news that French supply ships have sunk. He goes to take refuge in an abbey.

---

5. **Faulconbridge:** i.e., the Bastard

8. **Swinstead:** a town in northeast England (Since there is no record of an **abbey** in **Swinstead,** scholars argue that pre-Shakespearean accounts that place John's death at **Swinstead** are confusing it with the nearby town of Swineshead and its **abbey.**)

9. **supply:** reinforcement of troops

11. **Are:** i.e., is; **wracked:** ship-wrecked; **Goodwin Sands:** a dangerous shoal off the coast of Kent

12. **Richard:** i.e., the Bastard

13. **coldly:** without ardor or enthusiasm; **retire themselves:** retreat

16. **straight:** immediately, straightaway

5.4 While the English army continues to fight successfully under the Bastard, the rebel English nobles learn from the wounded French Count Melun that the Dauphin plans to murder them if the French are victorious. The rebels decide to return to John.

---

1. **stored:** supplied

Scene 3

Alarums. Enter ⌜*King*⌝ *John and Hubert.*

KING JOHN
How goes the day with us? O, tell me, Hubert.

HUBERT
Badly, I fear. How fares your Majesty?

KING JOHN
This fever that hath troubled me so long
Lies heavy on me. O, my heart is sick.

Hubert is sort of treated like a second messenger

Enter a Messenger.

MESSENGER
My lord, your valiant kinsman, Faulconbridge,
Desires your Majesty to leave the field
And send him word by me which way you go.

KING JOHN
Tell him toward Swinstead, to the abbey there.

MESSENGER
Be of good comfort, for the great supply
That was expected by the Dauphin here
Are wracked three nights ago on Goodwin Sands.
This news was brought to Richard but even now.
The French fight coldly and retire themselves.

The french being put against another country fended well

KING JOHN
Ay me, this tyrant fever burns me up
And will not let me welcome this good news.
Set on toward Swinstead. To my litter straight.
Weakness possesseth me, and I am faint.

They exit.

Scene 4

Enter Salisbury, Pembroke, and Bigot.

SALISBURY
I did not think the King so stored with friends.

The King's enemies always seemed greater than their friends

2. **Up:** i.e., forward

3. **miscarry:** are destroyed

5. **In spite of spite:** in defiance of defiance

6. **sore:** sorely, grievously

7. **revolts:** rebels

8. **happy:** fortunate

11. **bought and sold:** betrayed

15. **lords of this loud day:** i.e., victorious

16. **He:** i.e., the Dauphin

24. **quantity:** small piece, fragment

26. **Resolveth . . . figure:** loses its shape; **'gainst:** when exposed to

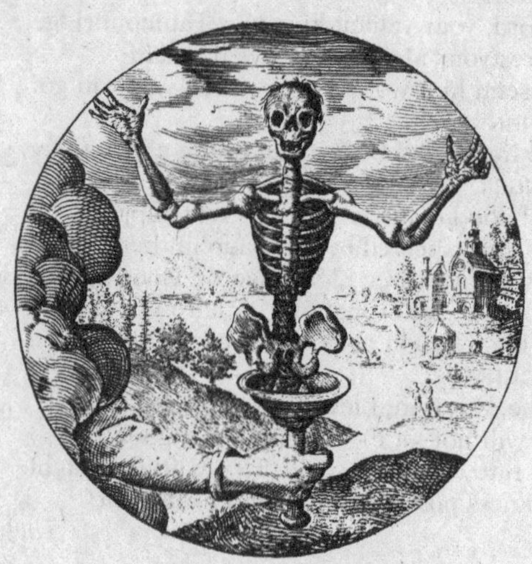

"Bare-ribbed Death." (5.2.180)
From George Wither, *A collection of emblemes . . .* (1635).

PEMBROKE
Up once again. Put spirit in the French.
If they miscarry, we miscarry too.

SALISBURY
That misbegotten devil, Faulconbridge,
In spite of spite, alone upholds the day.

PEMBROKE
They say King John, sore sick, hath left the field.

Enter Melun, wounded, ⌜led by a Soldier.⌝

MELUN
Lead me to the revolts of England here.

SALISBURY
When we were happy, we had other names.

PEMBROKE
It is the Count Melun.

SALISBURY
Wounded to death.

MELUN
Fly, noble English; you are bought and sold.
Unthread the rude eye of rebellion
And welcome home again discarded faith.
Seek out King John and fall before his feet,
For if the French be lords of this loud day,
He means to recompense the pains you take
By cutting off your heads. Thus hath he sworn,
And I with him, and many more with me,
Upon the altar at Saint Edmundsbury,
Even on that altar where we swore to you
Dear amity and everlasting love.

SALISBURY
May this be possible? May this be true?

MELUN
Have I not hideous death within my view,
Retaining but a quantity of life,
Which bleeds away even as a form of wax
Resolveth from his figure 'gainst the fire?

28. **use:** profit

30. **hence:** in heaven, in the hereafter

37. **ill:** evil; cruel; unlucky

38. **fine:** penalty; **rated:** (1) assessed; (2) severely reproved

39. **fine:** end

42. **respect:** consideration

43. **For that:** because

45. **In lieu whereof:** i.e., in return for which

46. **rumor:** clamor, din; **field:** battlefield

50. **beshrew:** curse

51. **favor:** appearance, look

53. **untread:** retrace

54. **bated . . . flood:** i.e., overflowing river that lowered and receded

55. **rankness:** swollen state

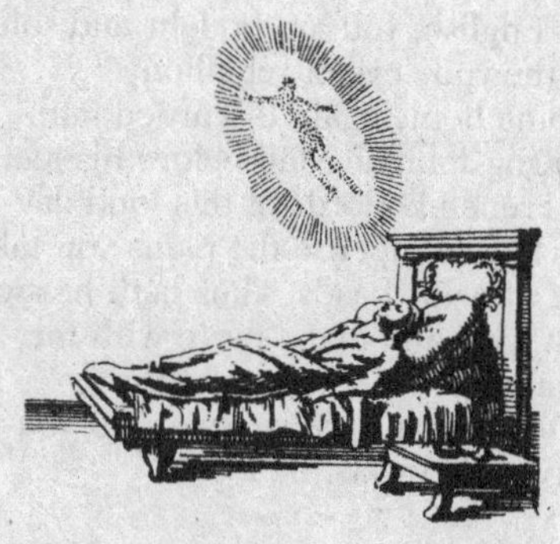

"And part this body and my soul." (5.4.48)
From August Casimir Redel, *Annus symbolicus* . . . [c. 1695].

What in the world should make me now deceive,
Since I must lose the use of all deceit?
Why should I then be false, since it is true
That I must die here and live hence by truth?
I say again, if Louis do win the day,
He is forsworn if e'er those eyes of yours
Behold another daybreak in the East.
But even this night, whose black contagious breath
Already smokes about the burning crest
Of the old, feeble, and day-wearied sun,
Even this ill night your breathing shall expire,
Paying the fine of rated treachery
Even with a treacherous fine of all your lives,
If Louis by your assistance win the day.
Commend me to one Hubert with your king;
The love of him, and this respect besides,
For that my grandsire was an Englishman,
Awakes my conscience to confess all this.
In lieu whereof, I pray you bear me hence
From forth the noise and rumor of the field,
Where I may think the remnant of my thoughts
In peace, and part this body and my soul
With contemplation and devout desires.

SALISBURY
We do believe thee, and beshrew my soul
But I do love the favor and the form
Of this most fair occasion, by the which
We will untread the steps of damnèd flight,
And like a bated and retirèd flood,
Leaving our rankness and irregular course,
Stoop low within those bounds we have o'erlooked
And calmly run on in obedience
Even to our ocean, to our great King John.
My arm shall give thee help to bear thee hence,
For I do see the cruel pangs of death

62. **intends:** maintains

5.5 The Dauphin rejoices that his forces have almost defeated the English. He then learns that Count Melun has died, that the English rebels have gone back to King John, and that his supply ships have sunk.

---

0 SD. **train:** attendants

1. **methought:** i.e., it seemed to me

2. **welkin:** sky

3. **measured:** traversed

5. **faint:** half-hearted, cowardly; **retire:** retreat; **bravely:** splendidly; **off:** i.e., **off** the battlefield

8. **tott'ring:** tattered; waving; **clearly:** free of all encumbrance

13. **fall'n off:** revolted, withdrawn from allegiance

14. **supply:** reinforcements; **which you:** i.e., for **which you**

16. **shrewd:** ominous; vile

20. **stumbling night:** i.e., **night,** during which people stumble

Right in thine eye.—Away, my friends! New flight,
And happy newness, that intends old right.
They exit, ⌜assisting Melun.⌝

Scene 5

Enter ⌜Louis, the⌝ Dauphin and his train.

DAUPHIN
The sun of heaven, methought, was loath to set,
But stayed and made the western welkin blush,
When English ⌜measured⌝ backward their own ground
In faint retire. O, bravely came we off,
When with a volley of our needless shot,
After such bloody toil, we bid good night
And wound our tott'ring colors clearly up,
Last in the field and almost lords of it.

Enter a Messenger.

MESSENGER
Where is my prince, the Dauphin?

DAUPHIN
Here. What news?

MESSENGER
The Count Melun is slain. The English lords,
By his persuasion, are again fall'n off,
And your supply, which you have wished so long,
Are cast away and sunk on Goodwin Sands.

DAUPHIN
Ah, foul, shrewd news. Beshrew thy very heart!
I did not think to be so sad tonight
As this hath made me. Who was he that said
King John did fly an hour or two before
The stumbling night did part our weary powers?

MESSENGER
Whoever spoke it, it is true, my lord.

22. **quarter:** watch, order

24. **adventure:** chance, hazard, venture

5.6 Hubert brings news to the Bastard that King John has been poisoned by a monk, and that, at the urging of his son Prince Henry, King John has pardoned the rebellious nobles. The Bastard, half of whose army has drowned, hastens to the dying king.

---

0 SD. **severally:** separately

2. **What:** i.e., who

3. **part of England:** i.e., English side

8. **perfect:** correct

9. **upon all hazards:** in spite of all perils

12. **Who:** i.e., whoever

14. **come one . . . Plantagenets:** a reference to his being Richard the Lion-heart's illegitimate son

15. **remembrance:** memory (Hubert chastises his own poor memory.)

19. **Sans compliment:** without formality or ceremony

An orchard. (5.7.10)
From Octavio Boldoni, *Theatrum temporaneum* . . . (1636).

DAUPHIN
Well, keep good quarter and good care tonight.
The day shall not be up so soon as I
To try the fair adventure of tomorrow.

They exit.

Scene 6

Enter Bastard and Hubert, severally.

HUBERT
Who's there? Speak ho! Speak quickly, or I shoot.
BASTARD
A friend. What art thou?
HUBERT Of the part of England.
BASTARD
Whither dost thou go?
HUBERT What's that to thee?
⌜BASTARD⌝
Why may not I demand of thine affairs
As well as thou of mine? Hubert, I think?
HUBERT Thou hast a perfect thought.
I will upon all hazards well believe
Thou art my friend, that know'st my tongue so well.
Who art thou?
BASTARD Who thou wilt. An if thou please,
Thou mayst befriend me so much as to think
I come one way of the Plantagenets.
HUBERT
Unkind remembrance! Thou and endless night
Have done me shame. Brave soldier, pardon me
That any accent breaking from thy tongue
Should 'scape the true acquaintance of mine ear.
BASTARD
Come, come. Sans compliment, what news abroad?

22. **Brief:** i.e., briefly

25. **very:** actual, true

28. **broke out:** i.e., sprang away

30. **you to:** i.e., yourself for; **sudden:** unforeseen, unexpected

32. **take it:** i.e., **take** the poison; **taste to:** i.e., act as taster for

33. **resolvèd:** resolute

34. **bowels suddenly burst out:** According to John Foxe's *Actes and Monuments* (1563), the monk who poisoned King John's wine and who "drank a great draft thereof" to encourage John to drink, died soon thereafter, "his guts gushing out of his belly."

35. **peradventure:** perhaps

37. **are:** i.e., have

42. **bear above:** endure beyond

43. **power:** forces; **this night:** last **night**

44. **Passing:** crossing

45. **These Lincoln Washes:** the estuary of the North Sea between Lincolnshire and Norfolk

46. **hardly:** with difficulty

HUBERT
Why, here walk I in the black brow of night
To find you out.

BASTARD
Brief, then; and what's the news?

HUBERT
O my sweet sir, news fitting to the night,
Black, fearful, comfortless, and horrible.

BASTARD
Show me the very wound of this ill news.
I am no woman; I'll not swoon at it.

HUBERT
The King, I fear, is poisoned by a monk.
I left him almost speechless, and broke out
To acquaint you with this evil, that you might
The better arm you to the sudden time
Than if you had at leisure known of this.

BASTARD
How did he take it? Who did taste to him?

HUBERT
A monk, I tell you, a resolvèd villain,
Whose bowels suddenly burst out. The King
Yet speaks and peradventure may recover.

BASTARD
Who didst thou leave to tend his Majesty?

HUBERT
Why, know you not? The lords are all come back,
And brought Prince Henry in their company,
At whose request the King hath pardoned them,
And they are all about his Majesty.

BASTARD
Withhold thine indignation, mighty ⌜God,⌝
And tempt us not to bear above our power.
I'll tell thee, Hubert, half my power this night,
Passing these flats, are taken by the tide.
These Lincoln Washes have devourèd them.
Myself, well mounted, hardly have escaped.

48. **doubt:** fear; **or ere:** before

5.7 As King John lies dying, surrounded by his newly loyal nobles and his son, Prince Henry, the Bastard brings him news of French victories and English losses. The Bastard then learns that Pandulph has brought an offer of peace from the Dauphin. After John dies, the Bastard and the nobles offer their allegiance to Prince Henry, soon to be crowned King Henry III.

---

1. **The life of all his blood:** i.e., his vital spirits, which in Shakespeare's day were thought to animate the body, being produced in the heart and carried by the **blood**

2. **touched:** infected, tainted; **corruptibly:** so as to be made putrid; **pure:** uncorrupted

4. **idle:** foolish, silly

5. **mortality:** mortal existence, life

10. **orchard:** garden (See picture, page 196.)

11. **rage:** rave, speak wildly

12. **patient:** calm

14–15. **Fierce extremes . . . themselves:** i.e., the most intense agonies, as they continue, are no longer felt by those who suffer them

17. **invisible:** i.e., invisibly, imperceptibly

19. **legions:** (1) vast hosts; (2) bodies of armed men

20. **hold:** stronghold, fortified place

Away before. Conduct me to the King.
I doubt he will be dead or ere I come.

Scene 7

Enter Prince Henry, Salisbury, and Bigot.

PRINCE HENRY
It is too late. The life of all his blood
Is touched corruptibly, and his pure brain,
Which some suppose the soul's frail dwelling-house,
Doth, by the idle comments that it makes,
Foretell the ending of mortality.

Enter Pembroke.

PEMBROKE
His Highness yet doth speak, and holds belief
That being brought into the open air
It would allay the burning quality
Of that fell poison which assaileth him.

PRINCE HENRY
Let him be brought into the orchard here.
⌜*Bigot exits.*⌝
Doth he still rage?

PEMBROKE He is more patient
Than when you left him. Even now he sung.

PRINCE HENRY
O vanity of sickness! Fierce extremes
In their continuance will not feel themselves.
Death, having preyed upon the outward parts,
Leaves them invisible, and his siege is now
Against the ⌜mind,⌝ the which he pricks and wounds
With many legions of strange fantasies,
Which in their throng and press to that last hold

23–26. **I am . . . rest:** a reference to the belief that the **swan,** a nonsinging bird, sings just before death **lasting:** everlasting

28. **indigest:** chaos, undifferentiated mass

29. **rude:** unfinished

30. **marry:** i.e., indeed

31. **nor:** i.e., or

33. **all my bowels:** the interior of my whole body

38. **fare:** (1) condition, welfare; (2) food

45. **cold comfort:** (1) the relief **cold** can provide; (2) inadequate consolation; **strait:** stingy

"The King . . . is poisoned by a monk." (5.6.27)
From John Foxe, *Actes and monuments* . . . (1632; image first published in the 1563 edition).

Confound themselves. 'Tis strange that Death should
  sing.
I am the cygnet to this pale faint swan,
Who chants a doleful hymn to his own death,
And from the organ-pipe of frailty sings
His soul and body to their lasting rest.

SALISBURY
Be of good comfort, prince, for you are born
To set a form upon that indigest
Which he hath left so shapeless and so rude.

⌜King⌝ John brought in, ⌜attended by Bigot.⌝

KING JOHN
Ay, marry, now my soul hath elbow-room.
It would not out at windows nor at doors.
There is so hot a summer in my bosom
That all my bowels crumble up to dust.
I am a scribbled form drawn with a pen
Upon a parchment, and against this fire
Do I shrink up.

PRINCE HENRY How fares your Majesty?

KING JOHN
Poisoned—ill fare—dead, forsook, cast off,
And none of you will bid the winter come
To thrust his icy fingers in my maw,
Nor let my kingdom's rivers take their course
Through my burned bosom, nor entreat the North
To make his bleak winds kiss my parchèd lips
And comfort me with cold. I do not ask you much.
I beg cold comfort, and you are so strait
And so ingrateful, you deny me that.

PRINCE HENRY
O, that there were some virtue in my tears
That might relieve you!

KING JOHN The salt in them is hot.
Within me is a hell, and there the poison

52. **unreprievable, condemnèd blood:** i.e., **blood** that, like a convicted criminal, has been **condemned** to die, without hope of a reprieve

53. **scalded . . . motion:** fired with my intense desire

54. **spleen:** eagerness

55. **set mine eye:** i.e., close my eyes

57. **shrouds:** ropes forming part of a ship's rigging

59. **My heart . . . it by:** a reference to the heartstrings, i.e., the sinews and tendons then thought to support the **heart** **stay:** support

62. **module:** image or counterfeit

63. **preparing hitherward:** i.e., **preparing** to come toward this place

64. **God He knows:** i.e., only **God knows; answer him:** encounter **him,** i.e., fight **him**

65. **best part of my power:** greater **part** of **my** forces

66. **upon advantage:** i.e., to achieve a favorable position

67. **all unwarily:** without any warning

72. **stay:** object of reliance, support

77. **still:** always

Is, as a fiend, confined to tyrannize
On unreprievable, condemnèd blood.

Enter Bastard.

BASTARD

O, I am scalded with my violent motion
And spleen of speed to see your Majesty.

KING JOHN

O cousin, thou art come to set mine eye.
The tackle of my heart is cracked and burnt,
And all the shrouds wherewith my life should sail
Are turnèd to one thread, one little hair.
My heart hath one poor string to stay it by,
Which holds but till thy news be utterèd,
And then all this thou seest is but a clod
And module of confounded royalty.

BASTARD

The Dauphin is preparing hitherward,
Where ⌜God⌝ He knows how we shall answer him.
For in a night the best part of my power,
As I upon advantage did remove,
Were in the Washes all unwarily
Devourèd by the unexpected flood.

⌜*King John dies.*⌝

SALISBURY

You breathe these dead news in as dead an ear.—
My liege! My lord!—But now a king, now thus.

PRINCE HENRY

Even so must I run on, and even so stop.
What surety of the world, what hope, what stay,
When this was now a king and now is clay?

BASTARD

Art thou gone so? I do but stay behind
To do the office for thee of revenge,
And then my soul shall wait on thee to heaven,
As it on earth hath been thy servant still.—

78. **stars . . . spheres:** In Ptolemaic astronomy each planet was carried around the earth in its own crystalline sphere; in this metaphor, the lords are figured as the planets circling King John as the earth. (See page xxxiv.) **stars:** planets **right:** proper

79. **powers:** forces

84. **Straight:** straightaway, immediately

85. **rages:** rushes furiously

90. **respect:** i.e., self-respect

91. **With purpose:** i.e., together with the Dauphin's **purpose; presently:** immediately

92. **rather:** sooner

93. **well-sinewèd to:** i.e., strong, firm, powerful in

95. **many carriages:** i.e., much military equipment (**Carriages** are literally wheeled supports on which cannons are mounted.)

99. **meet:** suitable; **post:** go in haste

100. **happily:** successfully

107. **happily:** felicitously

108. **lineal state:** power, greatness, pomp (of kingship) by **lineal** descent

Now, now, you stars, that move in your right spheres,
Where be your powers? Show now your mended
  faiths
And instantly return with me again
To push destruction and perpetual shame
Out of the weak door of our fainting land.
Straight let us seek, or straight we shall be sought;
The Dauphin rages at our very heels.

SALISBURY
It seems you know not, then, so much as we.
The Cardinal Pandulph is within at rest,
Who half an hour since came from the Dauphin,
And brings from him such offers of our peace
As we with honor and respect may take,
With purpose presently to leave this war.

BASTARD
He will the rather do it when he sees
Ourselves well-sinewèd to our defense.

SALISBURY
Nay, 'tis in a manner done already,
For many carriages he hath dispatched
To the sea-side, and put his cause and quarrel
To the disposing of the Cardinal,
With whom yourself, myself, and other lords,
If you think meet, this afternoon will post
To consummate this business happily.

BASTARD
Let it be so.—And you, my noble prince,
With other princes that may best be spared,
Shall wait upon your father's funeral.

PRINCE HENRY
At Worcester must his body be interred,
For so he willed it.

BASTARD Thither shall it, then,
And happily may your sweet self put on
The lineal state and glory of the land,

110. **bequeath:** transfer, deliver

111. **subjection:** homage, obedience

112. **like:** same

113. **rest without a spot:** i.e., remain in a state of unblemished allegiance

114. **kind:** gentle, benevolent; affectionate, loving

116–17. **but needful woe . . . griefs:** i.e., only such grieving as is required, since we have already grieved before **been beforehand with:** anticipated

120. **But:** except

121. **princes:** i.e., nobles (Salisbury, Pembroke, Bigot)

122. **the three corners of the world:** perhaps, **the** rest **of the world,** or, perhaps, **the** entire **world** (See longer note, page 221.)

123. **shock them:** encounter **them** in battle

King John lies dead of poison. (5.7.68)
From John Foxe, *Actes and monuments* . . . (1632; image first published in the 1563 edition).

To whom with all submission on my knee
I do bequeath my faithful services
And true subjection everlastingly. ⌜*He kneels.*⌝

SALISBURY

And the like tender of our love we make
To rest without a spot forevermore.
⌜*Salisbury, Pembroke, and Bigot kneel.*⌝

PRINCE HENRY

I have a kind soul that would give ⌜you⌝ thanks
And knows not how to do it but with tears.
⌜*They rise.*⌝

BASTARD

O, let us pay the time but needful woe,
Since it hath been beforehand with our griefs.
This England never did nor never shall
Lie at the proud foot of a conqueror
But when it first did help to wound itself.
Now these her princes are come home again,
Come the three corners of the world in arms
And we shall shock them. Naught shall make us rue,
If England to itself do rest but true.
They exit, ⌜bearing the body of King John.⌝

Longer Notes

1.1.0 SD. **the Chatillion of France: Chatillion** appears to be treated as a title, rather than as a proper name, in this Folio stage direction; in history, however, it was the proper name of a noble French family. There was in Shakespeare's time the English title "Chastilian," meaning "the owner of a castle."

1.1.10. **territories:** This word may refer to the regions named in line 11 **(Ireland, Poitiers** [i.e., Poitou], **Anjou, Touraine, Maine);** or it may refer to other regions left unnamed in this speech. In Act 2 Arthur is presented as laying claim to and John is presented as having in his control a number of different lands beyond England. The list at 2.1.155 leaves out "Poitiers" (i.e., Poitou); the list at line 509 restores "Poitiers" but omits "Ireland"; the one at lines 552–53 also includes "Poitiers" and omits "Ireland" but adds "Volquessen" (i.e., Vexin). Finally, at line 577 King John offers to create Arthur as Duke of Brittany, an offer implying that Brittany too is under the dominion of the English crown. Around the time this play was written, King John was represented as having had dominion over still other lands. John Taylor, in his 1630 *All the Workes . . .*, identifies King John as also "Duke of Normandy, Guyen and Aquitaine."

1.1.49. **expedition's:** Many editors argue for retaining the First Folio's "expeditious," on the grounds that the word could have meant "sudden." We could find no warrant in the *Oxford English Dictionary* or in the literature of the period for "expeditious" meaning "sudden," nor could we reconcile ourselves to allowing the First Folio's "expeditious charge" (i.e., "speedy expense") to stand. We have therefore accepted "expedition's charge," the reading of the Second Folio.

1.1.141 SP. **Bastard:** The Folio's shift in the speech-prefix designation of this character from "Philip" to "Bastard" coincides with Philip's decision to join the court as "the reputed son of Coeur de Lion" and to give up the name "Philip Faulconbridge." He is soon knighted and renamed "Sir Richard Plantagenet," and in the remainder of the play is variously addressed by other characters—sometimes as "Sir Richard," or "Richard," but also as "Philip" or as "Faulconbridge."

1.1.145–47. **That in . . . goes:** This emphasis on the thinness of the three-farthing coin is well-placed. This silver coin, worth only three-quarters of a penny, was itself quite **thin;** and Elizabeth's **face,** as represented on the coin, also looked pinched and **thin.** While the coin's picture of Elizabeth does not show her with a rose behind her ear, Elizabethan men and women sometimes adorned their ears with flowers.

1.1.174–77. **by chance . . . night:** Each of these expressions alludes to the Bastard's illegitimacy. "Something about," for example, suggests an indirect route, while "a little from the right" perhaps refers to the "bend sinister" that, in heraldry, signals bastardy. The phrases "in at the window, or else o'er the hatch" name two ways of illicit entry into a house (either through a window or over the bottom half of a divided door). One who "walk[s] by night" might be a suspicious person such as a thief.

1.1.213–22. **For he . . . rising:** In these lines the Bastard plays with the idea of using flattery or elaborate compliment and courtesy to accelerate his self-promotion. On the one hand, he suggests that he will have nothing to do with such affectations: "I will not practice to deceive." On the other hand, he acknowledges an inclination "to deliver / Sweet, sweet, sweet poison for the age's tooth." Then, although he says he will "avoid deceit," he nonetheless presents deceitful flattery in attractive terms when he says that it will "strew the footsteps of [his] rising"—just as, during this time period, rushes strewed in the path of great personages eased their steps.

1.1.238. **Philip Sparrow:** In John Skelton's early-sixteenth-century poem **"Philip Sparrow,"** a girl laments her pet sparrow's death. The name **Philip Sparrow** as a bird's name remained current in poetry of the 1580s and appears in Matthew Grove's 1587 *The most famous and Tragicall Historie of Pelops and Hippodamia. Whereunto are adioyned sundrie pleasant deuises, Epigrams, Songes and Sonnettes.* There, in "The restlesse estate of a Louer," the speaker imagines himself "A Phillip Sparow on [his lady's] fist" (line 89).

2.1.1 SP. **Dauphin:** The Folio's assignment of this speech and the one at line 18 to the Dauphin has been debated by editors. Some believe it odd that the Dauphin, the young heir to King Philip of France, should be the one to welcome an ally so important as the Duke of Austria. Arguing that King Philip should give the welcome, they reassign these speeches to him.

The editorial debate about these two speech prefixes involves a further problem at lines 150–58. There the First Folio is clearly in error, as will be explained below, and some editorial intervention into Folio speech assignments is unavoidable if the text is to be made intelligible. Editors who emend the speech prefixes at lines 1 and 18 seek to justify their emendation by pointing to these later lines, arguing that if the Folio can be in error later in the scene, then it can also be regarded as possibly in error in its speech assignments to the Dauphin at the scene's beginning.

In the Folio, lines 150–58 read as follows:

> *Aust.* What cracker is this same that deafes our eares
> With this abundance of superfluous breath?
> King *Lewis,* determine what we shall doe strait.
> *Lew.* Women & fooles, breake off your conference.
> King *Iohn,* this is the very summe of all:
> *England* and *Ireland, Angiers, Toraine, Maine,*
> In right of *Arthur* doe I claime of thee:
> Wilt thou resigne them, and lay downe thy Armes?
> *Iohn.* My life as soone: I doe defie thee *France.*

Obviously there is something amiss at line 152 when the Duke of Austria addresses a "King *Lewis,*" since there is no such character in the play (the King of France is "Philip" and the Dauphin is "Lewis," or "Louis"). According to some editors, there is also a problem with assigning the speech in lines 153–57 to *"Lew*[*is*]" the Dauphin, because King John responds to this speech by addressing King Philip (*"France"*) in line 158; these editors argue that King John must be responding to the character who has just spoken, and therefore they reassign the speech in lines 153–57 to King Philip.

Our approach to this speech-prefix problem—an approach that we do not pretend to be definitive—is to make only those changes to the Folio text that are necessary to make it intelligible to our readers. In the extensive history of debate concerning the speech prefixes in question, no one has advanced a compelling reason why the Dauphin Louis cannot offer the welcome to the Duke of Austria. We therefore keep the Folio speech prefixes for 2.1.1 and 2.1.18.

In addressing the problems at lines 2.1.150–58, we note first that since elsewhere in this scene the Folio sometimes uses "*King*" as the speech prefix for King Philip of France, it is possible that the Folio simply errs in setting "King" at line 152 in roman rather than the italic type needed for a speech prefix. We have therefore converted the word "King" in line 152 into a speech prefix for King Philip, and have otherwise left the Folio unchanged. We do not find it impossible that in line 158 King John should refuse to respond to the challenge from the Dauphin (lines 153–57) and instead address himself to his political equal "*France*" (i.e., King Philip, line 158).

2.1.5. **By this brave duke came early to his grave:** Richard did not actually come "early to his grave" at the hand of Austria, but was instead mortally wounded in a battle before the walls of the Viscount Limoges' castle; the Duke of Austria had earlier imprisoned Richard but had not killed him. In combining the Viscount Limoges with the Duke of Austria, Shakespeare's play follows a dramatic tradition begun in the two-part play *The Troublesome Raigne of Iohn, King of England.*

2.1.29. **that utmost corner of the West:** In ancient geography and mythology, the earth was conceived as a single landmass surrounded by the "river Ocean." Britain, in that conception, was cut off from the landmass of the known world and was thus beyond the end of the earth; it was often associated with the mythical islands of the Western Ocean, such as the Fortunate Isles and the Islands of the Blest. This view of England's geographical position continued long after the world was found to be round and lands far to the west of England were discovered. The term "utmost" or "uttermost" was used elsewhere to describe England's geographical position. Sir John Harrington wrote in 1591 that "Ariosto calls us 'ultima Ingle-terra,' the uttermost country." And John Selden uses the term "the utmost ends of the earth" in connection with the British Isles. (See Josephine Waters Bennett, "Britain among the Fortunate Isles," *Studies in Philology* 53 [1956]: 114–40.) The phrase **utmost corner of the West** seems therefore to describe England's geographical position as it was viewed in older cosmologies and as it continued to be described poetically.

2.1.66. **unsettled humors:** This phrase is figurative. John's men are called **humors,** a medical term in this period referring to the bodily fluids of blood, phlegm, black bile, and yellow bile; the balance or proportion of **humors** was thought to produce one's disposition, character, and mood. By referring to John's gentlemen soldiers as **unsettled humors,** Chatillion suggests that in none of them are the bodily fluids properly balanced or settled, with the result that the gentlemen are quite unstable.

The word **unsettled** may refer not only to the temperaments of John's gentlemen soldiers but also to their material situations. In this second sense, **unsettled** suggests that these men have yet to find a place or position in which they are willing to settle down. This sense is later developed in the lines that refer to them as having sold all they inherited in order to furnish themselves with the equipment for war, by means of which, whatever the risk, they hope to improve their lot in life: "Bearing their birthrights proudly on their backs, / To make a hazard of new fortunes here."

2.1.186–89. **Thy sins . . . womb:** These lines build on the Second of the Ten Commandments: "Thou shalt not make to thyself any graven image, nor the likeness of anything that is in heaven above, or in the earth beneath, nor in the water under the earth; thou shalt not bow down to them nor worship them. For I the Lord thy God am a jealous God, and visit the sins of the fathers upon the children, unto the third and fourth generation of them that hate me" (Exodus 20.4–5, as printed in the *Book of Common Prayer of . . . the Church of England,* 1559). Because the commandment is in the official prayer book of the Church of England, it can be referred to, as it is here, as the **"canon of the law"**—i.e., the rule of the church.

The passage also draws on the words of Psalm 51.5: "in sin hath my mother conceived me." In the psalm, these words are a general confession of sinfulness. When Constance uses the phrase **sin-conceiving womb** to attack Eleanor, she takes the words of the psalm and applies them to Eleanor's **conceiving** of her children, specifically (as we see in lines 191–97) her **conceiving** of John.

2.1.192–95. **he . . . her plague:** i.e., Arthur is punished because of Eleanor's **sin** (in accordance with the Second Commandment) and is punished by her and by John (who is Eleanor's own **sin** and **plague**).

2.1.195–96. **her sin his injury, / Her injury the beadle to her sin:** Among the possible meanings of **her sin his injury** are (1) the sinfulness of Eleanor is punished in Arthur; (2) John (**her sin**) is Arthur's punishment. The metaphor **Her injury the beadle to her sin** may be interpreted to mean that Eleanor's injuriousness whips John on to further cruelties. But because, in the course of this speech (lines 191–97)

Constance sometimes identifies Eleanor's **sin** as the conceiving of John, sometimes as John himself, and sometimes as a more general moral failure, it is possible to generate many possible meanings for lines 195–96.

2.1.302. **lioness:** This would be a particularly insulting term for Austria's wife, since the **lioness** had a reputation for lecherousness: "There is no beast more desirous of copulation than the **lioness**" (Topsell, *History of Four-footed Beasts,* 1607).

2.1.337 SP. **Citizen:** In the Folio this and four other speeches in this scene are assigned to *"Hubert"* (or *"Hub."*), and many editors equate this speaker with the Hubert who, beginning in 3.2, plays an important role in the action. They then either reassign to "Hubert" the earlier speeches that in the present scene the Folio assigns to a "Citizen" of Angiers or they follow the Folio in having the earlier speeches delivered by the anonymous Citizen and the later speeches in 2.1 delivered by Hubert. The basic premise underlying the decision to rename the Citizen "Hubert"—namely, that the *Hubert* who speaks from the walls of Angiers is the same character as the follower and confidant of King John later in the play—seems to us problematic in terms both of the play's characterization of the two and of the audience's ability to link an unidentified character in 2.1 with the character that is Hubert from 3.2 on. Nor do we see any distinction in the text between the two who speak in turn from the wall of Angiers—the nameless Citizen and the one the Folio names *Hubert.* We have thus followed those editors who use the name "Citizen" throughout the scene to designate the "speaker from the wall."

2.1.520. **shadow:** Here the Dauphin begins wordplay on **shadow, son,** and **sun** that extends over the next three lines as he develops his account of what he sees when he looks in Lady Blanche's eye. The lines are as follows:

> The shadow of myself formed in her eye,
> Which, being but the shadow of your son,
> Becomes a sun and makes your son a shadow.

In the first line, the Dauphin says that he sees a reflection of himself (**shadow of myself**) in the Lady Blanche's **eye.** This reflection, he tells his father in the second line, is only the insubstantial image (**shadow**) of Philip's **son.** In the third line, the Dauphin compliments the Lady Blanche by implicitly comparing her eye to the **sun,** which is so bright that he is reduced to a mere **shadow,** i.e., the dark figure cast on a surface by an object in sunlight.

3.1.77 SD. **hand in hand:** There are many ways of staging the gesture that links John and Philip in this scene. At several points (e.g., lines 107, 199, 236, 249–54, 271–72), reference is made to the kings standing arm in arm or hand in hand. Some directors have them already hand in hand when they enter at line 77, as we suggest in our stage direction. Others have them take hands at a later point; yet others have them enter hand in hand, then drop their hands and join them again later.

3.1.273–308. **So mak'st . . . weight:** In these lines, Pandulph argues that King Philip must break his agreement with King John because Philip cannot keep it without breaking his vow to support the Catholic Church, whose foe King John now is. Furthermore, Pandulph argues that Philip's vow to the church has precedence over any other vow, and that failure to keep his vow to the church will make Philip incapable of making or keeping any other promises.

3.3.44–45. **melancholy . . . thick:** According to Thomas Nashe in *Terrors of the Night* (1594): "the grossest part of our blood is the melancholy humour, which . . . still thickening as it stands still, engendreth many misshapen objects in our imaginations." Like Nashe, Robert Burton, in his *Anatomy of Melancholy* (1621), writes of **melancholy** as a humor, not a **spirit,** describing it as "cold and dry, thick, black, and sour." Burton describes **spirit** as "a most subtle vapor, which is expressed from the blood, and the instrument of the soul, to perform all his actions; a common tie or medium betwixt the body and the soul, as some will have it" (Part 1, section 1, memb. 2, subsection 2). See the discussion of **humors** in the longer note to 2.1.66.

3.4.1–3. **So . . . fellowship:** Many editors see much of this play as presenting religious strife in sixteenth-century Europe under the guise of King John's thirteenth-century story. This mention of an **armada,** for example, is seen as an allusion to the destruction by storm of the great Armada sent against Protestant England in 1588 by King Philip II of Spain, the leader of Catholic Europe. See Historical Background 2, page 232.

4.2.69 SD. **Enter Hubert:** It is possible that Hubert enters two lines earlier, just before John's capitulation at line 68, and that his presence affects John's decision to give in to the nobles' entreaty. The Folio text places the entrance at that point, and some editors argue that Hubert's presence during John's speech of capitulation makes it certain that John is being hypocritical. However, since the Folio so frequently prints entrances earlier than needed, our policy is to place entrance directions in proximity to the character's first speech on entering, and we maintain our practice at this point. Moreover, bringing Hubert on at the earlier point at which his entrance is printed in the Folio would narrow the interpretation of John's speech, a restriction we prefer to avoid.

5.7.122. **the three corners of the world:** The Bible sometimes refers to "the four corners of the world" (see, e.g., Isaiah 11.12); thus England may here be inferred to be one of the four **corners,** as it was explicitly said to be at 2.1.29: "that utmost corner of the West." Or these lines may imply a "three-nooked world," as in *Antony and Cleopatra* 4.6.6, in which *nook* means "corner."

Textual Notes

The reading of the present text appears to the left of the square bracket. Unless otherwise noted, the reading to the left of the bracket is from **F**, the First Folio text (upon which this edition is based). The earliest sources of readings not in **F** are indicated as follows: **F2** is the Second Folio of 1632; **F3** is the Third Folio of 1663–64; **F4** is the Fourth Folio of 1685; **Ed.** is an earlier editor of Shakespeare, beginning with Rowe in 1709. No sources are given for emendations of punctuation or for corrections of obvious typographical errors, like turned letters that produce no known word. **SD** means stage direction; **SP** means speech prefix; ***uncorr.*** means the first or uncorrected state of the First Folio; ***corr.*** means the second or corrected state of the First Folio; ~ stands in place of a word already quoted before the square bracket; ‸ indicates the omission of a punctuation mark.

1.1

5 *and hereafter in this scene.* SP QUEEN ELEANOR] Ed.; *Elea.* F

30. SD *Chatillion, Pembroke*] Ed.; *Chat., Pem.* F

43. God] Ed.; heauen F

49. expedition's] Ed.; expeditious F

49. SD *½ line later in* F

51 *and hereafter until line 135.* SP PHILIP FAULCONBRIDGE] Ed.; *Philip* F

51. subject‸ I,] ~, ~‸ F

55 *and hereafter.* Coeur de Lion] F (*Cordelion*)

57 *and hereafter.* SP ROBERT FAULCONBRIDGE] Ed.; *Robert.* F
62. certain] cerraine F
65. Thou] F ($\overset{u}{y}$)
81. yourself.] your selfe∧ F
137. rather:] ~∧ F
140. besides] F (beside)
151. I] F2; It F
163. wife's] F (wiues)
188. A] Ed.; *Bast.* A F
194. too respective] F2; two respectiue F
195. conversion.] ~, F
209. Pyrenean] F (Perennean)
214. smack] Ed.; smoake F
222. SD *5 lines later in* F
228 *and hereafter.* SP LADY FAULCONBRIDGE] Ed.; *Lady.* F
233. unreverent] F (vnreuerend)
243. well— . . . confess—] ~, . . . ~∧ F
244. he] Ed.; *omit* F
244. me.] ~∧ F
265. Thou] Ed.; That F

2.1

0. Act 2, scene 1] Ed.; *Scæna Secunda* F
0 SD *Austria . . . Arthur*] *This edition; Austria, Constance, Arthur* F
1 *and hereafter to line 153.* DAUPHIN] Ed.; *Lewis* F
35. that] F ($\overset{t}{y}$)
37 *and hereafter to line 79.* SP KING PHILIP] Ed.; *King.* F
37. work.] ~∧ F
45. blood.] ~, F
63. Ate] Ed.; Ace F
75. SD *2 lines later in* F
83. SD *King*] *K.* F

89 *and hereafter except line 152.* SP KING PHILIP] *Fran.* F
106. Geoffrey's.] ~∧ F
113, 175. From] Frõ F
114. breast] Ed.; beast F
121 *and hereafter except line 171.* SP QUEEN ELEANOR] Ed.; *Queen.* F
152. SP KING PHILIP] Ed.; King F
155. Anjou] Ed.; Angiers F
158 *and hereafter except 3.1.338 and 5.1.1.* SP KING JOHN] Ed.; *Iohn* F
159. Brittany] F (*Britaine*)
171. SP QUEEN ELEANOR] Ed.; *Qu. Mo.* F
195. plague; . . . sin∧ . . . injury,] ~∧ . . . ~: . . . ~∧ F
208. SD *Citizens*] Ed.; *a Citizen* F
223. French∧] ~. F
224. Confronts your] Ed.; Comfort yours F
261. invulnerable] F (involuerable)
268. roundure] F (rounder)
276. subjects.] ~∧ F
296. chevaliers!] ~∧ F
312. SP FRENCH HERALD] F (*F. Her.*)
318. earth] earrh F
324. SP ENGLISH HERALD] F (*E. Har.*)
337 *and hereafter.* SP CITIZEN] Ed.; *Hubert.* F
339. your] yonr F
353. water∧] ~, F
365. SD *aside*] *This edition*
378. Speak] Speeke F
384. SP CITIZEN] Ed.; *Fra.* F
418. town] Townc F
434. league,] ~: F
471. from motion] ftom motion F

474. SD *aside*] *This edition*
489. SP QUEEN ELEANOR] Ed.; *Old Qu.* F
489. match.] ~∧ F
509. Anjou] Ed.; *Angiers* F
526. SD *aside*] *This edition*
533. mine.] ~, F
534. aught] F (ought)
557. daughter] daughtet F
558. well.—Young princes,] ~∧∧~~: F
566. not,] ~∧ F
568. son? . . . knows.] ~, . . . ~? F
587. SD *All . . . exit.*] F (*Exeunt*)
600. that—] ~. F

3.1

0. Act 3, scene 1.] Ed.; *Actus Secundus* F
2. joined?] ~. F
40. have] heue F
65. Envenom] Euvenom F
72. stoop.] ~, F
77. SD *Enter . . . Attendants.*] Ed.; *Actus Tertius, Scœna prima. Enter King John, France, Dolphin, Blanch, Elianor, Philip, Austria, Constance.* F
112. God] Ed.; heauens F
120–21. thou coward] F ($\overset{u}{y}$ coward)
135 *and hereafter.* calfskin] F (Calues skin)
137, 139. SP BASTARD] F (*Phil.*)
149. Archbishop] Arshbishop F
154. task] Ed.; tast F
161. God] Ed.; heauen F
192. too. . . . right,] ~, . . . ~. F
202 *and hereafter.* SP QUEEN ELEANOR] Ed.; *Elea.* F
203. that,] ~∧ F

232. more,] ~? F
239. religious] religous
246. God] Ed.; Heauen F
253. ourselves] onr selues F
269. chafèd] Ed.; cased F
276. God . . . God] Ed.; heauen . . . heauen F
285. again;] ~, F
290. religion∧] ~: F
294. oath. . . . truth∧] ~∧ . . . ~, F
327. love.] ~, F
338. SP KING JOHN] F (*Eng.*)
338. thou] F (y^u)
339. that] F (y^t)
362. let's] le'ts F

3.2 4. SD *1 line earlier in* F.
11. SD *They exit.*] F (*Exit*)

3.3 0. Scene 3] Ed.; *not in* F

3.4 0. Scene 4] Ed.; *Scæna Tertia.* F
0. SD *Pandulph*] *Pandulpho* F
45. not] Ed.; *omit* F
65. friends] Ed.; fiends F
98. Remembers] Remembets F
112. world's] Ed.; words F
114. naught] F (nought)

4.1 14. Mercy] F ('Mercie)
35. Arthur] *Arthnr* F
86. God's] Ed.; heauen F
89. wince] F (winch)
102. God] Ed.; heauen F
102. mote] F (moth)
112. will,] ~∧ F
133. mercy-lacking] ~, ~ F
139. disguisèd] F (disguis'd)

4.2 1. again crowned] F3; against crown'd F

43. when] Ed.; then F
45. reformed∧] ~. F
61. exercise.] ~, F
69. SD *2 lines earlier in* F
75. Doth] F4 (Does); Do F
107. SD *2 lines earlier in* F
136. SD *2 lines earlier in* F
148. tràveled] F (trauailed)
211. embattlèd] F4; embattailed F
258. breath] F (breathe)
264. hand,] ~. F
265. blood.] ~, F
273. incensèd] incensəd F

4.3 11. Saint] F (S.)
36. beauty!] ~, F
41. precious-princely] ~ ∧ ~ F
42. beheld.] ~, F
47. height] F (heighth)
99. Salisbury] Salsbury F
111. life's] F (liues)
120. SD *Lords exit.*] *Ex. Lords* F
124. thou] F (yͧ)
150. up!] ~, F
151. royalty,] Ed.; ~? F
163. cincture] F (center)
167. SD *They . . . body.*] *Exit.* F

5.1 0. Act 5, Scene 1] Ed.; *Actus Quartus, Scæna prima.* F
1. SP KING JOHN] F (*K. Iohn.*)
30. God] Ed.; heau'n F
44. aught] F (ought)

5.2 3. precedent] F (president)
10. and] Ed.; and an F
36. grapple] Ed.; cripple F
43. thou] F4; *omit* F
53. with] wirh F

64. SD *1 line earlier in* F
66. God] Ed.; heauen F
80. propertied] proportied F
120. speak,] ~: F
121. King.] ~∧ F
136. these] F (this)
146. Englishman—] ~. F
154. mother England] Mother-England F
173. all∧] ~, F
177. legate] Lcgate F

5.3 9. the] rhe F

5.4 19. Saint] F (S.)

5.5 3. measured] Ed.; measure F
8. wound] F (woon'd)

5.6 6–7. BASTARD Why . . . Hubert] Ed.; Why . . . *Bast. Hubert* F
22. Brief] Brcefe F
26. swoon] F (swound)
41. God] Ed.; heauen F

5.7 1 *and hereafter.* SP PRINCE HENRY] *Hen.* F
18. mind] Ed.; winde F
21. that] F (y^{t})
23. cygnet] F (Symet)
64. God] Ed.; heauen F
93. sinewèd] F (sinew'd)
114. you] Ed.; *omit* F
116. time∧] ~: F

Historical Background

1. King John, Prince Arthur, and "borrowed majesty"

Shakespeare's *King John* depicts a period in history little more than a hundred years after William, duke of Normandy, conquered England in 1066. It thus reflects a time when the English monarch had dominion over extensive Continental holdings. William the Conqueror remained duke of Normandy (a large territory in France on the English Channel) while he ruled England as William I. During the reigns of William's sons (William II and Henry I) and his granddaughter (the Empress Matilda), the English monarch's Continental holdings were large but contested; they were extended and consolidated under Henry II, son of Matilda and Geoffrey of Anjou and father of John. Henry inherited Normandy, Anjou, Maine, and Touraine from Geoffrey of Anjou; he conquered Brittany, Toulouse, and the Vexin; and he acquired Aquitaine, Poitou, and Auvergne through marriage to Eleanor of Aquitaine.

When Henry II died in 1189, two of his four sons (Henry and Geoffrey) were already dead, and the crown and the extensive Continental territories passed peacefully to his eldest remaining son, who became Richard I. But when Richard died in 1199, there was genuine uncertainty about whether the monarchy belonged to Richard's younger brother, John, or to Arthur, the son of Geoffrey, the brother who would have succeeded to the throne had he lived. This uncertainty about the legal right to the throne was made more severe by Richard's having left the crown in one will to John, in another to Arthur.

In Shakespeare's *King John,* then, when King Philip of France charges that John's is but a "borrowed majesty" (1.1.4) and that John "sways usurpingly" the territories of "Poitiers [i.e., Poitou], Anjou, Touraine, Maine" (1.1.13, 11), Philip is not accusing the English monarch of ruling "usurpingly" over French territories. Instead, he is announcing France's support for Arthur's claim to be the legitimate king of England and thus to have dominion over all of the territories controlled by the English monarch. When, later in the play, the Dauphin, King Philip, and Constance charge King John with usurpation (2.1.9, 120–22), again the accusation is simply that John has unjustly supplanted Arthur as king of England and ruler of the territories belonging to the English crown.

2. King John and the Roman Catholic Church

Early in its first scene, *King John* gives us its first indication of what will become a central conflict in the play, namely John's ongoing struggle with the Roman Catholic Church. John's words about taxing "abbeys and priories" in order to raise money for his wars ("Our abbeys and our priories shall pay / This expedition's charge" [1.1.48–49]) reflect the historical king's arguments with the church over taxation and set the stage for John's dramatic confrontation in mid-play with Cardinal Pandulph, in which John is excommunicated for refusing to obey Pope Innocent III.

By the time Shakespeare wrote *King John,* the historical conflict between John and the church had given rise to contradictory images of the king. John's stance caused the early chroniclers of English history (who were themselves Roman Catholic churchmen) to paint him as an archvillain, but it gained him the veneration of Elizabethan Protestants, who saw him as a forerunner of the Tudor monarchs. John is, in fact, presented as a martyred hero in John Foxe's *Actes and Monuments of Martyrs* (1563).

While *King John* is in no way a Protestant tract (as are, in many ways, such earlier plays as John Bale's *King Johan* and the anonymous *The Troublesome Raigne of Iohn, King of England*), Shakespeare's play sometimes gives John language that echoes Protestant propaganda. When, for example, John replies to Cardinal Pandulph at 3.1.159–66,

> no Italian priest
> Shall tithe or toll in our dominions;
> But as we under God are supreme head,
> So, under Him, that great supremacy
> Where we do reign we will alone uphold
> Without th' assistance of a mortal hand.
> So tell the Pope, all reverence set apart
> To him and his usurped authority,

he uses the language of sixteenth-century attacks on the pope in calling him an "Italian priest" and referring to the pope's "usurped authority." In addition, John's claim that "we under God are supreme head" ties him rather specifically to King Henry VIII, the first king to call himself "supreme head" of the English church.

3. King John and "An Homily against disobedience and willful rebellion"

King John's representation of the events of John's reign becomes especially interesting when placed within the context of the Church of England's "Homily against disobedience and willful rebellion," published in 1587 under the authority of Queen Elizabeth and intended to be read aloud in every parish church. The general message of the homily is captured in the following sentence from Part 4: "[A]lmighty God doth abhor disobedience and willful rebellion, specially when rebels advance themselves so high, that they arm themselves with weapon and stand in field to fight against God, their prince, and their country . . ." (sig. [Nn7]).

Most of the homily's examples of disobedience and rebellion are from the Bible or from the histories of other countries, but its final example (and the only one from English history) centers on King John.

From "An Homily against disobedience and willful rebellion"

Now whereas the injuries, oppressions, raveny [i.e., robbery], and tyranny of the bishop of Rome, usurping as well against their natural lords the emperors as against all other Christian kings and kingdoms, and their continual stirring of subjects to rebellions against their sovereign lords . . . were intolerable; and it may seem more than marvel that any subjects would after such sort hold with unnatural foreign usurpers against their own sovereign lords and natural country; it remaineth that I declare the means whereby they compassed these matters . . . (sig. [Oo8]).

And to use one example of our own country: the bishop of Rome did pick a quarrel to king John of England [Margin: *King John*] about the election of Stephen Langton to the bishopric of Canterbury, wherein the king had ancient rights . . . the bishops of Rome having no right, but had begun then to usurp upon the kings of England and all other Christian kings, as they had before done against their sovereign lords the Emperors, proceeding even by the same ways and means, and likewise cursing king John, and discharging his subjects of their oath of fidelity to their sovereign lord. Now had Englishmen at that time known their duty to their prince set forth in God's word, would a great many of nobles and other Englishmen natural subjects for this foreign and unnatural usurper's [Margin: *Innocentius 3.*] vain curse of the king and for his feigned discharging of them of their oath and fidelity to their natural lord, upon so slender or no ground at all, have rebelled against their sovereign lord the king? Would English subjects have taken part against the king of England, and against Englishmen, with the French king and Frenchmen [Margin: *Philip French King. Lew. Dauphin of France.*], being incensed against this realm by the bishop of Rome? Would they have sent for and received the Dauphin of France with a great army of Frenchmen into the realm of England? Would they have sworn fidelity to him, breaking their oath of fidelity to their natural lord the king of England, and have stood under the Dauphin's banner displayed against the king of England? Would they have expelled their sovereign lord the king of England out of London, the chief city of England, and out of the greatest part of England upon the south side of the Trent, even unto Lincoln, and out of Lincoln itself also, and have delivered the possession thereof unto the Dauphin of France . . . ? Would they, being Englishmen, have procured so great shedding of English blood, and other infinite mischiefs and miseries unto England their natural country, as did follow those cruel wars and traitorous rebellion, the fruits of the bishop of Rome's blessings? Would they have driven their natural sovereign lord the king of England to such extremity that he was enforced to submit himself unto that foreign false usurper the Bishop of Rome, who compelled him to surrender up the crown of England into the hands of his Legate [Margin: *Pandolphus.*], who in token of possession kept it in his hands diverse days and then delivered it again to king John, upon the condition that the king and his successors, kings of England, should hold the crown and kingdom of England of the Bishop of Rome and his successors as the vassals of the said Bishops of Rome forever, in token whereof the kings of England should also pay a yearly tribute to said Bishop of Rome as his vassals and liegemen? Would Englishmen have brought their sovereign lord and natural country into this thralldom and subjection to a false foreign usurper had they known and had any understanding in God's word at all? . . . Would they by rebellion have caused this, trow [i.e., believe] you, and all for the Bishop of Rome's causeless curse, had they in those days known and understood that God doth curse the blessing and bless the curses of such wicked usurping bishops and tyrants, as it appeared afterward in King Henry the 8's days, and king Edward the 6. and in our gracious sovereign's days that now is, where neither the Pope's curses nor God's manifold blessings are wanting. But in King John's time, the Bishop of Rome understanding the brute blindness, ignorance of God's word, and superstition of Englishmen, and how much they were inclined to worship the Babylonical beast of Rome and to fear all his threatenings and causeless curses, he abused them thus, and by their rebellion brought this noble realm and kings of England under his most cruel tyranny, and to be a spoil of his most vile and unsatiable covetousness and raveny, for a long and a great deal too long a time (sigs. Pp2–[Pp3v]).

The Second Tome of Homilies . . . set out by the authority of the Queen's Majesty, and to be read in every Parish Church agreeably . . . (1587) [spelling modernized].

King John: A Modern Perspective

Deborah T. Curren-Aquino

BASTARD
And I am I, howe'er I was begot.
(1.1.180)

HUBERT
Who art thou?
BASTARD: Who thou wilt.
(5.6.11–12)

The distance between the Bastard's confident assertion of identity at 1.1.180 and the tentative response given to Hubert at 5.6.11–12 not only underscores a momentous change in the Bastard's sense of self but also highlights the play's own flux and mutability, for which Barbara Hodgdon's term "chameleonlike" is particularly apt.[1] "What's done is done" is not a possibility in the ever-shifting world of *King John,* where what is done is undone only to be done again. That Arthur lives when supposed dead and is dead when thought living is paradigmatic of the broken vows, the political vacillations, the semantic changes that undo words' meanings even as the words are uttered, and the rapid shifts in the odds of military success experienced by both the Bastard and Louis in the final scenes. The treacherous Goodwin Sands and the Wash, in which the Dauphin and the Bastard, respectively, lose supplies and men, carry metaphoric implications for the play as a whole, but especially for the changing "I" of individual speakers.

Throughout *King John,* as framed by the Bastard's two

remarks on identity, one finds a striking interest in the idea of self—whether as hereditary, social, physiological, geographical, or interior: "What men are you?" (1.1.50); "What becomes of me?" (3.1.37); "Thou dost forget thyself" (3.1.140); "I am not mad. This hair I tear is mine; / My name is Constance; I was Geoffrey's wife; / Young Arthur is my son" (3.4.46–48); "There's few or none do know me" (4.3.3); and so on. The verbal register is charged with speeches that say, in effect, "Pay attention to *me*," as characters plead, request, demand, or assume the right to be heard, often shouting down or interrupting others in an attempt to secure a place at the table of discourse.[2] Instead of Descartes' "I think, therefore I am," the philosophical mantra of *King John* may well be "I speak, therefore I am." But as Charles Taylor points out in his study of the modern identity,

> one cannot be a self on one's own. I am a self only in relation to certain interlocutors: in one way in relation to those conversation partners who were essential to my achieving self-definition; in another in relation to those who are now crucial to my continuing grasp of languages and self-understanding—and, of course, these classes may overlap. A self exists only within what I call "webs of interlocution."[3]

These defining interrelationships, with "*certain* conversation partners" (my emphasis), while present from the beginning of the play, become more pronounced in its second half as the structural dynamic shifts from "great massed public movements" to situations of "private intrigue . . . and private feeling" involving only two speakers, who incline more and more toward being "effects" on each other.[4] Shakespeare calls attention to this collaborative "self-fashioning" (to borrow Stephen Greenblatt's term) whereby voices are found, lost, and continually redefined through a series of "threshold moments"—each charting a rite of passage for the speaker involved. Such moments are by their nature transitional or "liminal" and therefore indicate flux.[5] Moreover, they mark a significant change away from *The Troublesome Raigne of Iohn, King of England* (hereafter *TR*), which served as a source for Shakespeare's play.[6] In *TR,* these moments are either completely absent, merely suggested, or, if present (as in the famous "blinding" sequence in 4.1), different in kind rather than degree. By making liminality a defining feature of *King John,* Shakespeare turns what was a polemic into a probing rite-of-passage play for characters and—because this is a history play—for England as well.

King John's most liminal figure is the Bastard, who functions in a series of transitional states on his way from country madcap to spokesman for England, a trajectory that anticipates Prince Hal's in the *Henry IV* plays. Even his name, in both the speech prefixes and dialogue, is the least stable of the characters' (he is addressed variously as Philip, Richard, and Faulconbridge). When we first meet the Bastard, he is legally no such thing, having both a first and a last name: Philip Faulconbridge. To the king's question "What men are you," he replies with an identification that, like the grammatical construction of his response, is fixed and static:

> Your faithful subject I, a gentleman,
> Born in Northamptonshire, and eldest son,
> As I suppose, to Robert Faulconbridge,
> A soldier, by the honor-giving hand
> Of Coeur de Lion knighted in the field.
>
> (1.1.51–55)

Civic duty, social status, local home roots, and—in keeping with a patriarchal world in which primogeniture governs inheritance—lineal position within a family are the defining terms of the speaker's "I." The one verb, "suppose," a parenthetical interruption varied later in the dialogue as "as I think" (lines 61, 136), is the only indicator of an interior identity: a self that is intelligent, mentally flexible, and open to inner dialogue. With his lively and irreverent "country manners" (160), realized in a stylistic signature of puns, proverbs, colloquialisms, and concrete and earthy diction, the Bastard quickly establishes in the ensuing paternity trial a rapport with John (never again so good-humored and relaxed as in this exchange) and especially Eleanor, both of whom detect a marked resemblance to the recently deceased Richard Coeur de Lion (87–92). The empirical evidence, coupled with her instinctive liking of this "madcap," leads the Queen Mother to ask a question requiring a choice, and by extension a risk:

> Whether hadst thou rather: be a Faulconbridge
> And, like thy brother, to enjoy thy land,
> Or the reputed son of Coeur de Lion,
> Lord of thy presence, and no land besides?
> (137–40)

Choosing mythic rather than merely respectable paternity, the newcomer to court publicly accepts his marginalized status as a bastard, albeit a royal one, and his speech prefix in the folio accordingly shifts from "Philip" to "Bastard." Pleased with his response, Queen Eleanor challenges him to be a soldier bound for adventure and martial glory. Within moments, the king, following his mother's lead (an early suggestion of John's dependence on her), gives the character now liminally caught between names—"Philip, my liege, so is my name begun"—a new name, thus formally registering a rite of passage: "Kneel thou down Philip, but rise more great. / Arise Sir Richard and Plantagenet" (162, 166–67). The rites of initiation by which he will grow into the legendary name are still to come.

The voice heard in the Bastard's "A foot of honor" soliloquy (188–222), the first of his four major speeches in the play (each marking off a phase of the action), is jauntily caught up in his newfound status, richer by title but poorer by land. Like those of the young gallants of Shakespeare's time forced to seek social advancement through means other than inherited estates,[7] the Bastard's is a "mounting spirit." Displaying a capacity for detachment, he assumes in the theater of his imagination the manipulable voice of "worshipful society" and momentarily abandons homespun, often bawdy, primarily monosyllabic bluntness ("pops me out," "fair fall the bones," "eel-skins," "Sir Nob," etc.) for sophisticated polysyllabic affectation ("respective," "sociable," "conversion," "accoutrement," etc.). His mocking performance of the upwardly mobile self he will need to fashion to ensure "the footsteps of [his] rising" reveals what will be the Bastard's modus operandi throughout the play: observation, not as distinct from participating in the world but as the key to being a player (213–14). Then, almost as though hearing and in the process editing himself, he consciously registers a difference between what he recognizes as an artificial and a natural self: he will observe the ways of the world and learn to "deliver / Sweet, sweet, sweet poison for the age's tooth," not "to deceive, / [But] to avoid deceit" (218–21). There is, then, an inner "I" inhabiting the "outward accoutrement" that promises us and himself not to be lost. What the Bastard does here, and what he will do more emphatically in the famous "Commodity" soliloquy (2.1.588–626), is, as Harry Berger observes about dramatic speech in general, to "speak . . . for his own ears, audit . . . monitor . . . his own speech, pronominally divid[ing] in two so as to become the receiver of his own messages."[8] With the hasty arrival of his mother, Lady Faulconbridge, the soliloquy abruptly stops and the Bastard reverts to his energetic and plainspoken manner (1.1.240–47). Gusto combines with conciliatory persistence (so different from the browbeating of *TR*'s Bastard at a comparable moment) to draw from Lady Faulconbridge the information he seeks: confirmation of his paternity. Boldly, with knighthood newly felt on his shoulder, he takes as his first quest the protection of a lady's good name, feistily vowing that "Who lives and dares but say thou didst not well / When I was got, I'll send his soul to hell" (279–80).

By the end of this initial rite of passage, in which two female interlocutors figure prominently, readers and audiences are disposed to like and trust this "good blunt fellow" with a gift for incisive observation and an obvious disdain for affectation. Certain traits—his skepticism and pugnacity, for example—first introduced in a comic mode will take on more depth and militancy in the course of the play. At the end, he will once again be the king's "faithful subject" but in a markedly different key. For that to happen, however, other thresholds must be crossed and the "webs of interlocution" must widen.

Like the "rash . . . fiery voluntaries, / With ladies' faces and fierce dragons' spleens" with whom he is associated in Chatillion's account of the newly arrived English forces, the Bastard enters Angiers "to make a hazard of new fortunes" (2.1.67–71). The voice that targets Austria, the man whom the play represents as responsible for killing the Bastard's father and who now arrogantly wears the celebrated lion's skin (see the longer note to 2.1.5, page 215), retains its impudence and proclivity for country proverbs (140–41) and colloquialisms (136, 138–39, 142–43). The threat to Austria will later be realized with savage brutality, but for now all is swagger (148–49). Absorbing what he sees and hears, the Bastard continues to manifest a capacity for assuming the habits (lexical and otherwise) of those around him. After the initial offstage battle, for example, in which he experiences the violence of war for the first time, he immediately responds to the two kings' talk of the "blood . . . cast away" and the "slaughter coupled to the name of kings" (348, 364) in a voice that, in the "Ha, majesty!" speech (365–76), begins to record what John Blanpied calls a "grating lust for violence and blood" that never fully disappears from his discourse.[9] Seeking validation from those more seasoned in the political ways of the world, the Bastard makes his mad military proposal (393–412) as a way of showing that he has picked up some of their "policy"—that is, the cunning associated with Machiavellian political strategy. His plan is frustrated by the Citizen's elaborately stated counterproposal—the expedient marriage of Blanche and Louis—but the Bastard once again deftly shifts linguistic register, repeating Louis' "drawn in the flattering table of her eye" in such a way that the Dauphin's artificial protestations of love are simultaneously exaggerated and mocked.

By the time the Bastard steps back from the action to comment on the "mad kings, mad world, and mad composition" he has just witnessed, he is no longer "green . . . and fresh in this old world" (3.4.148). The scorn permeating the "Commodity" soliloquy (2.1.588–626) suggests an older voice, harshly cynical in its penetrating assessment of a world governed by self-interest. The Bastard has made good on his earlier promise to "smack of observation": he has watched as a citizen robs God's "anointed deputies" of their majesty, forcing them to audition for the crown of England; he has been "bethumped" (487) with the rhetorical excesses of language meant to evade, "spin," and obfuscate the facts; and he has observed kings break faith for their own expediency. Structured as a syllogism with a major premise ("Commodity drives the world"), an implied minor premise ("I'm no different from those I've railed against"), and a conclusion ("Therefore I too will worship gain"),[10] the soliloquy reveals a keenly perceptive intelligence but not the mind of a philosopher given to logical, orderly predication of thought. This is a voice much too excited for introspective reflection, as the Bastard piles on examples (parataxis) and frequently repeats the same word in an initial position (anaphora): "that same purpose-changer, that sly devil, / That broker . . . That daily break-vow . . . That smooth-faced gentleman, tickling Commodity." Nouns and adjectives fly in a torrent. We are left with a sense of display rather than deliberation, of intense feeling rather than cognition. Then suddenly, reflexively, as though hearing himself with his own ears, he shifts to inner debate. Recognizing his human susceptibility to "the bias of the world," he candidly admits that while he may despise it, he cannot be a player in "this old world" and expect himself (or be expected) to avoid "break[ing] faith upon Commodity." In Michael Kahn's 1999 revival for the Shakespeare Theater in Washington, D.C., after delivering the line "Gain, be my lord, for I will worship thee!" (626), the Bastard not only followed in the direction of the wedding party but just managed to get through the gates of Angiers before they slammed shut. The speaker, having completed a crash course in realpolitik, had clearly crossed another threshold, in the process fashioning a new self: from soldier of fortune to Machiavel in the making. (Or so it seems; we never see him translate the slogan "Gain, be my lord" into action.)

In the next scene, framed by Constance and Blanche, the play's female victims of Commodity, the Bastard speaks very little; but that little, still in the tone of a mocking observer, allies him with Constance as he repeatedly appropriates her taunt to Austria to "hang a calfskin on those recreant limbs" (3.1.135–37, 139, 206, 230, 311). As we observe his taking up the cause of a woman in distress to challenge a mutual enemy, we are reminded of his earlier defense of Lady Faulconbridge. Though the Bastard is not present during the private exchange between the painfully incredulous Constance and a visibly uncomfortable Salisbury (3.1.1–77), he is onstage to hear the anguished cry of the bartered bride, with whom he had briefly connected in Act 2 (1.144–47, 526–32). In a riveting passage that has no counterpart in *TR* and that portends the increasing emphasis on pathos in subsequent acts, Blanche ceases to exist as a mere pawn in the political chess game awarding her to Louis and becomes a self in relation to others:

> The sun's o'ercast with blood. Fair day, adieu.
> Which is the side that *I* must go withal?
> *I* am with both, each army hath a hand,
> And in their rage, *I* having hold of both,
> They whirl asunder and dismember *me*.
> *Husband, I* cannot pray that thou mayst win.—
> *Uncle, I* needs must pray that thou mayst lose.—
> *Father, I* may not wish the fortune thine.—
> *Grandam, I* will not wish thy wishes thrive.
> Whoever wins, on that side shall *I* lose.
> Assurèd loss before the match be played.
>
> (3.1.341–51, my emphases)

In Blanche, as in Constance, politics as "parle" and "policy"—word games and strategies—assumes a human face, and this time the Bastard is there to observe it.

As the battle for Angiers resumes, King John, perhaps in recognition of the martial spirit on display in the previous act, officially gives the Bastard both military responsibility and a new name (for the first time explicitly acknowledging a personal bond of kinship): "Cousin [i.e., kinsman], go draw our puissance together" (354). The new name and responsibility usher in another rite of passage, as the Bastard's entry in 3.2 holding Austria's head makes clear. The Bastard has not only proved his mettle as a soldier, thus demonstrating his worthiness as Coeur de Lion's heir, but has also avenged his father's death. (In productions the actor typically dons the fabled lion's skin after the slaying of Austria.) We also learn (contrary to *TR*) that the Bastard, not John, has rescued Queen Eleanor from the French (3.2.6–9). Earning (offstage) the paternity that he had stumbled into in the first act, the Bastard will be addressed or described with increasing frequency as "cousin" (3.3.6, 17; 4.2.142, 165; 5.7.55), "coz" (3.3.18), and "kinsman" (4.2.173; 5.3.5).

When he exits at 3.3.18 to do the king's bidding (ransacking the abbeys to fill the royal coffers), the Bastard begins his longest absence from the stage. Resurfacing in 4.2—as typically happens after such absences in Shakespeare's plays—he will sound different. In *King John,* Shakespeare fills the interval between the Bastard's departure and return (essentially the middle of the action) with liminal moments for several characters. King John, Louis, Hubert, and Arthur each undergo a rite of transition, thereby becoming different conversation partners or presences from those the Bastard had encountered earlier. Their differences will affect his own self-definition.

Following the Bastard's exit and at the height of England's victory over France, King John experiences his first threshold moment, a transition that initiates the progressive diminution of his character. We know little about Hubert, the man in whom the king confides while Queen Eleanor and the captured Arthur stand off to the side, except that the king feels some kind of debt to a loyal follower (3.3.22–26). (Later we learn that the character has a sinister appearance [4.2.230–37, 268–69] and is not a nobleman [4.3.87–91].) But in *King John*, in contrast to *TR*, the newly arrived Hubert emerges as a key interlocutor for both John and the Bastard.

As the king hatches the deed that will precipitate his own undoing, the voice that had threatened France with "the thunder of [his] cannon" (1.1.26) and defied the church of Rome (3.1.153–66, 168–77) finds itself increasingly inarticulate. Whether his verbal awkwardness indicates conscience or a feeble attempt at Machiavellian cunning is not clear. Such utterances as "I had a thing to say, / But I will fit it with some better tune" (3.3.27–28) and "I had a thing to say—but let it go" (35), coupled with the periphrastic hinting at something ominous (36–49) and the wish to communicate "without eyes, ears, and harmful sound of words" (53), underscore the lack of specificity that characterizes John's discourse for the rest of the play. After being recrowned in 4.2, he promises the nobles that he will give them further reasons for this second coronation (43–44), but he never does. In the same scene, he says that he has a way to win back the allegiance of the traitorous nobles (175), but we never learn what it is. Finally, in 5.1, without any overt explanation, he surrenders the crown to and receives it back again from Pandulph; we are left to infer his rationale—i.e., that the cardinal has agreed to be a peace broker (5.1.6–14). Nowhere, however, is John's inexplicit mode more chillingly pronounced than in the Pinteresque exchange that effectively ends 3.3, a passage whose pauses and minimal predication have a tremendous psychological charge:

KING JOHN
Death.
HUBERT My Lord?
KING JOHN A grave.
HUBERT He [Arthur] shall not live.
(3.3.70–73)

Guy Hamel has observed that "the explanation of ways and means is not the strong suit of [*King John*]"; clearly, as Joseph Porter notes, John's speech, "the least . . . explicit of any Shakespearean monarch's," contributes greatly to the play's elliptical temper.[11] Language registers the exchange with the intuitively complicit Hubert as a liminal moment for John, the threshold crossed at "Enough. / I could be merry now" (74–75). The king who begins to lose his voice in this scene will surrender it to the Bastard at 5.1.79, becoming "almost speechless" by 5.6.28.

At the end of Act 3, shortly before the action moves back to England, the manipulative Cardinal Pandulph engages the political neophyte Louis in a pseudo-Socratic dialogue. The Dauphin is devastated over the French losses—Angiers, "divers dear friends slain" (3.4.7), and the capture of Arthur. He has also just witnessed Constance's moving transformation into grief personified, a woman on the verge of madness over the loss of her son. Watching his father, King Philip, rush off to prevent Constance from "some outrage" (108)—the first time anyone in the play attempts to bring comfort to another but not the last—Louis sinks in despair: "There's nothing in this world can make me joy. / Life is as tedious as a twice-told tale" (109–10). As Pandulph walks him through John's catch-22—if John keeps Arthur, he cannot keep him alive—the cardinal presciently foretells how an "act so evilly borne" will work to France's advantage: it "shall cool the hearts / Of all [John's] people" (152–53), leading them to revolt and rally to the side of the man whose recent marriage to Lady Blanche allows him to claim the English throne. Buoyed by this mentoring session (a continuation of the course in realpolitik that the Bastard had observed and summed up in Act 2), Louis becomes a man of action—the only foreign leader in Shakespeare's history plays to invade England. He will also emerge as a wily politician in his own right (5.2), proving a master of Machiavellian deceit in his treatment of the English lords and jarring the equilibrium of Pandulph as he finds the boy once so "green and fresh" no longer manipulable.[12]

The famous "blinding" sequence contains dual rites of passage for Arthur and Hubert. Though the historical Arthur was fifteen at the time of the play's action (*TR*'s is comparable in age), Shakespeare makes him seem much younger. Up until 4.1, with the exception of two pleas for his mother to be quiet and to be "content" (2.1.168–70, 3.1.44), Arthur had depended on others (Chatillion, King Philip, Constance) to speak for him or, like the proverbially well brought up child, had spoken when given permission to do so (2.1.12–17). But as he undergoes a harrowing experience, he speaks for himself and proves, on one level at least, to be his mother's son: he refuses to be silenced. Shakespeare's Arthur uses emotion rather than logic to argue with his would-be assassin, reminding Hubert of the times he, "a prince," had tenderly ministered to him, "knit[ting a] handkercher about [his] brows," holding his head, and trying to cheer him up (4.1.46–58). With a surprising sophistication that indicates his own education in the lessons of Angiers, Arthur acknowledges that his gestures of kindness might be construed as "crafty love" and "cunning"; implicitly, however, he disowns such motivation ("Do, an if you will"; 59–60). Arthur's voice (his "innocent prate," 27), to which Hubert is increasingly vulnerable (34, 35–39, 108); his frequent repetition of Hubert's name, which personalizes the voice-address relationship (9, 26, and ten other times); and his mounting fear and the pathos evoked by word and gesture (81–82, 84–92, 111–14) not only affect Hubert but also effect a change in him. No longer an object to be destroyed but a "self" performing, Arthur has become an "I" whom Hubert will not offend "for the wealth of all the world" (144; see also 135). "Gain" has clearly lost a follower. And, as so often in the play, when Hubert crosses his threshold at "Well, see to live" (134) his decision is abrupt, its motivation left unspoken.

Through the scene's interlocutory dynamic, Arthur and Hubert redefine themselves by discovering their true voices. Having learned to speak for himself in 4.1, Arthur two scenes later will take matters into his own hands as he tries to escape. Unlike his *TR* counterpart, who does not think beyond "gain[ing his] libertie" and who invokes the memory of his mother four times (at one point actually identifying himself as his "mother's sonne"), Shakespeare's Arthur never once mentions Constance; showing independence and practicality, he disguises himself as a shipboy (4.3.4) and is determined—if he makes the leap successfully—to "find a thousand shifts [stratagems] to get away" (7). At the point when the character in the source regresses, the "pretty child" in *King John* seems to advance in years at his final threshold. And Hubert, who had readily agreed to his king's hinted desires, will in their next exchange be able to lie to that same king for the sake of a greater good; he will refuse to take the blame for the supposed killing and will force John to accept his share of responsibility before announcing that Arthur lives, rebuking the king for his slanders (4.2.218–71). In his demonstration of compassion, honor, and courage, the man "marked by nature" to do an evil deed becomes paradoxically the first in the world of the play to act according to conscience, setting a precedent for such triumphs of ethical resolve as the Bastard's in 4.3 and Melun's in 5.4. For Hubert, the gentle self fashioned during Arthur's imprisonment, which is heard in his asides and to which he openly returns at the end of 4.1, has become the real self that Arthur greets joyfully: "O, now you look like Hubert. All this while / You were disguisèd" (4.1.138–39).

While King John, Louis, Arthur, and Hubert have been undergoing transitions onstage, the Bastard has had a threshold experience offstage. Traveling through the land, he has met conversation partners we never hear (except for the prophet's one line at 4.2.159) but who have had a palpable effect on him. The clarity of the world he had known—toothpicks, absey books, maids with puppy dogs, tangible proofs of military valor like a lion's skin and a severed head, countable sums of money—has been clouded by the uncertainty of strange fantasies, rumors, dreams, and prophecies. Having heard fear in the voices of the people, the Bastard, seemingly for the first time, finds himself unsettled, unsure of his world *and* his king. When he reports to John, he passes quickly over the news of the French invasion (the most important item for *TR*'s Bastard at the corresponding moment) to relate the rumor that weighs most heavily on his mind:

> Besides, I met Lord Bigot and Lord Salisbury
> With eyes as red as new-enkindled fire,
> And others more, going to seek the grave

> Of Arthur, *whom they say* is killed tonight
> On your suggestion.
>
> (4.2.168–72, my emphasis)

Choosing not to respond to the Bastard's implied question ("Is what I've heard true?"), John instead urges his "gentle kinsman" to bring the nobles back. Perhaps relieved to have his attention diverted to a clearly defined task, the Bastard returns to his energetic voice of the earlier acts in "The spirit of the time shall teach me speed" (184), but not before suggesting in his body language a hint of lingering doubt. John has been forced to repeat his order, formally exhorting his kinsman to "be Mercury . . . [and] set feathers to [his] heels" (182).

Upon the shattering discovery of Arthur's body in 4.3—the most crucial threshold experience for defining the Bastard, the one that will make possible the voice that closes the play—he maintains an outward control, thoughtfully raising the possibility of accidental death: "If that it be the work of any hand" (60). Skeptical restraint, however, quickly gives way to frenetic action as the Bastard impulsively and vigorously defends Hubert against the drawn swords of the nobles. After their exit, when the Bastard is alone with Hubert, the emotional floodgates open.

Because he needs to be convinced personally of Hubert's (and by extension John's) innocence, the Bastard furiously engages in an intense, highly charged interrogation. We have heard contempt and cynicism in his voice before, but nothing like the righteous anger and passion expressed here in the frenzied litany of "ifs" ("if thou didst this deed of death," "if thou didst kill this child," "if thou didst but consent / To this most cruel act," 123, 130, 132–33), the constant interruption of Hubert, the triple repetition of "damned" that in the Bastard's mind sends Hubert to hell, and the flourish of hyperbole by which the Bastard as prosecutor so shrinks the defendant that the smallest thread of a spider, a rush, a drop of water would be enough to execute him. With the Bastard emotionally spent—"I do suspect thee very grievously" (141) is somewhat anticlimactic—Hubert is allowed his defense. Taking each of the points in order—act, consent, and then, doing his interrogator one better, thought—Hubert's response makes it possible for emotions to quiet and the tempo to slow. In the grammatical and metrical pause separating the two parts of a shared monosyllabic pentameter ("I left him well. | Go, bear him in thine arms," 147), acquittal is won, a bond is forged, and introspection begins.

The "I am amazed, methinks, and lose my way" monologue may have a soliloquy-like feel but, as the directives to Hubert indicate, it is not quite a soliloquy. In addition to Hubert, there is the visually compelling conversational presence of the dead boy, with whom the Bastard seems in communion. Where observation led to satiric declamation in the "Commodity" soliloquy, the absorbing of a Pietà-like image—Constance's maternal grief now transferred to the distraught Hubert tenderly cradling Arthur—leads to reflection.[13] As he digests the implications of Arthur's death, the Bastard invests the boy with the life, truth, and right of England:

Go, bear him in thine arms.
I am amazed, methinks, and lose my way
Among the thorns and dangers of this world.
⌜*Hubert takes up Arthur's body.*⌝
How easy dost thou take all England up!
From forth this morsel of dead royalty,
The life, the right, and truth of all this realm
Is fled to heaven, and England now is left
To tug and scamble and to part by th' teeth

The unowed interest of proud-swelling state.
Now for the bare-picked bone of majesty
Doth doggèd war bristle his angry crest
And snarleth in the gentle eyes of peace.
Now powers from home and discontents at home
Meet in one line, and vast confusion waits,
As doth a raven on a sick-fall'n beast,
The imminent decay of wrested pomp.
Now happy he whose cloak and cincture can
Hold out this tempest. Bear away that child,
And follow me with speed. I'll to the King.
A thousand businesses are brief in hand,
And heaven itself doth frown upon the land.
(147–67)

While the syntax is clear and orderly (six complete and—until lines 160–64—simple or compound sentences make up the seventeen lines between "Go, bear him in thine arms" and "Bear away that child"), several stylistic features capture the speaker's inner turmoil: the lexical shift from abstractions ("royalty," "life," "right," "truth," etc.) to the sustained visceral imagery of dogs and ravens preying on England; the anaphora of the repeated "Now"; and the sensory eruption of the auditory ("snarleth"), the visual ("gentle eyes of peace"), the tactile ("bristle"), and the kinetic ("tug," "scamble," "part by th' teeth"). Pulsating metrical stresses, combined with (often alliterated) plosives, also suggest agitation (e.g., "Now for the bare-picked bone of majesty / Doth doggèd war bristle his angry crest," 156–57). Then, abruptly, the speaker shifts gears. Between the moral anguish of lines 148–64 and the practical directive to Hubert to "bear away *that* child" (the demonstrative adjective already indicating some emotional distance), the Bastard makes a conscious political choice to return to the very king just implicated in the confusion afflicting the country.

The decision to return to John becomes less jarring if we consider that the Bastard has been having an inner debate—and we have heard only one side. Once again, in a grammatical and metrical pause—"tempest. Bear away" (164)—the speaker seems silently to come to terms with the problem found in all of Shakespeare's histories: namely, how to distinguish between loyalty to the private figure who wears the trappings of authority (the body natural) and loyalty to the public representative of the country at large (the body politic). The clue to his decision to support the public rather than the private John appears in the repetition of "England"; the second time, the reference expands from a claimant to the throne (150) to the land (153), the realm that is on the verge of being torn apart. The Bastard had never spoken of England before. The land as a private holding that he had so lightly dispensed with in Act 1 ("I'll take my chance," 1.1.155) is in the process of becoming "home" (4.3.159), something to be protected from foreign as well as civil attack. We do not hear the panegyric poetry of John of Gaunt's "this blessèd plot, this earth, this realm, this England" (*Richard II*, 2.1.55–56), but we begin to sense a patriotism tempered by moral *and* political pragmatism. Fittingly, "land" as *patria* is the final word in a speech that concludes with the juxtaposition of political choice ("I'll to the King," 165) and a newly developing moral and spiritual awareness of displeased providential powers ("heaven itself doth frown upon the land," 167). However elliptically from the point of view of readers or audience, the Bastard has worked out the inner confusion mounting since his excursion through the land; in the process, he has fashioned a moral and civic self. As L. A. Beaurline astutely observes, Montaigne may provide the best gloss on the self emerging at the end of 4.3:

> The virtue assigned to the affairs of the world is a virtue with many bends, angles, and elbows, so as to join and adapt itself to human weakness; mixed and artificial, not straight, clean, constant, or purely innocent. Civic innocence is measured according to the places and the times. . . . We may regret better times, but not escape the present; we may wish for different magistrates, but we must nevertheless obey those that are here.[14]

Like Louis in 3.4, but to a different end, the Bastard has crossed an "Arthurian" threshold. Because Louis confronts the boy's death abstractly in Pandulph's political scenario, the rite of passage for him remains solely political. Emerging as a man of ambition and intrigue eager for "conquest and to win renown" (5.2.116), Louis will say to the English rebels in an effort to allay their pangs of guilt: "Come, come; for thou shalt thrust thy hand as deep / Into the purse of rich prosperity / As Louis himself" (5.2.60–62). In contrast, the Bastard, who feels Arthur's death deeply, experiences a moment of interior moral anguish that implicitly informs his political choice. Equally important is the difference in the "certain interlocutors" crucial to each of these characters' self-definition. Louis had Pandulph, labeled by one critic "the arch politician, the representative of super-commodity";[15] the Bastard had Hubert, the play's first victor over commodity—and the silent presence of Arthur, commodity's tangible human cost.

The king to whom the Bastard returns, with renewed purpose and with English place-names in his mouth (Kent, Dover Castle, London), is even weaker than in their previous encounter. Acutely aware of the country's need for a public image of strength and leadership (5.1.45–62), the Bastard is outraged at John's "happy peace" with Pandulph, seeing such an alliance as repeating the commodity-driven compromises made in Angiers (67–71). Ever the man of action, he calls attention to the "land" that has been growing in his own consciousness, and urges his "liege . . . to arms" (68, 75). As the Bastard grows in John's estimation, the king's self-regard diminishes to the point that he invests his kinsman with "the ordering of this present time" (79). The rite of passage that began with a journey through the land and now culminates in the Bastard's being named the king's surrogate is the most sustained treatment of liminality in the play, having its own beginning (3.3.18 to 4.2.137–84), middle (4.3), and end (5.1). The doubts that disturbed the Bastard in his travels and fierce interrogation of Hubert and that receive elliptical clarification in the climactic "I am amazed and lose my way" monologue moderate into the healthy skepticism of the prudent risk-taker keenly aware that "Our party may well meet a prouder foe" (5.1.82). Delivered as an aside, the comment further reveals a speaker who knows that in the voice of authority fear is best kept private.

As political responsibility and military leadership pass from the older generation of King John and King Philip to the younger generation of the Bastard and Louis, the two young men on parallel but morally contrasting trajectories confront each other directly for the first time. Although he mocks the Dauphin by referring to him as a "youth" (5.2.129), the Bastard is obviously delighted that the "beardless boy, / A cockered silken wanton" (5.1.71–72) he remembers from Angiers, is now so "willful-opposite" in standing up to the "halting legate" and refusing to "lay down his arms" (5.2.125, 177, 127). Like a good athlete competing with a respected rival, the Bastard is challenged by this interlocutory relationship to be at the top of his game, which in this instance means performing the voice of the king:

"Now hear our English king, / For thus his royalty doth speak in me" (129–30). This is not, however, the voice of the present king, who, even at his most defiant (with Chatillion, King Philip, and especially Pandulph), never spoke of "crouch[ing] in litter of your stable planks," or lying "like pawns locked up in chests and trunks," or "hug[ging] with swine" (141–43). We hear instead an imaging of royalty that reflects the Bastard's sense of how a king should speak. And he speaks it in his own voice—earthy, vigorous, and physical—with imagery from the country and words such as "cudgel" and "hatch" (139) that he alone employs. (For the Bastard's earlier use of "cudgeled" and "hatch," see 2.1.485 and 1.1.176.) Louis remembers this voice well from Angiers:

> There end thy brave and turn thy face in peace.
> We grant thou canst outscold us. Fare thee well.
> We hold our time too precious to be spent
> With such a brabbler.
>
> (160–63)

In the 1984 BBC production, the Bastard (George Costigan) waited until his encounter with Louis to don the lion's skin, the emblem of his father's courage. Fashioning for the first time "in his own person the 'concept of royalty,' "[16] Costigan's Bastard resurrected in the mind's eye the king whose memory haunts the play.

The martial leadership projected verbally in 5.2 translates into action as the Bastard "desires" John to leave the battlefield and is himself perceived by the enemy as "that misbegotten devil, Faulconbridge, [who] / In spite of spite, alone upholds the day" (5.4.4–5). By the time of the penultimate scene, however, something has changed. In a tense night episode, two men, both filled with anxiety and uncertainty, haltingly search each other out, each identifying the other by voice through a series of questions (5.6.1–18). What had been metaphoric for the Bastard in 4.3—a Dantesque sense of being lost in a dark wood—is now literal. The Bastard quickly recognizes his fellow speaker; that it takes Hubert longer might suggest that there is something new in the Bastard's voice and manner. His answer to Hubert's "Who art thou?"—"Who thou wilt. An if thou please, / Thou mayst befriend me so much as to think / I come one way of the Plantagenets" (11–14)—is general, vague, and, most important, malleable; as such, like the self emerging in the final lines of 4.3, it makes possible the more detached and inclusive voice that ends the play. For several scenes, the issue of genealogy that had occupied so much of the dialogue in the first two acts has been only implicit. Here, with just a touch of the humor that was initially a major part of his voice, the Bastard alludes to his paternity: his "way of the Plantagenets" is the marginal way, the way of bastardy. This more subdued humor, in conjunction with his lack of specificity, suggests a detachment from the "new-made honor" and newfound paternity he reveled in at 1.1.252–53, 260, 267–68, 277–78. Weary and dispirited (half his forces have been lost, 5.6.43–45), the man so boldly defiant with Louis has come up against the "prouder foe" that neither he nor the Dauphin (5.5.14–15) can control: Nature.

For the second time in the play the Bastard, feeling confused and unsettled, finds himself in a private encounter with the same interlocutor, Hubert, who now seeks him out to share the news about John's poisoning. Rebuking himself for not recognizing "any accent breaking from [the Bastard's] tongue," Hubert's "Brave soldier" reminds the Bastard of who he is (5.6.15–18). In a distant echo of his first soliloquy (1.1.207), the Bastard dismisses any "compliment" (19) and quickly presses for information in a series of direct questions that move rapidly from the general to the specific: "What news abroad?" (19), "How did he take it? Who did taste to him?" (32), and so on. Following his near-death experience in the Lincoln Washes (45–46), the Bastard comes back to life in the company of Hubert. His offstage realization that he is not invincible leads to an onstage moment of liminal reflection, as the man who had irreverently promised to pray for Queen Eleanor if he remembered to pray (3.3.14–16) suddenly prays in earnest: "Withhold thine indignation, mighty God, / And tempt us not to bear above our power" (5.6.41–42). In the presence of Hubert, the Bastard seeks deliverance from despair by invoking the traditional Christian belief that God does not send the human soul more than it can bear (1 Corinthians 10.13).[17] Suddenly, the action-oriented voice of the Bastard, appearing again without connectives, is back: "Away before. Conduct me to the King. / I doubt [fear] he will be dead or ere I come" (47–48). It is a voice always in search of something to do, a task to be performed, a direction in which to go—and once more Hubert, the Bastard's friend and the play's stellar example of moral conversion, is responsible for focusing the Bastard's mind, spirit, and energies.

The final scene into which the Bastard rushes is a cluster of rites of passage: John's transition from life to death, Prince Henry's transition to kingship, and the Bastard's transition from royal surrogate and image maker to the universal spokesman for all England. While able since 4.3 to distinguish between the public and private bodies of the king, the Bastard nevertheless retains a personal bond with the monarch who has called him "cousin" and "gentle kinsman"; the heat imaged in the Bastard's breathless greeting "O, I am scalded with my violent motion" (5.7.53) reinforces his link with the feverish John, who "shrink[s] up" like "a scribbled form . . . Upon a parchment . . . against this fire" (34–36). As a figure of intense human suffering (32–33, 38–44), the king who, for most of the play, had been on the receiving end of criticism invites comfort from those around him (although not always to his satisfaction, 44–46). In his last moments John compresses (and shifts among) the various stages thanatologists associate with dying—denial and isolation (6–9), anger (11, 38–46, 49–52), depression (30–36), and acceptance (12, 13, 55–62). At the king's death, the Bastard's question "Art thou gone so" (74), unlike Salisbury's and Prince Henry's abridged memento mori (70–73), shows that he feels the separation personally. Anticipating Horatio in *Hamlet* and Kent in *King Lear*, the Bastard desires to follow John in death; but in contrast to them, he promises first "to do the office . . . of revenge" (74–76). The bellicose vigor directed earlier at Louis and the rebels resounds in his challenge to the returned nobles (those "stars, that [now] move in your right spheres") to join with him "again / To push destruction and perpetual shame / Out of the weak door of our fainting land" (78–83). When suddenly informed that Pandulph has negotiated peace terms, the Bastard registers the beginning of his final transition. His statement "Let it be so" (101, like the earlier "I'll to the king" and "Away before") is the culmination of a self-fashioning that has repeatedly, often in the silence of an instant's pause, adapted to changing circumstances and conversation partners.

For major characters in Shakespeare, according to Marjorie Garber, failure to adapt means failure "to undergo a rite of passage" that brings with it "incorporat[ion] into a new identity or social role."[18] Determined since Act 1 to be a player, the Bastard is always open to "incorporation." His declaration of acceptance is immediately followed by his address to Prince Henry, suggesting an awareness of a new interlocutor in his conversational orbit, a sad and fragile young prince who might very well remind him of another young claimant to "the life, right, and truth" of England. (In performance the roles of Arthur and Prince Henry are sometimes doubled.) In the spatial proximity of the dead English king and his living heir, the father and his undisputed son, the Bastard observes a powerful image of continuity. This visual enactment of the ritual expression "The King is dead. Long live the King" crystallizes for him the issue that is so important to Shakespeare's history plays as a genre and that incites so much wrangling in this play in particular—the matter of legitimate succession and lineal heritage. (Michael Kahn, in the 1999 Washington, D.C., revival, had the Bastard and Hubert support John while Henry sat by John's feet; Karin Coonrod, in the 2000 production at New York's American Place Theater, had the Bastard embrace the dead king with one arm and the weeping prince with the other.) In an instant, the Bastard focuses attention on the young prince's imminent threshold moment: the "put[ting] on [of] / The lineal state and glory of the land" (107–8). Accordingly, the Bastard kneels to the "sweet self" of royalty before him and promises his "faithful services / And true subjection everlastingly" (110–11), thus setting an example for the nobles to follow.

In the Bastard's concluding speech, Shakespeare (as is typical of his approach to death and dying) emphasizes (again to quote Garber) "the survivor as one who needs to undergo rites of passage as much as do the dead. . . . In fact, rites of passage concerned with death in the plays are almost always related to a change in perception of those who survive, whether the survivor be an individual, a city or a state."[19] Since the end of 4.3, the Bastard has been filling a national need, shaping a self to fit the demands of the time. The present moment clearly requires a voice of gravitas, authority, and hope. Directly interacting with an emotional young prince, the Bastard picks up on Henry's "tears" to urge decorous but not excessive mourning (115–16); then, in an effort to embolden the son as he had the father, he begins what promises to be an unqualified panegyric (118–19). Almost immediately—as though taking in yet another compelling image—the speaker shifts to an exhortation that moves beyond Prince Henry to include the newly (and expediently) returned nobles (120–24). By way of the stubbornly intrusive "if" (the skepticism of Act 1 assuming its deepest register), the invincibility of an England that "never did nor never shall / Lie at the proud foot of a conqueror" changes from a given to a conditional dependent on something uncommon in the world of *King John:* moral integrity, now specifically translated into the constancy and fidelity of the English people, king and subjects alike.

The Bastard's "I am I, howe'er I was begot"—a comic forerunner of Coriolanus' tragic vow to "stand / As if a man were author of himself / And knew no other kin" (5.3)—is both true and false. There is certainly an "I" that remains in the speaking voice throughout—blunt, energetic, goal-oriented, pugnacious, and skeptical—but that same "I" is very much his father's son, as Eleanor's and John's comments on physical and behavioral traits, his own martial victories, and his projection of royalty before Louis indicate. It is also an "I" that the Bastard has fashioned and refashioned (often by fits and starts) through a series of threshold moments in relation to "certain" (often themselves changing) interlocutors, especially Hubert. The speaker's initial self-identification as the king's loyal subject in the first scene was pure formula, but his last before the dying John is something acutely and personally felt—a change grammatically indicated in the shift from the formal *"your* faithful subject" (1.1.51) to the more intimate *"thy* servant" (5.7.77). Here, as in his subsequent kneeling and promise of services to Prince Henry, the Bastard's self-identification is something he has lived and worked through—especially since the end of 4.3, when service to the king was subsumed into service to England.

The words from Charles Taylor quoted near the beginning of this essay go on to note that "the full definition of someone's identity . . . usually involves not only his stand on moral and spiritual matters but also some reference to a defining community."[20] For the Bastard and others, that defining community—one of the "webs of interlocution"—is England, itself engaged in a rite of passage. First narrowly equated with the ruling monarch (Chatillion's address "to the majesty . . . of England here" [1.1.3–4] and John's "Doth not the crown of England prove the King?" [2.1.282]), the name *England* begins to widen (ironically) during Louis' rite of passage when Pandulph talks about "all [John's] people" rising up in revolt and "ten thousand English" following the French (3.4.168, 178). As the Bastard travels through the land—a key transitional time for him—we hear of a prophet and "many hundreds treading on his heels" (4.2.152–54); soon the generalized image of the people takes on a degree of specificity in the newly converted Hubert's "old men and beldams in the streets," a blacksmith with his "hammer" and "iron [cooling] on the anvil," a tailor "with his shears and measure in his hand," and a "lean, unwashed artificer" (4.2.196, 204–7, 212). The dying Arthur, bequeathing his bones to England, distinguishes between the king whom he blames for his death and the land that will be his final resting place. As wayward sons return home in Act 5, England discovers children it never knew in secret Anglophiles like Count Melun, whose dying recollection of his English grandsire partially informs his own final rite of passage. The change, as the Bastard had begun to conceive when he saw Hubert bearing Arthur in his arms, is a growing consciousness of English sovereignty as national rather than dynastic: England as the people and the land. Fittingly, but in a radical departure from orthodox Tudor ideology, England at the end of *King John* is reimagined or "refigured" in the voice of the Bastard, the one speaker who has imitated and tried on other voices, who has listened to the people's rumors and fantasies, who has interacted with each of the play's women, and who, as a royal bastard with rights to the land as a whole but without any legal rights in reality, "speaks in the name of England because he himself has no name, upholds the 'unow'd interest' because he himself owns nothing."[21] Rather than being arbitrarily imposed on the speaker, the pronominal widening in the final speech as the Bastard shifts from "I" to the communal and patriotic "we/us" has been present since 5.1.68, when the speaker's newly developing appreciation of England as "the land" (4.3.167) became "our land" (repeated at 5.7.83).[22] The England of the second half of the play, where English place-names proliferate (Bury St. Edmunds, Kent, London, Dover, Swinstead, Worcester, the Goodwin Sands, and the Wash), appears to take on the Bastard's identity as "Who thou wilt," offered to Hubert at the beginning of 5.6. Increasingly fluid, dynamic, and diverse, "that white-faced shore . . . That water-wallèd bulwark" (2.1.23–27) becomes an isle of "sons and children," a "nation" that the tearful Salisbury wishes could be borne in "Neptune's arms" and sail like a ship to a foreign land where Englishmen would fight others rather than one another (5.2.25, 33–39). In Act 2 an English king and a French king speak for England. At the end, who speaks for England? "Bastards and else" (2.1.285).

King John, unlike *TR,* does not conclude with a coronation, the act that typically marks the end of a nation's mourning for its recently deceased monarch (though productions often show the crowning of Prince Henry). Without that formal ceremony, and as talk of tears and woe continues, the entire scene remains in the middle or transitional phase of the rite of passage associated with death—the mourning period between separation from that which was and incorporation into something new. That the Bastard and nobles kneel to Henry points in the direction of incorporation, as does the Bastard's plural inclusive voice. But his elegiac exhortation with its recalcitrantly loaded "if," delivered in the presence of a fragile boy-king surrounded by peripatetic nobles (not an image to instill confidence) and further qualified by the nonhistorical status of the speaker who emerges as the national conscience, maintains the sense of liminality to the very end.[23] The ending rushes not to closure, as some have suggested, but to another threshold, thus reinforcing the play's overall fluid, mutable temper.[24] Like the Bastard, whose threshold moments inform the play, and like the young prince at the threshold of kingship, England itself, caught up in the process of history, is presented as a work in progress.

---

1. Barbara Hodgdon, *The End Crowns All: Closure and Contradiction in Shakespeare's History* (Princeton: Princeton University Press, 1991), p. 29. Hodgdon locates the play's flux in its "politics of accommodation" (pp. 22–32); Virginia Vaughan in a constant pattern of frequent surprises and reversals of expectation ("Be-

tween Tetralogies: *King John* as Transition," *Shakespeare Quarterly* 35 [1984]: 407–20, esp. pp. 415–19); and Jane Donawerth in the repetition of oral images (tongue, mouth, ear, breath, etc.) that suggest the fluidity of language as spoken rather than as written (*Shakespeare and the Sixteenth-Century Study of Language* [Urbana: University of Illinois Press, 1984], pp. 165–88).

2. Examples include "Let me make answer" (2.1.122), "Hear me, O, hear me!" (3.1.116), "Now hear me speak with a prophetic spirit" (3.4.129), "Nay, hear me, Hubert" (4.1.87), "Do but hear me, sir" (4.3.125), "Let me have audience" (5.2.120), "Give me leave to speak" (5.2.164), and "No, I will speak" (5.2.165). See also the Bastard's constant interruptions of Robert Faulconbridge in 1.1.

3. Charles Taylor, *Sources of the Self: The Making of the Modern Identity* (Cambridge, Mass.: Harvard University Press, 1989), p. 36.

4. For the shift from a public to a private dynamic, see Alexander Leggatt, "Dramatic Perspective in *King John*," *English Studies in Canada* 3 (1977): 8; for speakers being "effects," see Harry Berger, Jr., "What Did the King Know and When Did He Know It: Shakespearean Discourses and Psychoanalysis," *South Atlantic Quarterly* 88 (1989): 813.

5. The notion of *liminality* was developed by Victor Turner, who defines it as "any condition outside or on the periphery of everyday life" (*Dramas, Fields, and Metaphors* [Ithaca: Cornell University Press, 1974], p. 47); see also his *Ritual Process: Structure and Anti-Structure* (Ithaca: Cornell University Press, 1969), pp. 94–130. In *Coming of Age in Shakespeare* (New York: Routledge, 1981), Marjorie Garber applies it, along with other anthropological concepts such as *threshold moments* and *rites of passage,* to a number of plays (not including *King John*). Rites of passage include three

phases: separation from a former identity, transition, and incorporation into a new role. *Liminality* relates specifically to the transition between a former identity and a new role as one confronts a threshold experience: "The act of crossing the threshold—of becoming a 'marginal person' or a 'liminary'—is both a danger and an opportunity, testing the individual's ability to grow and change" (p. 8).

6. The question of which text came first, the anonymous two-part *Troublesome Raigne* published in 1591 or Shakespeare's *King John* (for which almost every year between 1587 and 1598 has been offered as a possible date), is perhaps the most controversial topic in *King John* scholarship. Most hold that *TR* was Shakespeare's primary source; a minority view *TR* as the derivative play, related to *King John* either along the lines of a bad quarto (E. A. J. Honigmann's Arden edition [London: Methuen, 1954], pp. 174–76) or as a scenario-based transmission (L. A. Beaurline's New Cambridge *King John* [Cambridge: Cambridge University Press, 1990], pp. 206–9), with Holinshed's *Chronicles* serving as Shakespeare's primary source. (See "An Introduction to This Text," page l.) In the present essay, I treat *TR* as a source for *King John*. All references to *TR* are taken from Geoffrey Bullough's *Narrative and Dramatic Sources of Shakespeare* (1962; reprint, London: Routledge and Kegan Paul; New York: Columbia University Press, 1975), 4:1–151.

7. See Lawrence Stone, *The Crisis of the Aristocracy, 1558–1641*, abridged ed. (London: Oxford University Press, 1967), pp. 183–232, 258–60.

8. Harry Berger, Jr., *Imaginary Audition: Shakespeare on Stage and Page* (Berkeley: University of California Press, 1989), p. 101.

9. John Blanpied, *Time and the Artist in Shakespeare's English Histories* (Newark: University of Delaware Press; London: Associated University Presses, 1983), p. 105.

10. See Christopher Z. Hobson's detailed rhetorical analysis of the "Commodity" soliloquy in "Bastard Speech: The Rhetoric of 'Commodity' in *King John*," *Shakespeare Yearbook* 2 (1991): 95–114.

11. Guy Hamel, "*King John* and *The Troublesome Raigne:* A Reexamination," in *King John: New Perspectives,* edited by Deborah T. Curren-Aquino (Newark: University of Delaware Press; London: Associated University Presses, 1989), p. 44; Joseph Porter, "Fraternal Pragmatics: Speech Acts of John and the Bastard," in the same anthology, p. 136.

12. While the present edition follows the Folio in giving 2.1.1–11, 18, and 153–57 to the Dauphin rather than King Philip (see longer note on page 213), my reading of Louis reflects a theatrical tradition in which he remains essentially a cipher in the Angiers action until the marriage proposal, not really finding his voice until 5.2.

13. Geraldine Cousin notes how Deborah Warner's 1988–89 production for the Royal Shakespeare Company "used the absence of the women in the second half of the play to explore, through male characters, aspects of the mother-child relationship" (*Shakespeare in Performance: King John* [Manchester: Manchester University Press, 1994], pp. 128–29).

14. "Of Vanity," as cited in Beaurline, ed., New Cambridge *King John,* p. 57.

15. Gunnar Boklund, "The Troublesome Ending of *King John,*" *Studia Neophilologica* 40 (1968): 183.

16. Cousin, *Shakespeare in Performance: King John,* p. 97.

17. Because his prayer is made immediately after Hubert has announced the surprising return of Prince Henry in the company of the newly returned and pardoned nobles, James L. Calderwood and William

Matchett, among others, have suggested that the Bastard prays to be delivered from the alluring prospect of seizing power for himself. In rising above that temptation, he proves the worthiest heir to the legendary Coeur de Lion. See Calderwood's "Commodity and Honour in *King John*" (1960), in *King John and Henry VIII: Critical Essays,* edited by Frances A. Shirley (New York: Garland, 1988), pp. 142–44, and Matchett's "Richard's Divided Heritage in *King John,*" *Essays in Criticism* 12 (1962), pp. 250–52. But the speaker's sense of overwhelming woe—military losses, John's poisoning, and the image of a boy-king controlled by self-serving lords—offers at least as good a reason to pray urgently for strength.

18. Garber, *Coming of Age in Shakespeare,* p. 21.

19. Garber, *Coming of Age in Shakespeare,* p. 216.

20. Taylor, *Sources of the Self,* p. 36.

21. In a far-ranging essay dealing with medieval drama, the *Henry VI* plays, *Henry V,* and *King John,* Peter Womack insightfully discusses the "imagining" of England in Elizabethan drama. See "Imagining Communities: Theatres and the English Nation in the Sixteenth Century," in *Culture and History, 1350–1600: Essays on English Communities, Identities, and Writing,* edited by David Aers (Detroit: Wayne State University Press, 1992), pp. 91–145, esp. 111–26; the quoted passage appears on p. 126. See also Nina Levine's feminist approach to the topic in her chapter "Refiguring the Nation: Mothers and Sons in *King John,*" in *Women's Matters: Politics, Gender, and Nation in Shakespeare's Early History Plays* (Newark: University of Delaware Press; London: Associated University Presses, 1998), pp. 123–45. Ralph Berry was one of the first to note the play's progressive questioning of the initial fusion of nation and king ("*King John:* Some Bastards Too," in *The Shakespearean Metaphor: Studies in Language and Form* [London: Mac-

millan; Totowa, N.J.: Rowman and Littlefield, 1978], pp. 26–36).

22. As Womack persuasively argues, the Bastard "could not figure as a patriot in the first half of the play because there was, effectively, no *patria* to which such a role could refer, only the patently empty formalism of a monarchical rhetoric" ("Imagining Communities," p. 125).

23. In the 1999 Washington, D.C., revival, as the Bastard delivered the final lines near the front of the stage, the audience saw a newly crowned and royally garbed King Henry on an upper level surrounded by the nobles and (a textually interpolated) Pandulph. In the Coonrod production, the actor playing the Bastard ran off the stage into the audience after delivering his final speech, leaving the rest of the characters onstage. Was his work done? Had the "if" of uncertainty unsettled him once more? Where was he going? Was there a new task to be performed? Was he making good on his promise to follow John? Or was this a final way of highlighting his national incorporation as the voice of "the people"? In 1960 at Stratford, Ontario, Douglas Seale chose to have the funeral procession begin as the Bastard started his final speech. By the time he arrived at the concluding couplet, he was all alone, "solitary, friendless . . . and disillusioned" in a kind of perpetual "betwixt and between" state (Seale, "*King John* in the Modern Theatre," in *King John: The Laurel Shakespeare,* edited by Francis Fergusson and Charles Jasper Sisson [New York: Dell, 1963], p. 33). Both Coonrod and Seale, in different ways—one having the Bastard leave the action, the other having the action leave him—implicitly recognized that he existed outside the history enveloping the other characters. The two directorial choices also suggest that the Bastard might have more thresholds to cross.

24. See Virginia Vaughan, "*King John:* Subversion and Containment," in Curren-Aquino, *King John,* p. 73; also Sigurd Burckhardt, *Shakespearean Meanings* (Princeton: Princeton University Press, 1968), p. 134; and Robert C. Jones, *These Valiant Dead: Renewing the Past in Shakespeare's Histories* (Iowa City: University of Iowa Press, 1991), p. 57.

Further Reading

King John

Abbreviations: *KJ* = *King John; TR* = *The Troublesome Raigne of Iohn, King of England; 1H6* = *Henry VI, Part 1; 2H6* = *Henry VI, Part 2; 3H6* = *Henry VI, Part 3; R3* = *Richard III*

Barish, Jonas. "*King John* and Oath Breach." In *Shakespeare: Text, Language, Criticism: Essays in Honour of Marvin Spevack,* edited by Bernhard Fabian and Kurt Tetzeli von Rosador, pp. 1–18. New York: Olms Weidmann, 1987.

The topic of "oath breach" appears throughout the Shakespeare canon, but Barish contends that it receives "its most sustained and climactic treatment" in *KJ*. While most cases of breach of faith are plainly marked as reprehensible (e.g., King Philip's repudiation of his initial oath to Arthur and his later oath to John), the "blinding" episode in which Hubert reneges on his promise to murder Arthur demonstrates that there are occasions when "it is worse to keep an oath than to break it." Shakespeare's most complex and ambiguous treatment of the topic appears in the vacillation of the nobles whose vowed loyalties shift from John to Louis and back again to John; no matter how blameworthy their treacherous oath to support the Dauphin, "our antipathy" is mingled with "our sympathy." What Shakespeare shows in the "welter of swearing and unswearing" is that both the taking and breaking of oaths allow "of many gradations," and that in this area, as in others, the dramatist "remains a relativist."

Braunmuller, A. R. "*King John* and Historiography." *ELH* 55 (1988): 309–32.

Using Holinshed's *Chronicles*, Shakespeare's *KJ*, and the writings of Sir John Hayward, Braunmuller discusses the tensions between drama and historiography to focus a dual argument: (1) that for all their formal differences, whether as chronicle, play, or "new humanist" history, these texts employ similar techniques to create fictitious verbal structures; and (2) that "the truth claims" of these works and the truths they convey are "politically determined." To illustrate how the fictive *KJ* "reconceptualizes" the imaginative chronicle material lying behind it, Braunmuller examines Shakespeare's invention of the Bastard and the treatment of Arthur's death. He suggests that history writing and dramaturgy at the end of the sixteenth century may have been self-consciously reciprocal activities: "As Shakespeare and his fellow playwrights moved away from dramatizing the chronicles toward the kind of drama [*KJ*] is trying to be, they were . . . defensively and self-servingly admitting that plausibility" constitutes the chief means of "factifying" or authenticating "(hi)stories." Plausibility thus emerges as the only pertinent and available test of history writing. It is also, as Braunmuller notes, a dramatic test.

Bullough, Geoffrey, ed. "*King John.*" In *Narrative and Dramatic Sources of Shakespeare,* vol. 4, pp. 1–151, 1962. Rpt., London: Routledge and Kegan Paul; New York: Columbia University Press, 1975.

Bullough provides a complete text of the two parts of *TR* (the anonymous 1591 play widely assumed to be Shakespeare's primary source for *KJ*), summarizes Bale's *King Johan* (an analogue), and reprints excerpts from the following: the 1587 edition of Holinshed's *Chronicles* (a definite source), the 1583 edition of Foxe's

Actes and Monuments of Martyrs (a possible source), Hall's 1548 *Union of the Two Noble and Illustre Famelies of Lancastre and Yorke* (a probable source), and *The English Chronicle of Radulph of Coggeshall* (another analogue). Whether critics regard *TR* as the source for *KJ* (the majority position) or as the derivative play (the minority view), they generally agree that while the plot is essentially the same in both works, characterization and style are very different: the anonymous text is said to be more polemical than Shakespeare's, and also more explicit in matters of motivation (e.g., John's reasons for a second coronation [4.2] and for his later submission to Pandulph [5.1]). Bullough's scene-by-scene comparison of the two plays reveals divergences that include additions by Shakespeare (e.g., the Bastard's "foot of honor" [1.1.188–222] and "Commodity" soliloquies [2.1.588–626] and his "I am amazed, methinks, and lose my way" monologue [4.3.148–67], Blanche's lamentation at 3.1.341–51, the sequence in which John persuades Hubert to kill Arthur [3.3.20–76], and Constance's "mad" scene [3.4.17–107]); omissions (e.g., the Bastard's plundering of an abbey where he finds a nun hiding in an abbot's chest, an impeachment episode involving the nobles at St. Edmundsbury, and the full representation of John's poisoning by a monk); and variations (e.g., Shakespeare's foregrounding of interpersonal relationships over political ideology in the "blinding" episode, 4.1). The introductory comments also address the date of *KJ*, the contradictory medieval and Tudor images of John available to Shakespeare, and the origins of both the Bastard's character and the name Faulconbridge. Bullough concludes that *KJ* "helped Shakespeare to free himself from the conception of the History play as tragic or rhetorical drama, and to see the possibility of modulating in the same play from the broadly comic to the epic."

Burckhardt, Sigurd. "*King John:* The Ordering of the Present Time." In *Shakespearean Meanings,* pp. 116–43. Princeton: Princeton University Press, 1968. [The essay originally appeared in *ELH* 33 (1966): 133–53.]

In its questioning of Tudor orthodox ideology, *KJ* becomes a play about creating order (the modern position) rather than about discovering it (the classical view). Burckhardt contrasts *TR*'s and *KJ*'s respective treatments of the "blinding" episode (4.1) and Melun's reasons for revealing to the nobles Louis' planned treachery (5.4.41–44) to demonstrate that in *KJ* personal interaction and relationships are more important for ordering one's world than is traditional belief in an established hierarchy of fixed correspondences. The structure of *KJ* exposes the contradiction at the heart of Tudor doctrine: while the Elizabethan world picture and divine right theory demand one voice of authority, "of kings there are more than one." When royal and papal claims to ultimate authority are rejected, Shakespeare makes clear "that the whole beautiful structure crumbles: the divinity of kings, the duty of obedience, even the sanctity of oaths." Burckhardt's thesis—that "when he wrote [*KJ*], or quite possibly in writing it, Shakespeare was or became a 'modern'"—informs much of the play's post-1970 scholarship and performance history.

Cousin, Geraldine. *Shakespeare in Performance: King John.* Manchester: Manchester University Press, 1994.

In her introduction Cousin speculates on possible performances of *KJ* in the sixteenth and seventeenth centuries and offers background information on its popularity in eighteenth- and nineteenth-century theaters. She also addresses the "whys" of *KJ*'s infrequent appearance on the modern stage (e.g., lack of focus, thematic incoherence, too much declamation, and an episodic structure) and argues for the inherent stageworthiness and theatrical malleability of this "elusive" play. After looking at the nineteenth-century record (commenting specifically on the work of Kemble/Planché, Macready, Tree, and Mantell), she turns her attention to modern revivals and devotes the remaining chapters to the mid-century productions of George Devine at the Old Vic in 1953 and Douglas Seale at the Shakespeare Memorial Theatre in 1957, the radical reworkings by Buzz Goodbody and John Barton in the 1970s for the Royal Shakespeare Company (RSC), the "fundamentally conservative" 1984 BBC-TV *John* directed by David Giles, and Deborah Warner's "mould-breaking" achievement for the RSC in 1988–89, a production which the author praises for "its relevance to the late twentieth-century world."

Curren-Aquino, Deborah T., ed. *King John: New Perspectives*. Newark: University of Delaware Press; London: Associated University Presses, 1989.

The twelve essays making up the volume span a variety of critical interests and approaches: source study (Guy Hamel's "*King John* and *The Troublesome Raigne:* A Reexamination"), genre (Barbara Traister's "The King's One Body: Unceremonial Kingship in *King John*"), imagery and language (Dorothea Kehler's " 'So Jest with Heaven': Deity in *King John*"), theme (Joseph Candido's "Blots, Stains, and Adulteries: The Impurities in *King John*"), character (Michael Manheim's "The Four Voices of the Bastard"), historiography (Marsha Robinson's "The Historiographic Methodology of *King John*"), new historicism (Virginia Vaughan's "*King John:* A Study in Subversion and Containment"), feminism (Phyllis Rackin's "Patriarchal History and Female Subversion in *King John*"), speech act theory (Joseph Porter's "Fraternal Pragmatics: Speech Acts of John and the

Bastard"), performance history (Edward Brubaker's "Staging *King John:* A Director's Observations" and Carol J. Carlisle's "Constance: A Theatrical Trinity"), and perspectivism and closure (Larry Champion's "The 'Un-end' of *King John:* Shakespeare's Demystification of Closure"). Taken collectively, the essays suggest a deepening awareness of Shakespeare's complex experimentation with the dramatic genre of the history play. The volume includes a select performance history and a select bibliography.

Donawerth, Jane. "*King John:* Mutable Speech." In *Shakespeare and the Sixteenth-Century Study of Language,* pp. 165–88. Urbana: University of Illinois Press, 1984.

Where *Love's Labor's Lost* focuses on the graphic aspect of language, *KJ* emphasizes the oral dimension. The frequent repetition of words such as *tongue, mouth, ear,* and most notably *breath* signifies the transient, shifting, and vague qualities of language itself and is appropriate to a mutable world where verbal power is destructive rather than generative: "Language fails to be a social bond because [words come with little consequence], breath passes and vows are equally transitory." The ideas about language that Shakespeare gives voice to in the play support its larger purpose: that is, the study of "man as a political animal, not in the ideal Renaissance sense of the seeker after glory and knowledge infinite, but in the lesser sense of the vain striver after merely worldly power." Shakespeare has made the world of *KJ* credible, but he has not engaged our deep interest in it, partially because of his efforts to "embody in his style the defects in language that the characters perceive in their world." The concluding speeches suggest that Shakespeare "has written a play that is mainly an elegy for human hope."

Dusinberre, Juliet. "*King John* and Embarrassing Women." *Shakespeare Survey* 42 (1990): 37–52.

In this feminist study of *KJ*, Dusinberre draws on the play's performance history to examine the effect of the women on the men within the dramatic action and on the audience outside. Up until the end of Act 3, the central drive of the play (as shown in Deborah Warner's 1988 Royal Shakespeare Company production) is provided by its many "odd" female characters, a point not lost on the men who are embarrassed by this female domination and use it as a pretext for retribution against the women. Dusinberre relates her discussion of Eleanor, Lady Faulconbridge, Blanche, and Constance to the convention of having boy actors play the women's parts (as well as the role of Arthur): "In [*KJ*] Shakespeare gave the boy actors parts in which they might overact to their heart's content, stealing the stage from their betters, who are forced to stand around wondering how to quell them." Once the women leave the stage—once they are no longer there to challenge official discourse—Shakespeare loses interest, and the play "goes to pieces," never recovering "the energy associated with the new world of the [pre-Act 4] Bastard and the new generation: the boys. Or, in our terms . . . the women."

Grennan, Eamon. "Shakespeare's Satirical History: A Reading of *King John*." *Shakespeare Studies* 11 (1978): 21–37.

KJ, "more sui generis than a close relative" of Shakespeare's other histories, reveals a playwright sweeping away the "functional props" of the historico-dramatic world he had created in his *H6* plays and *R3*, while at the same time renewing his sense of what history means, thereby preparing "for the deeper, more demanding tasks of his second tetralogy." Grennan uses the siege of

Angiers depicted in both *TR* and *KJ* (2.1) to argue that the former is an exemplary *historia* (i.e., a coherent arrangement of historical facts designed to express a particular moral or political theme), while the latter is a critique of the humanist concept of history embodied in both *TR* and the first tetralogy. With its "faintly comic" isosceles triangle involving the Citizen and the rival kings and the Bastard's "wild counsel" to sack the city and then fight over its possession (lines 393–412), the Angiers scene compels a recognition of "an equilibrium so fastidious that it makes all objective decision impossible." The episode thus functions as an emblem of *KJ*'s emphasis on impasse or stalemate for its own sake rather than as "a stage in a predictable process." Essential to the play's status as a satirical history is the ironic transformation of the Bastard from agent of parody to a "puppet of patriotic meanings." The play's critical exposure of the nature of *historia* is best seen in its "most striking linguistic feature[,] . . . the continual trampling of objective meaning in a stampede of paradox and oxymoron."

Hibbard, G. R. "From Dialectical Rhetoric to Metaphorical Thinking: *King John.*" In *The Making of Shakespeare's Dramatic Poetry,* pp. 133–43. Toronto: University of Toronto Press, 1981.

Hibbard's interest lies in those moments when characters make new discoveries about either their situations or themselves. At such times verbal expression becomes rich in images and metaphors that "do not merely beget one another . . . but unite to form a coherent whole and make something hitherto but half apprehended . . . clear, concrete, and dynamic." By way of illustration, Hibbard engages in a detailed analysis of the Bastard's "I am amazed" monologue (4.3.148–67) in which the character voices his confusion in metaphors that "exploit . . . ambiguities and double meanings." What Shakespeare evolves through a rapid, associational shifting from image to image is "a way of writing that is also a way of thinking and of comprehending." While such speeches and the John–Hubert sequence in 3.3 look ahead to the great tragedies, *KJ*'s dominant mode of declamatory speech, most impressively heard in Constance, looks back to the earlier histories. The play thus suggests "something of a poetic dramatist's workshop . . . in which [Shakespeare] reassesses old techniques and tries out new ones."

Hodgdon, Barbara. "Fashioning Obedience: *King John*'s 'True Inheritors.'" In *The End Crowns All: Closure and Contradiction in Shakespeare's History*, pp. 22–43. Princeton: Princeton University Press, 1991.

The first half of Hodgdon's intertextual study of "closural form" in *KJ* provides a literary analysis of the play's "politics of accommodation," particularly as it dominates the last third of this "chameleonlike" history, which constructs its close through a "semblance of ideological neutrality." While conventional methods and the use of proverbial tags suggest an orthodox conclusion in the legitimate succession of Prince Henry, the closing scene's "particular bricolage of rhetorical signs of ending can also be read as a bastard form, a last figure for [*KJ*'s] initial questions concerning plural claims on royal legitimacy." The choice of the marginally historic figure of the Bastard to deliver the final speech for the kingdom "discloses the historical limits of subversion at the fictional limits of the play." Evoking an England identified more with the power of the body politic than with the concept of the King's two bodies, the Bastard offers "not a mirror for magistrates, but a complex, even refractory, mirror for subjects." The second half of the chapter discusses how one of Shakespeare's "bleakest" succession scenes has been realized in performance, with an emphasis on the 1974 Barton and 1988 Warner revivals, both for the Royal Shakespeare Company. Barton created a "black-comedy spectacle," while Warner configured "a starkly demystified compromise."

Levine, Nina S. "Refiguring the Nation: Mothers and Sons in *King John*." In *Women's Matters: Politics, Gender, and Nation in Shakespeare's Early History Plays*, pp. 123–45. Newark: University of Delaware Press; London: Associated University Presses, 1998.

While Shakespeare's early histories (*1*, *2*, and *3H6*, *R3*, and *KJ*) rewrite the Tudor chronicle record so as to acknowledge the importance of women in ensuring patrilineal succession, Levine contends that they also "generate a critique of patrilineal inheritance and legitimacy" that speaks to the Elizabethan present in which the plays are "situated." The chapter on *KJ* attends to several of the more radical succession tracts circulating in the 1590s to illustrate similarities between the John–Arthur succession debate and the one permeating the waning years of Elizabeth's reign. In a reading that goes beyond Rackin's (see below) to suggest a more radical Shakespeare, Levine claims that *KJ* "contest[s], as well as validate[s]" its own authorizing patriarchal structure by (1) replacing fathers with mothers as the agents who confer power and legitimacy in representations of succession, and (2) decentering the orthodox representation of the monarchy as exclusively figured in the heroic warrior king. Through their subversive questioning of legitimacy and law, the vocal mothers of *KJ* translate the traditional image of the patriarchal monarch into that of "a dependent son, whose power and authority rest with his mother." In the closing image of a fragile, weeping

Henry III (who recalls the tearful, powerless Arthur) and in the assigning of the final patriotic speech to the Bastard, Shakespeare continues rather than resolves his radical interrogation of patrilineal succession and refigures the image of the nation-state as inclusive and iconoclastic. "Evoking the nation's desire for a mother even as it voices a nostalgic yearning for a patriotic and patriarchal past, *KJ* may also register both the anxieties and the possibilities prompted by the unsettled Elizabethan succession."

Machiavelli, Niccolò. *The Prince* (1513). Ed. and trans. Robert M. Adams. 2nd ed. New York: W. W. Norton, 1992.

In this famous political treatise, Machiavelli draws on his experience as a member of the Florentine government in order to present his conception of the kind of strong leader and tactics required to impose political order for the good of the unified Italy he envisions. Because Machiavelli separates politics from ethics and is more concerned with ends than with means, his name has become identified with all that is cynical and even diabolical in state affairs. In Shakespeare's England, this exaggeratedly negative reputation gave rise to the conventional villain known as the Machiavel. In the scholarship on *KJ*, critics have observed Machiavellian traits in John, Queen Eleanor, the Bastard, King Philip, Pandulph, Louis, and the nobles. While John has been called an "incompetent" or "would-be" Machiavel, who pales next to the artful Richard III and Bolingbroke, the Bastard is often regarded (like Hal/Henry V) as an example of the "attractive," "new," and "legitimized" or "redeemed" Machiavel. As examples of Machiavellian tenets and strategies, critics often single out the Bastard's line "Smacks it not something of the policy?" (2.1.412) and his "Commodity" soliloquy, John's indirection with Hubert in 3.3, and the arguments Pandulph uses to manipulate King Philip (3.1) and Louis the Dauphin (3.4).

Rackin, Phyllis. "Patriarchal History and Female Subversion." In *Stages of History: Shakespeare's English Chronicles*, pp. 146–200, esp. pp. 178–91. Ithaca, N.Y.: Cornell University Press, 1990. [Includes material from "Anti-Historians: Women's Roles in Shakespeare's Histories" (*Theatre Journal* 37 [1985]: 329–44) and "Patriarchal History and Female Subversion in *King John*," in Curren-Aquino above.]

Observing that the issue of legitimacy is nowhere more central in Shakespeare's English histories than in *KJ*, Rackin examines the paradoxical role of women who ostensibly have no voice within the patriarchal historiography of the Renaissance but who nonetheless manage, by their very presence as "keepers of the unwritten and unknowable truth" of biological legitimacy, to subvert the patriarchal historical record. To illustrate both the "arbitrary and conjectural nature of patriarchal succession" (1.1.119–32) and "the suppressed centrality of women to it," Rackin discusses the different ways in which Philip Faulconbridge in Holinshed, *TR*, and *KJ* learns the identity of his biological father: only in *KJ* "is he required to receive his paternity at the hands of women," one who guesses the truth (Queen Eleanor) and one who verifies it (Lady Faulconbridge). In none of Shakespeare's other history plays do the women enjoy such important and varied roles: Eleanor as the "Machiavellian dowager," Constance as the relentless and lamenting mother, and Blanche as the traditional female site "for the inscription of a patriarchal historical narrative." In the morally ambiguous world of *KJ* where nothing is conclusive, patriarchal authority is constantly subjected to "skeptical feminine interrogation." The image of dismemberment in Blanche's lament (3.1.342–45) embodies "the many divisions that characterize this play . . . the most troubling of all Shakespeare's English histories."

Shirley, Frances A., ed. King John *and* Henry VIII: *Critical Essays*. New York: Garland, 1988.

The first part of this volume contains twelve selections dealing with the performance history and criticism of *KJ* spanning the years 1770 to 1974. Those relating to the play's stage life are Eugene M. Waith's essay "*King John* and the Drama of History" and excerpts from Francis Gentleman's *The Dramatic Censor or Critical Companion*, Thomas Davies' *Memoirs of the Life of David Garrick, Esq.*, William Hazlitt's *A View of the English Stage*, and Arthur Colby Sprague's *Shakespeare's Histories*. The critical studies are taken from William Hazlitt's *Characters of Shakespeare's Plays*, E. M. W. Tillyard's *Shakespeare's History Plays*, Caroline F. E. Spurgeon's *Shakespeare's Imagery and What It Tells Us*, Adrien Bonjour's "The Road to Swinstead Abbey: A Study of the Sense and Structure of *King John*," James L. Calderwood's "Commodity and Honour in *King John*," M. M. Reese's *The Cease of Majesty*, and Robert L. Smallwood's introduction to the New Penguin edition of *KJ*. The Waith, Bonjour, and Calderwood selections are among the most frequently cited and reprinted essays in the scholarship on the play. Waith focuses on *KJ*'s theatrical success in the eighteenth and nineteenth centuries when the emphasis was on the play's emotionally charged scenes and passionate characters like Constance; he questions the appropriateness of the twentieth century's more cerebral approach to the play. Both Bonjour and Calderwood address the issue of dramatic unity: for Bonjour it inheres in "a deliberately contrasted evolution[:] . . . [the] decline of a hero [John]—

the rise of a hero [the Bastard]"; for Calderwood, in a testing of commodity (scheming self-interest) and honor (loyalty in general but in its highest form loyalty to the good of England), a theme with implications for the qualities needed in a king.

Vaughan, Virginia. "Between Tetralogies: *King John* as Transition." *Shakespeare Quarterly* 35 (1984): 407–20.

KJ replaces the first tetralogy's sense of history as continuing process with an "intense focus on the political present—the here and now of decision-making." This focus, along with Shakespeare's increasing awareness that "political questions are seldom as easy to answer as the traditional hierarchical model suggests," convinces Vaughan that *KJ* marks an important transition between the two tetralogies. She observes in the first half of the play the presentational mode characteristic of the first tetralogy (set speeches, emblematic scenes, stylized language, unified perspective, didacticism); in the second half she detects an experimentation with the more sophisticated representational mode associated with the second tetralogy (personalized conflicts, divided loyalties, multiple perspectives, and increasing ambiguity and flux). In contrast to *TR*, *KJ* "probes rather than pronounces"; as a result, "politics becomes embedded in personal relationships rather than abstract ideas." Vaughan attributes what she and others (see Burckhardt above) regard as the play's unsatisfactory ending to a "rush to closure" in which Shakespeare abruptly returns to presentational tactics in the Bastard's final patriotic speech: Shakespeare's withdrawal "from the tensions and reversals which animate the play" leads to a solution "imposed from above, not within," the solution being the "standard formula of chronicle history."

Warren, W. L. *King John.* 2nd ed. Berkeley: University of California Press, 1978.

In what is generally considered to be the standard biography of King John, Warren reassesses the king's reign under the following chapter headings: "The Genesis of a Sinister Reputation," "Gaining a Kingdom," "Losing a Duchy," "King of England," "King versus Pope," "King John and the Barons," "The Road to Runnymede," and "The Road to Newark." Warren concludes that "the monster of personal depravity portrayed by [medieval chroniclers] must be dismissed forever. . . . It was uncertainty and not 'superhuman wickedness' . . . that darkened the years of John's reign. . . . One of his greatest enemies was his own impatience. . . . He had the mental abilities of a great king, but the inclinations of a petty tyrant."

Weimann, Robert. "Mingling Vice and 'Worthiness' in *King John.*" *Shakespeare Studies* 27 (1999): 109–33.

According to Weimann, the Vice tradition associated with the medieval morality play and Tudor interlude offered Shakespeare a way of negotiating and "digesting" the socially sanctioned gap between the "worthy" matter of history and the "unworthy" theatrical space in which that matter was staged—that is, the distance between the "represented locale in the world-of-the-play and the location of playing-in-the-world of Elizabethan London." To illustrate his thesis, the author concentrates on the Bastard's mingling of the Vice's frivolity and the humanistic hero's worthiness. As both commentator and participant, presenter and representer of character, the Bastard appropriates the Vice's performative energy, impudence, and direct rapport with the audience (see, e.g., the "foot of honor" and "Commodity" soliloquies) to emerge as "a vital medium in the conflation of past significance and performed meaning." In him, the antics of the irreverent Vice "are domesticated in a seminal representation of the unruly self in 'worshipful society.'"

Shakespeare's Language

Abbott, E. A. *A Shakespearian Grammar.* New York: Haskell House, 1972.

This compact reference book, first published in 1870, helps with many difficulties in Shakespeare's language. It systematically accounts for a host of differences between Shakespeare's usage and sentence structure and our own.

Blake, Norman. *Shakespeare's Language: An Introduction.* New York: St. Martin's Press, 1983.

This general introduction to Elizabethan English discusses various aspects of the language of Shakespeare and his contemporaries, offering possible meanings for hundreds of ambiguous constructions.

Dobson, E. J. *English Pronunciation, 1500–1700.* 2 vols. Oxford: Clarendon Press, 1968.

This long and technical work includes chapters on spelling (and its reformation), phonetics, stressed vowels, and consonants in early modern English.

Houston, John. *Shakespearean Sentences: A Study in Style and Syntax.* Baton Rouge: Louisiana State University Press, 1988.

Houston studies Shakespeare's stylistic choices, considering matters such as sentence length and the relative positions of subject, verb, and direct object. Examining plays throughout the canon in a roughly chronological, developmental order, he analyzes how sentence structure is used in setting tone, in characterization, and for other dramatic purposes.

Onions, C. T. *A Shakespeare Glossary*. Oxford: Clarendon Press, 1986.

This revised edition updates Onions' standard, selective glossary of words and phrases in Shakespeare's plays that are now obsolete, archaic, or obscure.

Robinson, Randal. *Unlocking Shakespeare's Language: Help for the Teacher and Student.* Urbana, Ill.: National Council of Teachers of English and the ERIC Clearinghouse on Reading and Communication Skills, 1989.

Specifically designed for the high-school and undergraduate college teacher and student, Robinson's book addresses the problems that most often hinder present-day readers of Shakespeare. Through work with his own students, Robinson found that many readers today are particularly puzzled by such stylistic devices as subject-verb inversion, interrupted structures, and compression. He shows how our own colloquial language contains comparable structures, and thus helps students recognize such structures when they find them in Shakespeare's plays. This book supplies worksheets—with examples from major plays—to illuminate and remedy such problems as unusual sequences of words and the separation of related parts of sentences.

Williams, Gordon. *A Dictionary of Sexual Language and Imagery in Shakespearean and Stuart Literature.* 3 vols. London: Athlone Press, 1994.

Williams provides a comprehensive list of the words to which Shakespeare, his contemporaries, and later Stuart writers gave sexual meanings. He supports his identification of these meanings by extensive quotations.

Shakespeare's Life

Baldwin, T. W. *William Shakspere's Petty School.* Urbana: University of Illinois Press, 1943.

Baldwin here investigates the theory and practice of the petty school, the first level of education in Elizabethan England. He focuses on that educational system primarily as it is reflected in Shakespeare's art.

Baldwin, T. W. *William Shakspere's Small Latine and Lesse Greeke.* 2 vols. Urbana: University of Illinois Press, 1944.

Baldwin attacks the view that Shakespeare was an uneducated genius—a view that had been dominant among Shakespeareans since the eighteenth century. Instead, Baldwin shows, the educational system of Shakespeare's time would have given the playwright a strong background in the classics, and there is much in the plays that shows how Shakespeare benefited from such an education.

Beier, A. L., and Roger Finlay, eds. *London 1500–1700: The Making of the Metropolis.* New York: Longman, 1986.

Focusing on the economic and social history of early modern London, these collected essays probe aspects of metropolitan life, including "Population and Disease," "Commerce and Manufacture," and "Society and Change."

Bentley, G. E. *Shakespeare's Life: A Biographical Handbook.* New Haven: Yale University Press, 1961.

This "just-the-facts" account presents the surviving documents of Shakespeare's life against an Elizabethan background.

Chambers, E. K. *William Shakespeare: A Study of Facts and Problems.* 2 vols. Oxford: Clarendon Press, 1930.

Analyzing in great detail the scant historical data, Chambers' complex, scholarly study considers the nature of the texts in which Shakespeare's work is preserved.

Cressy, David. *Education in Tudor and Stuart England.* London: Edward Arnold, 1975.

This volume collects sixteenth-, seventeenth-, and early-eighteenth-century documents detailing aspects of formal education in England, such as the curriculum, the control and organization of education, and the education of women.

De Grazia, Margreta. *Shakespeare Verbatim: The Reproduction of Authenticity and the 1790 Apparatus.* Oxford: Clarendon Press, 1991.

De Grazia traces and discusses the development of such editorial criteria as authenticity, historical periodization, factual biography, chronological development, and close reading, locating as the point of origin Edmond Malone's 1790 edition of Shakespeare's works. There are interesting chapters on the First Folio and on the "legendary" versus the "documented" Shakespeare.

Dutton, Richard. *William Shakespeare: A Literary Life.* New York: St. Martin's Press, 1989.

Not a biography in the traditional sense, Dutton's very readable work nevertheless "follows the contours of Shakespeare's life" as he examines Shakespeare's career as playwright and poet, with consideration of his patrons, theatrical associations, and audience.

Fraser, Russell. *Young Shakespeare.* New York: Columbia University Press, 1988.

Fraser focuses on Shakespeare's first thirty years, paying attention simultaneously to his life and art.

Schoenbaum, S. *William Shakespeare: A Compact Documentary Life*. New York: Oxford University Press, 1977.

This standard biography economically presents the essential documents from Shakespeare's time in an accessible narrative account of the playwright's life.

Shakespeare's Theater

Bentley, G. E. *The Profession of Player in Shakespeare's Time, 1590–1642*. Princeton: Princeton University Press, 1984.

Bentley readably sets forth a wealth of evidence about performance in Shakespeare's time, with special attention to the relations between player and company, and the business of casting, managing, and touring.

Berry, Herbert. *Shakespeare's Playhouses*. New York: AMS Press, 1987.

Berry's six essays collected here discuss (with illustrations) varying aspects of the four playhouses in which Shakespeare had a financial stake: the Theatre in Shoreditch, the Blackfriars, and the first and second Globe.

Cook, Ann Jennalie. *The Privileged Playgoers of Shakespeare's London*. Princeton: Princeton University Press, 1981.

Cook's work argues, on the basis of sociological, economic, and documentary evidence, that Shakespeare's audience—and the audience for English Renaissance drama generally—consisted mainly of the "privileged."

Greg, W. W. *Dramatic Documents from the Elizabethan Playhouses*. 2 vols. Oxford: Clarendon Press, 1931.

Greg itemizes and briefly describes many of the play

manuscripts that survive from the period 1590 to around 1660, including, among other things, players' parts. His second volume offers facsimiles of selected manuscripts.

Gurr, Andrew. *Playgoing in Shakespeare's London*. Cambridge: Cambridge University Press, 1987.

Gurr charts how the theatrical enterprise developed from its modest beginnings in the late 1560s to become a thriving institution in the 1600s. He argues that there were important changes over the period 1567–1644 in the playhouses, the audience, and the plays.

Harbage, Alfred. *Shakespeare's Audience*. New York: Columbia University Press, 1941.

Harbage investigates the fragmentary surviving evidence to interpret the size, composition, and behavior of Shakespeare's audience.

Hattaway, Michael. *Elizabethan Popular Theatre: Plays in Performance*. London: Routledge and Kegan Paul, 1982.

Beginning with a study of the popular drama of the late Elizabethan age—a description of the stages, performance conditions, and acting of the period—this volume concludes with an analysis of five well-known plays of the 1590s, one of them (*Titus Andronicus*) by Shakespeare.

Shapiro, Michael. *Children of the Revels: The Boy Companies of Shakespeare's Time and Their Plays*. New York: Columbia University Press, 1977.

Shapiro chronicles the history of the amateur and quasi-professional child companies that flourished in London at the end of Elizabeth's reign and the beginning of James'.

The Publication of Shakespeare's Plays

Blayney, Peter W. M. *The First Folio of Shakespeare.* Hanover, Md.: Folger, 1991.

Blayney's accessible account of the printing and later life of the First Folio—an amply illustrated catalog to a 1991 Folger Shakespeare Library exhibition—analyzes the mechanical production of the First Folio, describing how the Folio was made, by whom and for whom, how much it cost, and its ups and downs (or, rather, downs and ups) since its printing in 1623.

Hinman, Charlton. *The Norton Facsimile: The First Folio of Shakespeare.* 2nd ed. New York: W. W. Norton, 1996.

This facsimile presents a photographic reproduction of an "ideal" copy of the First Folio of Shakespeare; Hinman attempts to represent each page in its most fully corrected state. The second edition includes an important new introduction by Peter W. M. Blayney.

Hinman, Charlton. *The Printing and Proof-Reading of the First Folio of Shakespeare.* 2 vols. Oxford: Clarendon Press, 1963.

In the most arduous study of a single book ever undertaken, Hinman attempts to reconstruct how the Shakespeare First Folio of 1623 was set into type and run off the press, sheet by sheet. He also provides almost all the known variations in readings from copy to copy.

Key to Famous Lines and Phrases

. . . new-made honor doth forget men's names.
[*Bastard*—1.1.193]

Sweet, sweet, sweet poison for the age's tooth.
[*Bastard*—1.1.219]

Sir Robert might have eat his part in me
Upon Good Friday and ne'er broke his fast.
[*Bastard*—1.1.241–42]

. . . that pale, that white-faced shore,
Whose foot spurns back the ocean's roaring tides . . .
. . . that utmost corner of the West.
[*Austria*—2.1.23–29]

. . . all th' unsettled humors of the land—
Rash, inconsiderate, fiery voluntaries,
With ladies' faces and fierce dragons' spleens—
Have sold their fortunes at their native homes,
Bearing their birthrights proudly on their backs,
To make a hazard of new fortunes here.
[*Chatillion*—2.1.66–71]

. . . like a jolly troop of huntsmen come
Our lusty English, all with purpled hands,
Dyed in the dying slaughter of their foes.
[*Eng. Herald*—2.1.333–35]

. . . I was never so bethumped with words
Since I first called my brother's father Dad.
[*Bastard*—2.1.487–88]

That smooth-faced gentleman, tickling Commodity,
Commodity, the bias of the world.
[*Bastard*—2.1.601–2]

I will instruct my sorrows to be proud,
For grief is proud and makes his owner stoop.
[*Constance*—3.1.71–72]

Bell, book, and candle shall not drive me back
When gold and silver becks me to come on.
[*Bastard*—3.3.12–13]

Grief fills the room up of my absent child.
[*Constance*—3.4.95]

Life is as tedious as a twice-told tale,
Vexing the dull ear of a drowsy man.
[*Dauphin*—3.4.110–11]

I should be as merry as the day is long.
[*Arthur*—4.1.20]

To gild refinèd gold, to paint the lily,
To throw a perfume on the violet, . . .
Is wasteful and ridiculous excess.
[*Salisbury*—4.2.11–16]

So foul a sky clears not without a storm.
[*King John*—4.2.110]

Nay, but make haste, the better foot before!
[*King John*—4.2.178]

I am amazed, methinks, and lose my way
Among the thorns and dangers of this world.
[*Bastard*—4.3.148–49]

. . . now my soul hath elbow-room.
[*King John*—5.7.30]

This England never did nor never shall
Lie at the proud foot of a conqueror . . .
. . . Naught shall make us rue,
If England to itself do rest but true.
[*Bastard*—5.7.118–24]